Syria from Reform to Revolt

Modern Intellectual and Political History of the Middle East
Mehrzad Boroujerdi, *Series Editor*

Syria from Reform to Revolt, VOLUME 1

Political Economy and International Relations

Edited by
Raymond Hinnebusch
and Tina Zintl

 SYRACUSE UNIVERSITY PRESS

Contents

Tables and Illustrations

Tables

Figures

Syria from Reform to Revolt

1

Introduction

RAYMOND HINNEBUSCH
AND TINA ZINTL

When Bashar al-Asad smoothly assumed power in July 2000, just seven days after the death of his father, observers were divided on what this new head of state would mean for the country's foreign and domestic politics. On the one hand, it seemed everything would stay the same: an Asad on top of a political system controlled by secret services and Ba'thist one-party rule. On the other hand, it looked like everything would be different: a young president with exposure to Western education who, in his inaugural speech, emphasized his determination to modernize Syria.

This book examines Syrian politics in the first decade of the twenty-first century, from Bashar al-Asad's accession to the outbreak of the revolt against his regime in early 2011. It looks at the strategies and practices of authoritarian upgrading that matured under Bashar al-Asad and were successfully deployed to counter the multiple crises threatening the Syrian regime during the decade while also identifying in these same practices the seeds of the 2011 revolt. This introductory chapter aims to provide the reader with a broad survey of the main trends that provide the context for the subsequent chapters, particularly the political economy background. It discusses the vulnerabilities and dilemmas built into the Syrian regime as it was constructed, primarily under Hafiz al-Asad after 1970, with which his son had to deal after his succession; it surveys the strategies pursued by Bashar al-Asad and examines the consequences of these strategies. Thereby, it also identifies some of the seeds of the 2011 revolt in these strategies.

1

Authoritarian Upgrading

According to Volker Perthes's assessment (2004), Bashar al-Asad's project was to "modernize authoritarianism" in Syria. This ambition was certainly congruent with similar projects across the region, transitions documented in the literature as a movement from an originally populist form of authoritarianism to "post-populist" (Hinnebusch 2006), neoliberal (Guazzone and Pioppi 2009), or "new" (King 2009) authoritarianism; or to "liberalized autocracies" (Brumberg 2002). Authoritarian power was now used to pursue economic liberalization and to shift the social base of regimes to new "networks of privilege" (Heydemann 2004) and privatization-generated crony capitalism. The parallel literature on hybrid regimes and competitive authoritarianism (Schedler 2006) stressed how limited political liberalization and manipulated electoral competition paradoxically facilitated authoritarian persistence (Kassem 2004; Lust-Okar 2004; Pripstein-Pousousny 2005) and allowed regimes to foster social forces supportive of economic liberalization (Glasser 2001). The literature on "authoritarian upgrading" stressed strategies and techniques by which authoritarian regimes tapped new resources, diversified their legitimacy bases and constituencies, and reregulated state-society relations (Heydemann 2007).

However, what has since become clear from the 2011 Arab uprisings is that, corresponding to each shorter-term gain for regimes from the changes documented in this literature, themselves meant to correct previous vulnerabilities in populist authoritarianism, there have been cumulative *long-run costs*, generating *new* vulnerabilities. Arguably these costs help explain the overthrow of presidents in Egypt and Tunisia and the collapse or near collapse of regimes in Libya and Yemen, and the even more ruinous civil war in Syria.

Yet, during the decade from Bashar al-Asad's succession to the presidency up to the beginning of the so-called "Arab Spring" in early 2011, Syria was considered a prime case of a stable and fairly successful authoritarian regime. It seemed to engineer an effective transition from statist authoritarianism to a somewhat more flexible and more "modern," though still exclusionary, political system. During this time Bashar al-Asad mastered several severe crises, most notably Syria's international isolation after the Iraq war, Syria's expulsion from Lebanon, and Israeli wars against Syrian allies Hezbollah and Hamas. In spite of these external pressures, the regime simultaneously proceeded with the economic liberalization it saw as essential to diversifying its economic base while controlling the initially high expectations for positive change by a sluggish yet steady pace of sociopolitical reforms that kept alive or at least sedated these hopes. This "authoritarian upgrading" was characterized by a variety of political and economic measures, all bolstering al-Asad's rule and making it seem up-to-date with the globalized world. This volume details how al-Asad junior attempted, building on the system he had inherited from his father, to reproduce the regime's power and legitimacy (part one), to reconstruct its social base (part two), and to cope with manifold regional and international challenges (part three).

The Inheritance: Regime Construction and Built-in Vulnerabilities

The Syrian Ba'thist state was, from its beginning in a 1963 coup by radical officers, a construct in which the techniques of state consolidation simultaneously built into the regime certain vulnerabilities that it had to continually counter, including persistent opposition, ongoing foreign policy challenges, and chronic economic problems. These vulnerabilities can be seen in several features of regime construction and adaptation.

First, the regime rose out of the deprived countryside and carried out a "revolution from above" against the landed oligarchy and urban merchant class. In the process it consolidated a popular base of support incorporated into regime institutions, but it also excluded and alienated those who had previously controlled private wealth and property and whose remnants regularly exported their capital rather than investing in Syria. The regime put in their place a public sector centered on their nationalized assets plus a land-reform peasantry supported by state cooperatives. The core of the regime was an alliance between the Ba'thized army and the Ba'th Party, which soon turned into an elaborate political apparatus presiding over corporatist organizations that cut across sectarian cleavages and incorporated the regime's middle-class–peasant/worker constituency.

This incorporation rested on a populist social contract in which the regime's constituency traded loyalty for jobs and social entitlements. This revolution initially led to the modernization of and considerable upward mobility from the countryside, reduced social inequalities, and appreciably raised Syria's human development index; but it also built into Syria's political economy a bias in favor of consumption over investment and also, in raising living standards, encouraged a spurt of population growth that soon exceeded economic development, leading in time to frustrated expectations among new generations (Hinnebusch 2001).

Second, although initially wracked by factional conflict, the new regime was stabilized when Hafiz al-Asad constructed a presidential system above army and party and backed by a core elite commanding these institutions, drawn from his close comrades, kin, and fellow sectarians in the minority 'Alawite community. While stabilizing the state, the cost of this approach was a gradual deterioration into neopatrimonial rule: the party turned from an ideological movement into institutionalized clientalism, with key loyalists co-opted through various forms of patronage, corruption, and exceptions to the law that undermined economic development, enervated capital accumulation, and debilitated the fiscal capabilities of the state, and hence were unsustainable without continual access to various forms of rent. Moreover, the domination of the elite by 'Alawite ex-rural officers provoked resentment and rebellion by elements of the Sunni majority, notably the merchant-clergy complex represented by the Muslim Brotherhood, which led several urban antiregime rebellions, including the early 1980s insurrection that rocked the northern cities and was brutally repressed, and successfully so, because the army held firm to the regime, Damascus remained quiescent, and the rural constituency of the Ba'th remained loyal. Especially after this rebellion, the regime proliferated multiple intelligence agencies and praetorian units, such as the presidential guards, to protect the regime. These special units had to be kept loyal through tolerance of their extortions from the public and immunity from the law.

Third, from its very construction, the legitimacy of the Syrian Ba'th regime depended on its nationalist defiance of Israel and its Western backers, with the struggle over Palestine and the Golan legitimizing the construction of a national security state. Syria's role as a front-line state entitled it to considerable Arab aid in the 1970s, which enabled the consolidation of Hafiz al-Asad's regime but also fueled the overdevelopment of the state relative to its economic base. Once aid declined and the public sector was exhausted as an engine of capital accumulation, evident from the economic crisis of the late 1980s, economic growth barely kept up with population, resulting in burgeoning youth unemployment. By the 1990s a consensus emerged in the regime that private investment was the only solution to the exhaustion of Syria's statist economy, but the elite was divided over how far and how fast to proceed. Indeed, this regime was highly resistant to economic liberalization: the Ba'th Party institutionalized a populist ideology distrustful of the private sector; regime insiders reaped wealth from their control of the state and their ability to extort a share of wealth from private business; the business class benefited from state contracts and thus did not welcome a state withdrawal from the market; and the political legitimacy of the regime rested on its provision of subsidized food and employment to its plebeian constituency.

Finally, the regime's main adaptations under Hafiz to the economic crisis were austerity in the 1980s that starved the public sector and ran down social benefits, wage freezes that together with inflation slashed the earning power of the state-employed middle class, and a drop in military spending from about 18 percent of gross national product in 1976–88 to 7 percent in the 1990s (Huuhtanen 2008). Even as the regime was thus targeting its own constituents, state import monopolies were turned over to the private sector and a new investment law was promulgated to entice private and foreign investment. These measures revived the private sector as an engine of growth, thus appeasing the bourgeoisie, parts of which were incorporated into the regime support base. In this late Hafiz period, however, the regime continued to carefully balance between its old constituencies and its emerging new ones.

Succession, Struggle for Power, and Legitimizing Discourses of Bashar al-Asad's Rule

Bashar al-Asad's project, on his accession to power, was to further open up the Syrian economy and adapt it to the age of globalization through measures such as modernization of the banking system, opening of a stock market, and promotion of the Internet. Initially he had to share power with the "old guard" that was wary of change while also facing demands for political liberalization from democracy activists. Asad's struggle to consolidate power therefore took place at several levels: intraregime, state-society, intraregional, and international.

At the elite level, Asad sought to overcome resistance to his reform project and centralize power in the presidency in an extended struggle with an old guard entrenched in the party "politburo," the Regional Command. As detailed in Raymond Hinnebusch's contribution to this volume (chapter 2), Bashar al-Asad accomplished this goal by using presidential powers to retire the elder generation, inserting his loyalists in the army and security forces, and engaging in a tug-of-war with the party over control of government, legislation, and implementation of economic reform. His strategy was to co-opt moderate economic reformers into government, while inside the party he also engineered a turnover in leadership and cadres that culminated in the 2005 Tenth Regional Party Congress. As a result power was concentrated in the presidency and the Asad family at the expense of the old-guard centers of power. But in uprooting the regime barons, Asad inadvertently weakened the regime itself. The party, the regime's connection to its constituency, was also weakened: it was infiltrated by elements with conflicting orientations, and the reduction in benefits for members eroded recruitment.

Parallel to his subordination of the party and the old guard, Asad continued to co-opt into his coalition reforming technocrats and businessmen that supported his economic reforms, and thereby he significantly altered the regime's social base (see part two). In some ways this shift in constituencies re-empowered authoritarianism through the incorporation of previously hostile capitalist elements into the regime coalition; moreover, dependent on the regime for business opportunities such as contracts and licenses, for the disciplining of the working class, and for the rollback of populism, these elements had no interest in a democratization that could have allowed the losers in the process (workers, peasants, state employees) to block economic liberalization. At the heart of the regime coalition emerged a new class of "crony capitalists"—the rent-seeking alliances of political brokers (led by Asad's mother's family, the Makhloufs) and the regime-supportive bourgeoisie that thrived on the combination of limited economic liberalization and profitable partnerships with external investors. Thus the regime aimed to survive the incremental transition to a (partial?) market economy by creating its "own" crony capitalists, at the cost, however, of discouraging more productive capital.

The ideological discourse promoted by the regime sought to derive legitimacy from dual bases, as Aurora Sottimano and Samer Abboud show in chapters 3 and 4. For the regime's traditional constituency and the general public, the "old" nationalist discourse was deployed, amid US and Israeli threats to Syria, to fend off calls for political reform (see analysis below under the heading Inside-Outside Dynamics for further details). For its new bourgeois constituency and international donors, there was the "new" discourse of economic modernization and reform. Both authors dissect the regime's attempt, by positing the goal of reform as a "social market economy," to reassure *both* those fearing the abandonment of the populist social contract and those keen for reform. Their analyses show that, in practice, this concept had little content, and regime policy was little distinguishable from neoliberalism with its priority on capital accumulation and growth to the neglect of equality and distribution. Investment and employment responsibility were shifted to the private sector, and although the state in principle recognized its responsibility to invest in health, education, and social security, fiscal austerity obstructed it from taking action in these fields; rather, the regime tried to get private charities and NGOs (nongovernmental organizations) to take responsibility for social protections. The Chinese model of spreading the private sector and the market while retaining a reformed public sector was in principle embraced but in fact the public sector was not reformed, was run down, and was partially privatized by turning over enterprises to private management (Lust-Okar 2006). The sector ceased to provide employment and pensions that Syrians were used to relying on. The managers of the new private banks and businesses earned high salaries, and taxation became regressive as income tax reductions for the rich were compensated for by cuts in subsidies on food and heating oil, inflicting hardship on low-income citizens. A new labor law ended what "reformers" considered "overprotection" of workers even though the labor movement had always been very weak in the private sector. Investment did flow into Syria but it was predominately in tertiary sectors (only 13 percent of investment after 2000 was in manufacturing) and did not provide nearly enough jobs to compensate for cuts in public employment.

Sociopolitical Consequences:
Restructuring the Regime's Social Base

At the societal level, Bashar al-Asad faced several waves of dissidence, beginning with the Damascus Spring (2001) and breaking out again in 2005, that demanded an end of the emergency law and a multiparty system with competitive elections. The regime was readily able to contain the secular liberal opposition, centered in the professional classes, which suffered from fragmentation, resource scarcity, and relative isolation from mass society. However, Najib Ghadbian's chapter (chapter 5) documents how, over time, opposition alliances emerged across the secular-Islamist divide and also incorporated Kurds (as the Arab majority groups acknowledged their rights), seeking to counter the regime's claim that there was no viable opposition to it except Islamist extremism and Iraqi-like civil war. But they failed to create a mass movement that could drive political reform. Asad tried to legitimize his shutdown of the Damascus Spring of 2001 by arguing that Western democracy could not just be imported and that democratization had to build upon social and economic modernization rather than precede it; he attempted to discredit the second 2005 wave by accusing the opposition of treasonous association with the parallel Western siege of Syria. The opposition tried to use new global media such as satellite TV, which the regime countered by jamming—triggering, literally, a "proxy war" when the opposition used foreign proxy servers to circumvent the digital barricade.

The main political innovation accompanying the liberalization of economic policy was the reversal of the former populist bias in the regime's corporatist system: investors got increased access to policy-makers while the popular syndicates, which formerly represented workers and peasants, were now used to demobilize them. At the same time, as Tina Zintl details in chapter 6, efforts were made to co-opt urban middle-class civil society through the establishment of several development-promoting NGOs under the patronage of Syrian First Lady Asma al-Asad. With the decline of regime patronage resources, co-optation was restructured in a more "efficient," elitist way toward entrepreneurs and professionals, especially those with purely technocratic, that is, non-regime-threatening, international connections. A parallel strategy was the creation of a Ministry of Expatriates to encourage the return of migrants from the West who helped to shift discourse in favor of the reformist camp. Their influence can, for example, be traced in the licensing of several private universities, some founded in cooperation with foreign partners that attracted home and employed foreign-educated Syrians. This fostering and co-opting of secular segments of Syrian society aimed at balancing the increasing parallel rise of a moderate, nonpolitical Islamic civil society that the regime also sponsored. Thus the regime was able to balance above a divided civil society.

Iconic of another double strategy of the regime, a typical manifestation of "authoritarian upgrading," was the mixed message to which students in Syria's schools were exposed: on the one hand, the party-affiliated Revolutionary Youth Union still organized them and they still recited the party's socialist slogans; on the other hand, the president's wife encouraged "young entrepreneurs" to think about setting up their own businesses. In chapter 7 Mandy Terc details how volunteerism and entrepreneurial activities among the upper strata were encouraged to fill the gap left by the decline of the states' developmental role and social services and as a regime-friendly alternative to the Islamist charity networks that had proliferated under the regime's tolerance. But the activities of the upper-class youth organizations, she recounts, reflected the massive accumulated inequalities of wealth that had become conspicuous under Bashar al-Asad. The empowerment of private schools, universities, and medical facilities for the new rich paralleled the running down of public services for ordinary citizens and the changing social base of the regime. Especially ironic is that the most prestigious elite school was the American one, its highly Westernized, internationalized, and English-speaking students displaying a patronizing attitude toward the popular classes. Terc's snapshot suggests why the urban upper classes aligned with the regime and the peripheries with the revolt against it.

Regime-Islamist relations were central to the regime's authoritarian upgrading, too. The Ba'th regime developed an ambivalent relationship with Syria's Islamist milieu, traditionally the strongest concentration of opposition to it that had mounted a major insurrection in the early 1980s. Paolo Pinto shows in chapter 8 how, particularly after that rebellion, Hafiz al-Asad sought a modus vivendi with Islamist currents. In particular, he struck an alliance with moderate Sufi Islam, notably through the appointment of Ahmad Kuftaro as Grand Mufti, which enabled Kuftaro to expand his *naqshbandiyya* Sufi order and his al-Nur Institute in Damascus. Also, Muhammad Sa'id al-Buti, a moderate Islamic preacher with a wide following who opposed Muslim Brotherhood attacks on Ba'th Party officials and 'Alawites in the late 1970s, played a vital role in bridging the gap between the Sunni community and the regime and, in return, was given exceptional access to the media.

The influence of Islam increased toward the end of the Hafiz period and continued under Bashar, evident in the plethora of Islamic organizations, primary schools, colleges, charitable associations, conservative attire, mosque attendance, and domination of bookstores by Islamic literature. A liberal modernist movement, Tajdeed (Renewal), was led by Shaykh Muhammad Habash, who was elected to parliament. Also highly influential were the "sisters" of Shaykha Munira al-Qubaysi, officially recognized by the state in May 2006, which spread Islamic teaching among wealthy Damascene women. This mainstream Islam was largely nonpolitical, preaching the need to concentrate on the *dawa*, rejecting violence and intolerance, calling for constructive criticism within the system, and mobilizing around nonpolitical issues such as alcohol-free public spaces and opposition to liberal reforms of the Syrian family law (Khatib 2011).

Bashar al-Asad opened a new phase of relations based on further accommodation with moderate Islam as a counter to both radical Islamists and the secular opposition. This shift was reflected in the (temporary) lifting of a government ban on teachers' and students' wearing full-face veils, the release of imprisoned Muslim Brotherhood activists, public celebrations of Islamic feast days, and co-optation of more Islamist intellectuals and businessmen into parliament (ibid.). While the outlook of the 'ulama, recruited from the suq merchant class, was sharply at odds with Ba'thist socialism, it was convergent with the regime's new neoliberal tangent: Most 'ulama, at least in the cities, professed a bourgeois ethic that despised begging, rejected state interventions in the economy, and saw the acquisition of wealth as a sign of God's favor, with only a minority of 'ulama expressing solidarity with the poor (Pierret forthcoming). The 'ulama were permitted to preach Islamic economics and to manage the growing charities and financial institutions allowed by the regime to attract money from the Gulf. Bashar also made a concerted effort to build alliances with the interlocked business and religious elite of formerly oppositionist Aleppo, which benefited from the economic opening to Turkey that brought in new investment. Finally, during the height of the Western pressures on Syria over Iraq and Lebanon, the regime was also able to mobilize religious-tinged patriotism under the slogan "God protects you, Oh Syria" (see chapter 8).

Accommodation of Islam was paralleled by efforts to control it. Most 'ulama were financially independent of the state, but the regime controlled the appointments of top positions, such as muftis and imams of the big mosques, and took advantage of the fragmentation of the Islamic public sphere, for example between Damascus and Aleppo, and among multiple networks of preachers, Sufi orders, conservative imams, and modernists, further dividing them by favoring some and repressing others. The state also regulated financial flows to Islamic charitable associations. Accommodation with the regime accorded Islamic groups the freedom and resources to spread their networks but it also risked loss of credibility with the public. Because the boundaries between what was prohibited and what was permitted were not clear, Islamic actors needed brokers in the regime while, in parallel, the regime was also divided between conservative Islam-friendly elements and secularists; as such, alliances cut across the regime-society divide, including between branches of the security services and Islamist groups or clerics, diluting regime-Islamic polarization (Donker 2010). The downside for the regime was that Salafi Islam tended to expand at the expense of the traditionally dominant Sufi tendency (ICG 2011). Having encouraged Islamism, the regime itself began in 2008 to reintroduce limits on it, for example, on public displays of piety and wearing of the full-face veil in state educational institutions, as well as to extend controls over Islamic institutions and charities, even including the Kuftaros. This action, however, sparked a mobilization of Islamist leaders that forced a partial backing down, particularly once the uprising began (Khatib 2011).

The regime's policies undermined secularism and empowered an Islamic current that could never be wholly trusted by a minority-dominated regime; yet, these developments also alarmed secularists, women, and minorities, who therefore looked to the regime for protection. Rania Maktabi's research on the struggle over Syria's personal status law exposes both the benefits and the risks for the regime of its simultaneous empowerment of rival secular and Islamic constituencies (chapter 9). In the first five years of Bashar al-Asad's presidency, the women's union and educated woman activists, no doubt encouraged by the Westernized First Lady, used Syria's adhesion to the UN convention on elimination of discrimination against women to promote liberal reform, including a campaign against femicide. Conservative Islamic religious leaders led a backlash that extracted the formation of a secret committee on revising the personal status law whose proposals would have marked a regression even compared to Syria's 1953 law. Women, secular intellectuals, and liberal clergy mobilized against it via the Internet, forcing the government on the defensive. In this conflict, an 'Alawite-led regime had, in taking a position, to guard against charges of Islamic impiety; but it was also bolstered by the secular backlash against the Islamists' overly conservative proposal. The stand of the Ba'thist women's union and the Ministry of Justice on opposite sides of this controversy exposed how contrary interests had colonized different branches of the regime, allowing it to both co-opt and mediate rival forces.

The most dramatic outcome of Bashar al-Asad's decade as president was the virtual abandonment of the regime's historic plebeian constituency, especially its rural component. Myriam Ababsa details in chapter 10 the consequences of the terrible drought of 2007–9, comparable to that of 1958, which is widely considered to have been responsible for the breakup of the United Arab Republic. She shows that the drought was not just owing to the lack of rainfall but also to corrupt mismanagement, leading to a drying up of groundwater due to overpumping. It led to a mass exodus from villages in the Jezira to the suburbs of the big cities. At the same time, she argues, the privatization of the land of state farms allowed tribal elites and urban entrepreneurs to reestablish larger holdings in the age-old process of buying up the small plots of peasants lacking the means to cultivate their lands. Although more research on the issue is needed, it seems likely that, in neglecting the system of agricultural planning, subsidized inputs, and support prices developed in the 1970s, the regime was left unprepared to cope with the worst effects of the drought. Yet in addition to drought and mismanagement it appears that with population growth on fixed land, the burgeoning younger generations who did not inherit land were increasingly excluded from the regime system of cooperatives and subsidies, hence from its rural constituency.

The urban lower and middle classes were similarly negatively affected. Poor neighborhoods around the cities expanded inexorably with the influx of rural victims of the droughts but also because of Iraqi refugees. Though the Iraqi refugees' crisis was dealt with fairly successfully, as Muhammad Kamel Doraï and Martine Zeuthen demonstrate in chapter 12, the massive influx and prolonged sojourn of these refugees had a considerable influence on Damascus's urban fabric. In parallel, urban real estate speculation unleashed by the influx of capital from the Gulf countries, together with an end to rent controls as part of a liberalization of the market, also drove up the cost of housing for the middle strata.

Overall, during the first decade of the twenty-first century, the regime's authoritarian upgrading was fairly effective in diluting the opposition by co-opting modernizing technocrats and using parliamentary elections, albeit boycotted by many, to incorporate urban notables, while activists were kept off balance by shifting redlines as to what was permitted and by attempts to sow distrust among them. Yet, in the long run, divisions became too deep and co-optation was too shallow, so the ability of Bashar al-Asad to balance above, and to control, Syrian politics and society became ever more limited toward the end of the decade.

Inside-Outside Dynamics: Accessing Legitimacy and Rent

As Carsten Wieland shows in chapter 11, there is always a link between the international and the domestic in Syria. The first link is the need to generate external rent and other economic resources. Bashar al-Asad's domestic economic liberalization was initially to be empowered by a tilt toward a West-centric foreign policy manifest in an opening to Western Europe that would create the conditions for an influx of investment. However, the international context for this project rapidly deteriorated owing to the collapse of the peace process with Israel and the parallel souring of Syrian-US relations. To fill the gap left by the dimming of prospects for foreign investment, Syria pursued an opening to Iraq, which boosted its earnings from receipt of oil through the Syrian-Iraqi oil pipeline, but at the cost of antagonizing Washington. Syria not only opposed the US war on Iraq but also facilitated the passage of anti-US fighters through its territory; given the arousal of the Syrian public against the US invasion, the regime had no choice but to oppose it even had it wished to bandwagon with Washington. Syria was saved from US retribution by the costs of America's occupation of Iraq, but US-imposed sanctions, aiming to economically isolate Syria, discouraged Western investment and caused difficulties for the financial services and telecommunications industries by which the regime sought to propel the globalization of the Syrian economy. Relations with Europe were another temporary casualty of the regime's foreign policy, after the assassination of Lebanese Prime Minister Rafiq al-Hariri in 2005 was blamed on Syria. The European Union had become Syria's main trading partner in the 1990s after the end of the Soviet bloc, but the increasingly united Western front against Syria underlined the political vulnerability of this West-centric trade concentration and accelerated Syria's efforts to diversify trade relations. After the Iraq war, during the height of Western political and military pressure, Syrian foreign trade actually increased significantly, albeit shifted toward China, Iran, and Turkey under bilateral trade agreements as well as toward the Arab world under the Greater Arab Free Trade Association (GAFTA).

The regime was also fortunate that the years of pressure from without were good years for oil exports, whose value doubled between 2000 and

2005 because of high prices and oil trade with Iraq, enabling the regime to build up a reserve of official foreign assets of around US$17 billion, an economic security buffer that reached 68 percent of GDP in 2002. However, urgency was given to economic reform by the projected exhaustion of Syria's oil reserves, threatening the fiscal base of the state. The regime thus made a concerted drive to evade Western isolation by attracting Arab, expatriate, and non-Western investment: new laws liberalized trade and foreign exchange, reduced tax rates, opened most fields to private investment, allowed capital repatriation, and relaxed labor protections. The introduction of private banking and a stock market aimed to mobilize savings for investment, notably from expatriates. In fact, the proportion of GDP generated in the private sector steadily rose and foreign direct investment (FDI) boomed, reaching $1.6 billion in 2006.[1] In 2005, the year the regime experienced its most extreme isolation from the West, Syria was the fourth largest recipient of Arab investment. Investment inflows drove a private-sector boom in trade, housing, banking, construction, and tourism. The economy grew at a rate of 5 percent in 2006 and at 4 percent in 2007 as well as in 2008 despite declining oil output. The inflow satisfied the crony capitalists around the regime, and improved tax collection enabled the treasury to extract a share of this growth (Abboud 2009; Huuhtanen 2008; Leverett 2005, 86–87).

The other main connection between inside and outside is that successes in foreign policy and resistance to external enemies have always been pivotal to generating legitimacy for the regime while foreign policy failures have eroded that legitimacy, as Sottimano's and Pinto's contributions indicate. Asad's stand against the Iraq war won him a windfall of political capital that helped consolidate his regime. The fall of Saddam Hussein's regime was, however, the occasion of demands by the loyal opposition for a national unity government to resist US imperialism, which the

---

1. United Nations Conference on Trade and Development, *World Investment Report 2004–2006*. According to official Syrian figures in 2005, 36 percent of all investments in Syria (licensed by the Investment Bureau) were foreign. "Foreigners Represent a Third of All Investments," *Tishreen*, Mar. 18, 2006.

regime declined to accommodate, arguably a first missed opportunity to begin political liberalization when it enjoyed rising nationalist credentials. The Iraq war also stimulated an Islamic revival, which the regime used to strike a détente with the main opposition, Islamic forces. Additionally, the chaos and sectarian conflict in Iraq, together with the fear—ignited by the Kurdish riots of 2004 and by the rise of Islamic militancy—that the "Iraqi disease" could spread to Syria, led the public to put a high premium on stability. The influx of Iraqi refugees was, as detailed by Doraï and Zeuthen in chapter 12, highly visible in certain quarters of Damascus, and also the confessional instability in Lebanon underlined the regime's message that security and stability take precedence over freedom. This message generated for the regime what might be called "legitimacy because of a worse alternative."

However, the continuing US pressures on Syria to cut off the flow of fighters to the Iraqi resistance, the Hariri Tribunal indictments, Syria's growing international isolation, and especially its forced and humiliating 2005 evacuation of Lebanon, encouraged the opposition to think the regime might be vulnerable to pressure for reform or even regime change. This situation induced them to join ranks with exiles, including the Muslim Brothers and purged former vice president Khaddam (once the senior Sunni Ba'thist in the regime), as well as the opposition in Lebanon to promulgate the "Damascus Declaration" demanding political reform. The regime resolutely rebuffed this demand as treasonous, being unwilling to experiment with internal changes under external threat. The opposition petered out, having little resonance with the Syrian public at this time and divided between a minority willing to be associated with the United States, who were discredited, and a majority that was not. Indeed, the association of democracy discourse with the US project of regional hegemony and its negative demonstration effects in Iraq and Lebanon diluted the extent to which it might otherwise have empowered Syrian civil society against authoritarianism. Thereafter the regime's nationalist legitimacy was replenished after its Hezbollah ally successfully resisted Israel's 2006 attack on Lebanon. With Syria's identity as a "confrontational state" in the conflict with Israel deeply ingrained in public thinking, as Sottimano's chapter shows, Israeli attacks on Lebanon and Gaza shocked the Syrian population into rallying behind Asad. Likewise, the regime's championing of the Palestine cause and the basing of Hamas's external leadership in Damascus was popular domestically, as Valentina Napolitano illustrates in chapter 13. In parallel, Hezbollah's 2008 power play in Beirut demonstrated the futility of trying to isolate Syria and broke the Western siege of Damascus, with French President Sarkozy leading Syria's rehabilitation and the Bush administration departing office. Asad's success in breaking international isolation might have provided the confidence and occasion for an opening to the opposition, but, instead, the regime appears to have seen it as an opportunity to move against dissent. As Carsten Wieland points out, this was another lost opportunity to broaden the base of the regime by co-opting secular nationalist opposition at a time when regime nationalist legitimacy was high.

Each of the following chapters details a different aspect of authoritarian upgrading under Bashar al-Asad's first decade, 2000–2010. While each of the measures taken by the regime and detailed in the chapters was meant either to fix vulnerabilities inherited from regime formation under Hafiz al-Asad or to respond to new challenges posed in a globalizing world, each of them also had its costs as well. Their costs and the new vulnerabilities that regime policies generated can be seen as the *seeds* of the uprising. Additionally, however, the nature of the regime, its upgrading strategy, and the reaction to it by different societal actors also explain the peculiar *tangent* the uprising took, one that, by contrast to other cases, led not to a fairly quick removal of the incumbent president, but rather to an increasingly violent civil war. In the following chapters the authors will, after treating a particular aspect of the 2000–2010 decade, also point to its consequences for the uprising. These findings will be summarized in the conclusion, which seeks to relate the 2000–2010 period to what unfolded beginning in 2011.

PART ONE

Reproducing Power and Legitimacy

2

President and Party in Post-Ba'thist Syria

From the Struggle for "Reform"
to Regime Deconstruction

RAYMOND HINNEBUSCH

For the first five years of Bashar al-Asad's presidency, the Ba'th Party was a rival center of power, slowing Bashar's reformist agenda. A struggle for power ensued over control of the levers of state power, that is, the military, security forces, and government. The president ultimately prevailed and the old guard was swept from power, replaced by Asad loyalists, a watershed in steering the country into a "post-Ba'thist" period in which the old system was dying but had not been replaced by an effective new system of governance. While by the second half of the decade Bashar had strengthened the presidency (and the Asad clan), he had weakened the regime as a whole, since Asad's new elites lacked the stature and the clientele networks of the old guard. Simultaneously, Asad's weakening of the Ba'th Party enervated the regime connection to its former rural base, leaving it dependent on the loyalty of the new elites generated by "economic reform."

Regime Formation and the Historic Role of the Ba'th Party

The Ba'th Party played the decisive role in the rise of the Syrian regime that Bashar al-Asad inherited in 2000. In the 1950s and 1960s, the party recruited a generation of activists, many from minority, peasant, or rural

21

petit-bourgeois families, some of whom went into the army. The party's capture of the army enabled its 1963 seizure of power, and party officers used their control of the army military organization to dominate the party after 1966. The party was crucial to giving the Ba'th regime, besieged in the cities, a rural power base and was a key mobilizational instrument in the carrying out of its revolution from above, especially in the countryside.

Hafiz al-Asad's coup ushered in the consolidation of the Ba'th regime. Asad concentrated power in a "presidential monarchy" above the party. He used his control of the army to free himself of Ba'th ideological constraints and placed a core of largely 'Alawite personal followers in the security apparatus to give him autonomy of the army. Secure in control of the party and army, he appeased the private bourgeoisie through limited economic liberalization and fostered a state-dependent new bourgeoisie to create another leg of support. At the top of the power pyramid, elements of the Damascene Sunni bourgeoisie entered into tacit alliances with 'Alawite military elites, the foundation of a new class, while at the base the party and its auxiliaries incorporated a popular following from both Sunni and non-Sunni villages; thus, Asad built a cross-sectarian, cross-class coalition, whose effectiveness proved itself in defeating the major Islamic fundamentalist uprising of 1978–82. To stabilize the regime, Asad also depended on external resources: Soviet arms to build up the army and Arab oil money with which he expanded the bureaucracy and co-opted the bourgeoisie. The legitimacy of his regime was in good part based on its relative success in the struggle with Israel, beginning with the 1973 Arab-Israeli war (Dawisha 1978; Hinnebusch 2001, chap. 4).

Under Hafiz, the party still played a pivotal role in the regime, albeit subordinated to the presidency. Under the 1973 constitution it was accorded a privileged leading role that later became a matter of controversy. Though high policy was the prerogative of the president, he normally concentrated on foreign and security policy and left the details of economic matters to be decided between the party and government technocrats. Nor was the party, in contrast to Egypt's flimsy state parties, a mere creation of the regime, having had a long history as an ideological movement before coming to power. In power, it developed an elaborate institutionalized apparatus, based on Leninist practices of selective recruitment and indoctrination of militants from the lower and lower-middle strata, which penetrated schools, factories, and villages and was linked to society by an array of corporatist "popular organizations" (*munazzamat sha'biyya*) of peasants, youth, women, and workers. These organizations, which were given privileged access to decision-makers denied to the bourgeoisie until the 1980s, accorded popular sectors some means to resist creeping economic liberalization measures damaging to their interests. Generally, the Ba'th Party institutionalized the regime's populist-statist thrust: it incorporated constituencies that, initially possessed of little property, had a stake in statist policies—a big public sector, cooperative agriculture, populist regulation of the market—which was part of the "social contract" on which regime legitimacy was contingent. As an elite recruitment pathway (along with the army) for peasant youth and minorities, the party sustained the initial cleavage between the social composition of the Ba'th state and the recovering bourgeoisie, the main social force pushing for economic liberalization, notably from the 1980s.

After 2000, Bashar al-Asad found the party the main obstacle to his economic "reforms," but he could not readily shunt it aside: it remained the regime's main connection to the provinces and villages, its original power base; additionally, the 'Alawite dominance of the ruling elite made the party all the more crucial to the regime's capacity to sustain support among Syria's Sunni majority.

Regime Power Structures

The Syrian Ba'th regime, and the presidency that heads it, rested on three overlapping pillars of power: the party apparatus, the military-police establishment, and the ministerial bureaucracy. The president, also party general secretary and armed forces commander in chief, held the legal and political reins of all three pillars of power, had numerous powers of command and appointment, and was the main source of policy innovation. Second only to the presidency in policy-making power was the Ba'th

Party's "Regional Command" (RC) (*al-qiyadah al-qutriyah*),[1] the top collegial leadership body, roughly divided between senior military commanders, the most powerful cabinet ministers, and top party apparatchiks. It endorsed policy initiatives and controlled the party apparatus, which systematically penetrated other institutions of state and civil society. The Council of Ministers (cabinet or government) was headed by a prime minister jointly appointed by the president and the RC, and assembled some thirty ministers who implemented policy through the ministerial bureaucracy. The regime manipulated the composition of the parliament, with a majority of the seats reserved for candidates of the Ba'th Party; hence parliament normally approved the initiatives of the executive branch. Under Bashar al-Asad the presidency became the origin of a spate of economic reform proposals, often delayed by the party but eventually approved by parliament and formally, although in practice often ineffectively, implemented by the Council of Ministers through the state bureaucracy.

The military was a main pillar of the regime. When in 1963 Ba'th officers brought the party to power, they inevitably became an equal partner in the new military-party state. However, Hafiz al-Asad, with a foot in both (as a former air force commander), became the first Syrian leader to maintain firm control over the military. As legal commander in chief, the president controlled appointments and dismissals of senior officers. In presidential guard units or special forces primarily charged with regime defense, appointments were based on political loyalty to and ('Alawite) sectarian or family affiliation with the president. 'Alawite Ba'th officers also held a disproportionate number of top operational commands, especially of coup-making armored units. The Ba'th Party's military organization exercised political control over military members and gave them some voice in party institutions, with about one-third of the members of the party Regional Congress representing the military branches (Drysdale 1979, 359–73).

---

1. "Regional," in Ba'th parlance, denotes the institutions of Syria, a *region* of the wider Arab nation. The Ba'th Party also has "national" institutions at the Pan-Arab level, which in theory but not in practice are superior to its regional bodies.

The regime maintained multiple intelligence or security services (*mukhabarat*), whose function was surveillance of possible threats to the regime from external enemies, the opposition, the army, and each other; they vetted all candidates for office and promotion, kept files on everyone's peccadilloes and loyalty, and, after the Islamist insurgency of the 1970s and 1980s, assumed extralegal powers. While they were instruments through which the president controlled the other regime power centers and while they were formally supervised by the RC Office of National Security, they were centers of initiative in political matters and powerful political brokers in their own right whose support ambitious politicians and prominent businessmen sought. The president, however, periodically removed security chiefs to prevent them from establishing fiefdoms autonomous of his control or when they pushed their self-aggrandizement too far.

The top party organ was the fifteen-member Regional Command, Syria's top collective leadership; it presided over the party apparatus through an array of offices for internal party organization and finance that administered the branches in the regions, while military and security bureaus oversaw those in these services. In addition, bureaus for peasants and agriculture, economy, education, workers, and youth controlled the wider society. Each office of the Regional Command had a subordinate counterpart at the provincial branch and subbranch levels, constituting a vertical line of command throughout Syria through which the party supervised the bureaucracy at all levels of the administration as well as the popular syndicates to ensure they operated within the party line.

The Regional Command was selected from the Syrian Regional Congress (made up in 2005 of 1,200 delegates), a main arena in which intraregime ideological and later bureaucratic conflicts were compromised, elite turnover engineered, and the stamp of approval given to major new policies. The Regional Congress also elected a Central Committee, whose ninety members included party functionaries, ministers, senior military officers, security barons, governors, heads of syndicates, and university presidents, and was in many ways the political elite assembled.

The party organization was a pyramid rising on a base consisting of more than 11,000 cells (*halaqat*) grouped in about 1,400 basic units (*firaq*) located in villages, factories, neighborhoods, and public institutions.

These units formed 154 subbranches at the district (*mintiqah*) or town level, and were further grouped into eighteen branches (*furu'*) in the provinces (*muhafazat*), big cities, and major institutions (such as universities). A parallel structure of branches existed inside the army and security services. Under party rules, party organs convened every five years, starting at the base level, to pass resolutions and elect delegates to higher-level assemblies, culminating in the national-level policy-making Regional Congress. In this process, ambitious local politicians needed a patron at the top to move up very far in the party hierarchy, but also had to cultivate constituents to win the local-level election needed to catch the attention of higher-ups; as such, delegates to various-level congresses sometimes arrived armed with resolutions reflecting the wishes of their constituents, and the leadership reports to the congresses, which formed the basis of their debates, sometimes incorporated such input from below. In the 1980s, however, and especially after the Muslim Brotherhood rebellion, elections ceased to turn on issues, official candidates were nominated from above and dissidents purged, alternative candidates ceased to be tolerated, and the security forces became pivotal to vetting and sponsoring candidates and neutralizing activists' attempt to challenge incumbent officeholders. From the mid-1980s to 2000, the cycle of party elections was put on hold, with incumbents frozen in office and inner-party life largely deadened until Bashar al-Asad revived it in the late 1990s.

Presidential Succession and the Intra-elite Struggle for Power

Bashar al-Asad's rise to power completed the process Hafiz had begun of establishing his son as his successor. For the first time since the revolution, the president did not have a significant previous history in party politics. Yet the succession was collectively engineered by the regime elite who, holding the top party and army positions, closed ranks to preserve regime stability and prevent an intra-elite power struggle, with the initial decrees investing Bashar with power issued by the senior Ba'thist and First Vice President Abdul Halim Khaddam and Defense Minister Mustafa Tlas. As an Asad, Bashar reassured the 'Alawites, was expected to defend his father's heritage, and, politically inexperienced, was not thought to threaten the incumbent elite. He was, moreover, initially dependent on their support, which was given on the condition that he share power with them. Among the public, especially the younger generation, he was popular, seen as uncorrupted and, in fact, he came to power with an agenda to modernize the regime (Lesch 2005). However, when during the Damascus Spring (2001), opposition activists, whom Bashar had encouraged in order to strengthen his hand in pushing a reformist agenda, began to challenge the regime itself, he realized his dependency on the party to sustain his authority.[2] As a result, while under Hafiz the party had been firmly subordinated to the presidency, in the vacuum left by his death its power briefly revived. A balance of power between the presidency and the party, in which each both needed and constrained the other, spelled a certain revival of institutions after Hafiz's personal rule.

Indeed, the 2000 elections to the long-delayed Ninth Ba'th Party Regional Congress, which had begun before Hafiz's death, both reflected and defined this power balance. Bashar had used his father's party authority to liberalize the elections in a process called "consulting" (*istinass*) in which congresses at lower levels nominated *several* candidates for the executive posts of their organizations and the RC chose leaders from among these. Bashar hoped to use liberalized elections as a way of calling corrupt figures in the old guard to account, injecting new blood into the party, and inserting his own allies into leadership positions. However, while the membership took the opportunity to remove many leaders that had been in office for the long years in which there had been no elections (five standing ministers lost reelection and two-thirds of the Central Committee were newcomers), they were replaced by local notables and careerists, albeit of a younger generation, rather than activists committed to reform; an alarmed Bashar stopped the elections at the branch-level congresses and co-opted a Regional Congress and Regional Command in a compromise between various power centers.

Importantly, those not returned in the elections were the once powerful intelligence bosses and close associates of Hafiz, Ali Duba (Military

---

2. *Middle East International*, Sept. 1, 2000, 15.

Intelligence) and Muhammad Khuli (Air Force Intelligence), men whose networks had reached into every corner of society, while newcomers included younger Republican guard officers and friends of Asad, Mahar al-Asad, and Manaf Tlas. Twelve of the twenty-one members of the RC were newcomers. Also important was the fall of Izz ad-Din Nasser, a Khaddam associate who had made the trade unions a formidable base of power from which he built a fiefdom in the public sector industry; his fall signaled a loss of power for organized labor and the public sector industry, notably their ability to obstruct economic liberalization, but it also marked the weakening of the patronage network that had tied the organized working class to the regime. The election of newcomers Foreign Minister Farouk al-Shara' and Prime Minister Mustafa Miro ratified their arrival at the top of state institutions. The new RC was split between supporters of Vice President Khaddam, Prime Minister Miro, and Bashar; Bashar's men, having reached their positions more from his patronage than from support within the party machine, lacked stature and were, to an extent, isolated within the RC by the old guard. Then, the death of the former president in June 2000 opened the way for the congress to elect Bashar as party general secretary, enabling the Regional Command to subsequently nominate him for election by parliament as president.[3]

The Struggle for "Economic Reform"

Bashar al-Asad set out to make the presidency an instrument of major internal reform, something that his father, who built the system to conduct foreign policy, largely did not attempt. However, the separation of power between presidency and RC meant that Asad could only decide some issues unilaterally, and where RC approval was required and there was no consensus, policy-making was paralyzed; hence a struggle for power between the presidency and the RC over reform inevitably emerged.[4] In

3. *Middle East International*, Sept. 1, 2000, 15; *Daily Star*, June 15, 2000; *UPI*, June 26, 2000.
4. "Interview with Syria's President," Jan. 12, 2003, nytimes.com/2003/12/01.

this struggle, the presidency had enormous constitutional powers, above all appointment/promotion and dismissal/retirement powers over the bureaucracy and the military, which enabled Asad to gradually retire old-guard officials and bring in a younger generation more beholden to him. Three-quarters of the top sixty-odd officials in political, security, and administrative ranks were replaced by the end of 2002 (Perthes 2004).

The first key to power for Asad was to secure control of the security forces and the military. Hostile members of the old guard had been purged before his father's death, allowing Bashar to appoint their successors, including his brother-in-law Asef Shawqat, while a survivor, Bahjat Sulayman, became Bashar's key ally. In the army the president exercised his uncontested power to retire the older generation and promote younger, second-rank 'Alawite officers who were beholden to him.[5] As the coercive pillars of the state were secured, the contest shifted to the administrative and political institutions. However, the president enjoyed no comparable power of appointment over the party (where posts were nominally elective), and his proposals for an extraordinary congress to enable new elections were blocked by the RC. Nor could his control of the coercive apparatus readily be used against the party, which he referred to as analogous to resorting to a nuclear weapon. This situation shifted the struggle for reform to control of the government (that is, the Council of Ministers and career bureaucracy).

The incongruence between the generational and ideological change in the presidency and the considerable continuity in the party leadership was reflected in struggles between the president and the party RC over appointment of the four governments from 2000 to 2005. In each case, Asad sought to bring in younger, technocratic, less corrupt or ideological, and more liberal ministers, either non-Ba'thists or Ba'thist reformers. However, the Ba'thist share of ministerial portfolios never declined, indicative of the very incremental nature of elite circulation. This reflected the fact that the presidency and the RC shared powers over appointment of governments. Asad managed to negotiate an increase in his own relative

---

5. *Middle East International*, July 14, 2000, 10–12.

powers under which the presidency would present the RC with three names for each cabinet post, which it would reduce to two for each, leaving the final choice to the president. Choices of ministers were made on the basis of loyalty but also on such criteria as confessional and regional balance (for example, a proportion of Damascene Sunnis); representation of the various parties in the pro-regime alliance of parties, the National Progressive Front (NPF); and the need for competent "technocrats" in ministries requiring specialized expertise.

In Bashar al-Asad's first cabinet reshuffle after assuming the presidency, when the RC was still able to insist on its share of posts, the outcome reflected its split between partisans of Miro, Khaddam, and Asad, and heads of most politically crucial ministries remained veterans, including Defense Minister Tlas and Foreign Minister al-Shara'. The number of Ba'thists was reduced to nineteen and political independents increased from five to seven.[6] The main change was the replacement of the veteran economic team headed by Economy Minister Muhammad al-Imadi with "modernizers": Ghassan al-Rifai, a World Bank economist, became minister of economy and foreign trade, and Muhammad al-Atrash, a graduate of British universities and a non-Ba'thist social democrat, became minister of finance; Isam al-Zaim, a French-educated leftist, was appointed minister of industry with a mandate to reform the public sector, which, lacking a power base of his own, he would find impossible. East Europe–educated Ba'thist Muhammad al-Hussein, head of the party economic bureau, became deputy prime minister for economic affairs, well positioned to restrain any overly liberal enthusiasms on the part of al-Rifai.[7] A close associate of Asad in the Syrian Computer Society, Saadallah Agha al-Qal'a, became minister of tourism, the revival of which would be a main thrust of the regime's new concentration on promoting the tertiary sector.

Asad soon became disillusioned with Miro, who, in his view, used his position to foster a coterie of crony capitalists enriching themselves on monopoly licenses for delivery of goods to Iraq. He took the crisis

6. *Middle East Intelligence Bulletin*, Dec. 2001.

7. *Syria Comment*, Friday, Oct. 8, 2004.

generated by the fall of the Iraqi Ba'th in March 2003 to highlight the need for change; parliament, under his ally and Miro's emerging rival, Speaker Naji al-Otri, sharply criticized the cabinet's performance, enabling Asad to get RC approval to dismiss it and designate Otri to form a new government. Otri initially presented a list with only five Ba'thists (including al-Shara' and Tlas) and dominated by liberal technocrats, many of them Syrian exiles; to strengthen his hand against the party, he tried to marshal support from the NPF parties and the chambers of commerce and industry. But the RC demurred, saying that one could not end the party role in government and launch major liberalization at a time of external threats (from the US presence in Iraq). It insisted on negotiating a final list with Bashar, and the balance of votes in the RC was such that Bashar had to accept this outcome.

As a result, the share of portfolios held by the Ba'th Party in the September 2003 government actually increased. Naji al-Otri (also a member of the RC) became prime minister, but Rifai's Ministry of Economy and Foreign Trade was stripped of its control of the strategic banking sector, the liberalization of which was the centerpiece of the government's effort to launch a market economy and which was transferred to the empowered Ministry of Finance under Ba'thist RC member Muhammad al-Hussein; Hussein also remained deputy prime minister for the economy in charge of the cabinet economic committee. Clearly the party, even though of a younger, more pragmatic generation, was to stay in charge of the key drivers of reform. A year after it took power, Otri's government was reshuffled. Major changes in the military/security sector included the appointment of General Hassan al-Turkmani as defense minister, in place of old-guard stalwart Mustafa Tlas, who had retired but who retained his post as head of the party military bureau. Neoliberal Economy Minister Ghassan al-Rifai lost his post but independent reformer Abdallah al-Dardari became minister of planning and was later elevated to deputy prime minister for economic affairs, becoming Asad's point man for driving ahead economic reform. Ba'thist liberal reformer Mahdi Dakhallah, editor of *al-Ba'th*, replaced Khaddamist Ahmad al-Hassan as information minister; from this time, Vice President Khaddam saw himself as marginalized from the levers of power (OBG 2003).

Another struggle revolved around the relationship of party and government. Under the existing semi-Leninist system, the party, through its specialized offices, supervised the workings of government to ensure its conformity with party ideology and policy; but in practice, as ideology declined, this supervision turned into patronage—the right of party leaders to appoint clients in government and, in return for various approvals, to extract payoffs from those doing business with government. In order to liberalize the economy, Asad had to end this intervention; but insofar as this meant an end to party patronage it risked undermining both the loyalty of the party and its ability to co-opt clients, and it was naturally resisted by party apparatchiki.[8] Nevertheless, in July 2003, Asad issued a decree that appointments to government offices and the public economic sector would henceforth be based on merit rather than party affiliation; initiatives in policy-making would be conceded to the government, with the party's role reduced to approving or amending these. The party was to cease intervention in the economy and day-to-day administration, although it would be surprising if informal intervention did not continue. Asad's initiative meant shifting power from the party to the government, hence from the regime's rural power base to the educated urban classes. Another prong of reform was an anticorruption campaign that had several purposes. It was a way of threatening members of the old guard who had been involved in corrupt activities for years with exposure if they resisted the president. Asad encouraged the press to do investigative reporting that exposed corruption, at least among middle-rank officials, as a way of enforcing some accountability. This effort aimed to put some limits on the rent-seeking that deterred significant productive investment.

The president increasingly monopolized the initiative in proposing new legislation within the cabinet, but the proposals had to be approved by the party and ratified by parliament, which had been relatively empowered with the end of the dominant Hafiz presidency and was controlled by the Ba'th Party. They responded to Asad's proposals with amendments or counterproposals that the president often vetoed, with the result that

8. *Economist* (US), Nov. 18, 2000; *Financial Times*, Aug. 26, 2003.

reformist legislation might be watered down to such a degree that it was ineffectual. Another problem was that implementing reform depended on a bureaucracy staffed by Ba'thists that lacked the outlook and technical capabilities to understand and undertake reform. Thus a massive corpus of new laws and decrees was churned out by the cabinet, but much went unimplemented for various reasons, partly obstruction by vested interests, partly the lack of professional cadres with the ability to do so, partly the lack of proper conditions in society. Regarding the latter, for example, a decree on the return of certain properties taken from landlords in the Jezira during the 1970s could not be implemented because peasants now in effect occupied the land and nobody was prepared to confront them. In an effort to renovate the civil bureaucracy, Asad issued a decree mandating retirements at the age of sixty, a measure that set off a massive turnover in senior ranks.

The Struggle over Reform of the Party

Ultimately the stalemate between president and the RC could not be resolved without a showdown within the party itself. The old guard continually delayed major reforms, insisting that only the next party congress could give them the stamp of ideological and party legitimacy. Hence the Tenth Party Congress scheduled for 2005 was widely seen as a watershed that would approve more significant, even radical, reform if the reformers could manage its preparation; in this regard, Asad, as party general secretary, was able to appoint his ally Ghayyath al-Barakat as organization secretary (in charge of congress preparation) and also moved to replace many secretaries of lower-level executive committees by requiring retirement of incumbents at age sixty. A preparatory committee eliciting the opinion of the membership on reform issues opened a wide-ranging debate in the party ranks, meant to encourage a climate of change. Those pushing hardest for reform were primarily urban intellectuals who did not hold posts with influence over state patronage, while rural party members who benefited from the Ba'th revolution, on the other hand, were less receptive to change. A key episode in the debate was the call of General Ibrahim al-Ali, a veteran 'Alawite officer, commander of the People's Army and member of the party's Central Committee, during an interview on Syrian TV, for the dismissal of RC leaders who opposed reform. This provocative intervention suggested that Asad had the support of key elements of the 'Alawite security forces, who had long been thought to oppose economic reform, with which he could intimidate opponents in the party; simultaneously in the press, Asad's supporters launched a campaign identifying his opponents as corrupt.[9]

Hopes were high as the congress met that it would ratify major changes. The fall of the Ba'th in Iraq and Syria's forced withdrawal from Lebanon highlighted the costs and obsolescence of the party's traditional Pan-Arab ideology. The liberal minister of planning, Abdallah al-Dardari, was counting on elimination of socialism from the party's program to allow a move toward a market economy.[10] Both party members and democracy activists agreed on the need for political liberalization to generate unity against outside threats. Among political reforms expected were ending the martial law in effect since 1963; suspending Law 49 outlawing membership in the Muslim Brotherhood; granting citizenship to approximately 100,000 Kurds who were permanent residents of Syria; abolishing Article 8 of the Syrian constitution, which gave the Ba'th a permanent monopoly of power; and a enacting a party law allowing opposition parties.

While considerable debate over Syria's future was allowed in the state-controlled press,[11] that certain "redlines" could still not be crossed was indicated by arrests of secular intellectuals who were advocating a coalition with the Muslim Brotherhood and by the unsolved murder of a prominent Kurdish Muslim religious leader who had spoken for Kurdish political rights and aligned with the Brotherhood. Any opposition figures that were seen to cooperate with the United States in its campaign of pressure on Syria would disqualify themselves for inclusion in any more liberal political order (Rabil 2005). Skeptics predicted that the congress would merely topple "several elderly, corrupt figures" as scapegoats for

---

9. *Tishreen*, Apr. 25, 2005; *al-Ba'th*, Apr. 7, 2005; *Syria Comment*, Feb. 27, 2005.

10. *Syria Comment*, Mar. 23 and 26, 2005.

11. *al-Thawra*, May 17, 2005.

past failures and rubber stamp arrangements dictated behind the scenes by the security forces.[12]

Elections for the Regional Party Congress (starting at lower-level congresses) began in April 2005. The security services, apparently loyal to Asad, played their normal role in vetting candidates for election, and reformers, alarmed at their lack of success, mounted a petition complaining that the corruption of the elections was excluding them; this complaint brought the inclusion of some 150 reformist delegates, including women, intellectuals, economists, and law professors in the congress.[13] The congress was held June 6–9, 2005. In his opening speech to the 1,221 delegates, President Bashar al-Asad disabused those expecting him to lead a major revision of Ba'thism, insisting its ideas were valid although their implementation had fallen short. He defended Arabism, which he described as under siege from the West, and, strikingly for a leader hitherto associated with an Internet revolution in Syria, denounced the manipulation of international communications by the United States against Arab identity as aiming to destroy any capacity for resistance to its hegemony. Yet he appeared to suggest that Syrian interests had to be prioritized and that Syria would refrain from Pan-Arab entanglements, an acknowledgment of the costs of its involvement in Lebanon and Iraq.[14]

After three days of sometimes acrimonious debates in three committees (organizational, economic, and political) on the reports and recommendations presented by the leadership, the congress issued its resolutions. It endorsed what it called a "social market economy"—in opposition to a neoliberal "market economy"—through gradually opening up the Syrian market and privatizing certain fields of the economy, hitherto a taboo. Political liberalization would cautiously be deepened. The emergency law would not be abolished, but limited in its application to times of actual emergency such as wartime. The interference by the security services in such details as approval of licenses to open businesses was to be curtailed

12. al-Nahar (Syria), May 25, 2005.

13. Nicholas Blanford in Christian Science Monitor, June 17, 2005.

14. Megan K. Stack, Los Angeles Times, June 7, 2005; Syria Today, June 6, 2005.

as a step in reversing their pervasive influence in society. A review of an old census could lead to granting citizenship to at least some of Syria's stateless Kurds (Sid-Ahmad 2005; St. John 2005) No mention was made of dropping Article 8 of Syria's constitution, but a new party law was promised that would allow formation of other parties, providing they were not formed on the basis of some identity other than Arabism: specifically neither Islamic nor Kurdish parties would be legalized. But the Syrian Social Nationalist Party, which historically had a popular base that could compete with the Ba'th, was admitted to the NPF. What was envisioned was some form of the highly controlled multiparty system that had been in existence in other Arab states for decades.[15]

Reformist Ayman Abdel-Nur provided the most nuanced explanation for the limits of reform (Pace 2005). The party, he claimed, was a heterogeneous movement incorporating all the diverse groups of Syrian society, from Islamists to trade unionists to businessmen, hence its resolutions inevitably expressed a "lowest common denominator" and were bound to be general, even vague. In the congress, reformers had argued that without liberal market reforms Syria could not attract investment and, with oil exports set to decline, would otherwise have no way of providing employment for its burgeoning population. The worker and peasant contingents of the party had resisted such reforms that they saw as privileging the private sector and that would inevitably sacrifice acquired labor rights. The leadership, at a time of external threat, prioritized avoidance of a split that a hard reformist line would have provoked. Yet the party that had slowed down economic reform for five years had now apparently embraced and legitimized it, even if the vagueness of the reform resolutions meant that there were bound to be many future conflicts over their exact meaning and extent. In fact, at the economic level the climate was changed: foreign investment as well as what could be called crony capitalism had been given the green light, with bureaucratic obstructions to investors no longer to be tolerated. On the other hand, even the very modest political reforms

15. "Syria: Congress Conundrums," Oxford Business Group, June 15, 2005; *Der Spiegel online*, "Prying Open Syria," June 15, 2005.

suggested by the congress were not implemented, neither a new party law, nor citizenship for stateless Kurds, nor an end to the emergency law. This outcome is because, evidently, the regime believed pressures on it to reform had been relieved since, in the second half of the 2000–2010 decade, the foreign siege of Syria dissipated and the internal opposition was decimated in a wave of repression. Ironically, under pressure from the uprising after 2011, presidential decrees quickly delivered on these shelved promises and even a new constitution was ratified in 2012. However, reforms that, before 2011, would have been considered major breakthroughs toward a political pluralization congruent with advancing economic pluralization were now seen by protestors as too little, too late.

More significant than policy change was the wholesale fall of the old guard engineered at the congress. The biggest change was the resignation of First Vice President Khaddam, the second most important man in the country, who, as one of Hafiz's closest political allies, had been at the center of power for thirty-five years. He had been on increasingly bad terms with Bashar and increasingly marginalized from his power base by the president. He announced he would step down when he was slighted by the selection of Farouk al-Shara' over him to head the congress political committee and after a sharp debate with Shara' over responsibility for the debacle in Lebanon. While Khaddam had competently presided over the Lebanon file for decades (and had close relations with the assassinated Lebanese premier, Rafiq al-Hariri), it was those under whose watch the killing of Hariri was used to deprive Syria of its Lebanese prize—Asad and Shara'— who profited; indeed, rumor had it that the killing of Hariri was part of a struggle between Khaddam's and al-Asad's respective Lebanese networks. Later, another Khaddam client, Ghazi Kannan, who had been Syrian pro-consul in Lebanon and had been appointed interior minister after Syria's withdrawal, was revealed to have shot himself in his office, possibly after an attempted conspiracy against the president. Also removed were former Prime Minister Miro, Vice President Zuhayr Masharqa, former Defense Minister Mustapha Tlas, Assistant Secretary General of the RC Sulayman Qaddah, and former Speaker of Parliament Abd al-Qadir Qaddura. The average age gap between the young president and these retired barons was thirty years. The anticorruption campaign may have enabled Asad to subtly threaten the old guard that they could be brought to account for their illicit wealth if they did not go quietly. Asad took advantage of the strong desire for change both within and without the party and the perception that the old guard were obstructing it (Moubayed 2005). With the removal of the last major Sunni barons in the inner circle, Bashar's personal power was consolidated. Those remaining on the RC were Foreign Minister Farouk al-Shara', the lone surviving political figure whose prominence predated Bashar's presidency; Prime Minister Muhammad Naji al-Otri; and Finance Minister Muhammad al-Hussein. Newcomers included the new Speaker of Parliament Mahmud al-Abrash, Defense Minister Hassan al-Turkmani, and Minister of Expatriate Affairs Bouthaina Shaaban. Old-guard military barons and intelligence bosses including 'Alawite generals Ali Aslan, Adnan Badr Hasan, Shafiq al-Fayyad, and Ibrahim al-Safi were removed from the Central Committee while Bashar's two peers, his brother Maher and Manaf Tlas, were reelected to it. The other major change came one week after the conference when Asad replaced Bahjat Sulayman, the powerful director of interior security, thought to have been his main patron in the security services, signaling his independence of such support. In 2007, Bashar al-Asad was inaugurated for a second seven-year term, his personal power consolidated without resorting to violence and through ostensibly legal and institutional means.

The congress had satisfied pent-up demands within the party for upward mobility that had been blocked by the decades-long hold of the older generation on top power positions. The new leadership elected at the conference included only a minority of ardent reformers, but lacked long-accumulated vested interests to protect and was, therefore, thought less likely to obstruct reform as the old guard had done. Resistance in the party to the president's initiatives did thereafter decline, but did not disappear; indeed, Regional Secretary Muhammad Said Bukheitan soon emerged as a conservative defender of party prerogatives against the reformers and, in 2010, in preparation for the Eleventh Regional Congress, Asad dissolved party leadership committees to ensure they could not promote conservatives over reformers in the elections to the congress.

However, Asad was able to bypass remaining party resistance by shifting power to state institutions, notably the cabinet and its technocrats, at the expense of Ba'th Party apparatchiks. The former were left free to follow a neoliberal agenda, in reality undiluted by the idea of a social market economy endorsed by the congress, owing to its failure to lay down a model or strategy for transition to such an economy (Seifan 2010a); this perhaps deliberate vagueness allowed the government to do what it pleased. The elimination of the main opposing centers of power did not, however, eliminate the inertia and hostility of the underqualified, poorly motivated bureaucracy charged with carrying out reform; Asad's strategy was to prioritize the reform of education in order to produce the more qualified cadres needed in government, a strategy that, however, in practice meant encouraging new private universities that sprang up, often associated with expatriate capital. It was also unclear whether the young Turks moving up into power positions vacated by the old guard were more amenable to reform or less corrupt than those they replaced. Moreover, Asad lacked a political movement to energize reform since the Ba'th Party could not readily be transformed into a liberal party and was increasingly debilitated, but he neither sponsored nor allowed formation of alternative pro-business parties that could have pushed for economic reform.

Indeed, in the process of removing the old guard, Asad destroyed the old patronage networks that had linked many constituents, especially Sunnis, to the regime, and his replacements, having no comparable stature or resources, could not substitute for them; these weak figures could not challenge Asad, but equally they were of limited use to him in controlling regime and society. As a result, the president's ability to implement, as opposed to promulgate, policy through regime institutions did not noticeably increase.

In addition, the fall of the old guard was paralleled by a concentration of power in, not just the presidency, but also the presidential family. The tendency of Asad to rely on his kin in place of the purged old guard seemed to simply transfer opportunities for rent-seeking from the latter to the former.[16] Crony capitalist tycoon Rami Makhlouf increasingly faced no competition in monopolizing profitable economic sectors as well as

16. *Syria Comment*, Mar. 2, 2005.

opportunities being made possible by economic liberalization, by covert privatization, and by the influx of tertiary investment from the Gulf that the regime encouraged. This perhaps reflected the fact that in the stage of "crony capitalism" that intervenes in the transition from statism to market capitalism, survival of the incumbent political elite is dependent on its fostering of loyal regime-connected crony capitalists. The cost was that those marginalized from such opportunities, that is, less well-connected elements of the Sunni business class, were alienated. Thus, even as the regime was changing its social base from the popular classes to the business class, it was also narrowing its support among this newly emergent class base.

Yet the concentration of power did not necessarily result in the desired elite cohesion, even within the presidential family; thus intelligence failures and pressures on the regime from the Hariri Tribunal appear to have led to cleavages between the president and his sister, Bushra, and her husband, intelligence boss Asef Shawqat, who was put under house arrest, although he was later restored as deputy chief of staff of the army.

In conclusion, the debilitation of the party marked a very dangerous move toward a family rather than a party regime. Already the inheritance of the presidency by Bashar al-Asad had marked, for critics, a transition toward *jumlukiyya* (republican monarchy). As long as party institutions shared power with the presidency, this transition was not yet wholly the case, but after 2005, as the family—mainly Bashar, but also his siblings and cousins—concentrated power in its hands, the president could no longer credibly evade responsibility for the discontent accompanying so-called "economic reform."

The Party Bases and Reform

Through the 1980s, the Ba'th Party was overwhelmingly composed of teachers, state employees, peasants, workers, and soldiers, with only 1–2 percent from upper-strata backgrounds; it therefore incorporated into the regime an alliance between the state-employed middle class and the working classes, with around 60 percent of membership from the latter. Among leadership cadres, the lower middle class dominated, with a quarter having higher education (compared to only 3.36 percent of the overall membership) and nearly half having secondary education, with the education level rising with each level in the party hierarchy. From the 1980s, there was a drive to increase the recruitment of professionals who had hitherto escaped incorporation, and in 2003 higher education was made a requisite for election to leadership positions, indicative of Bashar al-Asad's drive to put "modernist" elements in charge of the party apparatus. The proportion of peasants, 16.5 percent (297,000), approximately 33 percent of total peasants, had remained roughly constant from 1980 (17.63 percent). However, if students, whose social origins are indeterminate, are excluded from the count, the proportion of peasants had steadily *declined* from 35 percent in 1980 to 28 percent in 1984 to 25 percent in 1990. This decline was indicative of the urbanization of Syria and the drive to recruit from the professional and bureaucratic classes, and it signaled an erosion of the traditional rural-centeredness and plebeian character of the party, although many of the former were likely to be sons of peasants.

By the time of Bashar al-Asad's succession, the party had reached 1,815,597 members (18 percent of the adult population, up from 8.36 percent in 1984), of whom 406,047 were "active members" with voting rights and the rest "supporting members." Sixty-seven percent of the members were below thirty, reflective of Syria's young population profile. Thirty-six percent of members were students and 61 percent of total students were party members, mostly in the supporting category and many purely nominal and a function of the advantages of membership for access to university places, scholarships, and the military academy. Women constituted 34.56 percent of the membership, most in the supporting-member category, but an increase of more than 400 percent since 1985, reflective of a rise in education and employment among younger women (ABSP 1985; 1990).

Inevitably, as the Ba'th seemingly turned, especially in the 1990s, from an ostensibly ideological party into a more all-inclusive mass party, many members could no longer be assumed to be committed to party ideology or even necessarily to the regime. The regime's overt promise of special privileges to members and its tolerance of the abuse of party position for private ends inevitably attracted a growing proportion of *intihaziyin* (opportunists), while more ideologically committed elements had left the party in the late 1970s and 1980s, disillusioned by the anti-Palestinian intervention in Lebanon and by elite corruption. By the time of Hafiz's death, top party leaders had used political office to enrich themselves, constituting a class of new rich with a stake in the status quo and not the least interest in political reform; they were mirrored at the local level by local party bosses that had not faced election in one and one-half decades.

By 2000 widespread discontent in the party bases at the corruption of the leadership benefited Asad's drive against the old guard. There was also an ideological crisis as traditional Ba'thism was gradually abandoned by the regime; aware of the vacuum, Bashar set up party commissions to debate ideological reform. An opinion poll taken of Ba'th Party members in 2004 (whose reliability is uncertain) suggested a palpable shift in member attitudes from the 1970s when they were relatively congruent with the party's secular nationalist-populist ideology. Reputedly, roughly 25 percent of members said they would vote for Muslim Brotherhood or Muslim Brotherhood–backed candidates in an election, and another 25 percent reported they would vote "Islamic-Nationalist"; reputedly in some Sunni villages the regime was actually perceived as 'Alawite (that is, not Ba'thist, hence not "ours" but "theirs"). The introduction of "prayer rooms" into the offices of what had been a fiercely secularist party was indicative of the accommodation with Islamism inside the party itself. So also was the Islamic-tinged nationalism propagated by the regime under the banner of "resistance" against Israel, in concert with Hezbollah and Hamas, and to the US invasion of Iraq. On the other hand, among the new-generation party members, and especially in the urban areas and among the sons of the elite, there was little ideological resistance to economic liberalization. Far from being mistrustful of business, as Ba'thist militants formerly were, many were keen for it, and their stand on liberalization depended on whether they calculated it would increase their opportunities or would threaten their monopolies and inside connections. Thus the party was being penetrated by the diverse orientations, social cleavages, and contradictions of Syrian society as a whole, relatively unmediated by common ideological orientation. Under Bashar al-Asad, the end to obligatory ideological education in universities and secondary schools together with the reduction in privileges for party members in access to university places (while four new private universities opened, largely free of Ba'thist influence) gradually shrank the student base of recruitment for the party. The decline in public jobs and other kinds of patronage reserved for party members and the parallel stress on merit recruitment to government office spelled a shift of power from the party to the government, and hence from the rural areas to the educated urban classes. Members began falling away, hollowing out the party's local organizations.

Ba'thi corporatism also lost its populist character. Under Hafiz, as economic liberalization began, the chambers of commerce, representative of regime-connected business interests, began to acquire regularized access to decision-makers, notably to the prime minister, in a way comparable to that long enjoyed by the worker and peasant unions, but the latter continued to enjoy their special connection to the party apparatus. Bashar al-Asad, conscious of a pressing need to encourage investment, deliberately began to open up privileged access for businessmen directly to the presidency; a new Ministry of Expatriates was also created to explicitly foster and satisfy expatriate investors. At the same time, the trade unions lost the privileged power position they had enjoyed in the late Hafiz period under influential party boss Izz ad-Din Nasser. As long as the power balance between president and party lasted, workers and peasants retained the clout to obstruct liberalizing measures overtly favoring investors. Even after the balance shifted toward the presidency, however, he could not effectively use the weakened party apparatus to impose neoliberal discipline on workers and peasants.

Conclusion

The Ba'th Party was a decisive factor in the rise of a new elite in Syria, in the consolidation of the Hafiz al-Asad regime, and in the durable populist thrust given to government power for decades. Notably in the 1980s, however, the party degenerated into a clientalist network and a shield against accountability. After the 2000–2005 period of rivalry between presidency and party, Bashar al-Asad reasserted the dominance of the former over the latter and attained a freer hand to further empower other institutions of the state such as the government and parliament—albeit firmly under his leadership. The party's former performance of key functions in the political system, notably political recruitment to high office, approval of policy, and interest articulation for the regime's constituency, sharply contracted, leaving it unable to restrain the regime's turn to neoliberal policies; but, increasingly debilitated, neither could it mobilize support for nor help implement economic reform. The regime remained dependent on it to control society where its networks had traditionally cut across sectarian and class cleavages and incorporated a constituency, but this capacity was declining.

Indeed, the party's precipitous decline both as an instrument for fostering ideological conformity and as a patronage network left the regime increasingly susceptible to Islamic counter-mobilization. Under the pressure of the uprising, the party split, with many Sunni rurals abandoning it. Symptomatic of the regime's disconnect from its rural base, the uprising began in long-time party stronghold Der'a, as the regime's security forces targeted protestors, many of whom would have been family or friends of several traditionally pro-Ba'th families, such as the Zubis, who themselves ended up on different sides in the civil war. Still, it is likely that the remnants of the Ba'th network still provided the regime with more linkage to society during the uprising than, for example, Libya's no-party state had done, and that linkage helps explain its greater survival capacity; according to Sami Moybayed, "The regime wanted [party members] to realize that if [the regime elite] goes, everything will go with them. Only then would [party members] fight, as one body, for regime survival. The regime tapped into the Baath reservoir for support and got plenty of it" (Lund 2013). Indeed, the party appears to have adapted to the conditions of civil war by metamorphosing into an armed militia.

Nevertheless, while Bashar al-Asad saw the Ba'th Party as an obstacle to his power consolidation and economic reforms, as he perhaps insufficiently appreciated, it was also a key to the stability of the regime he inherited. Its marginalization and debilitation therefore opened the door for the possible deconstruction of the regime the party had once created.

3

Locating the "Social" in the Social Market Economy

SAMER N. ABBOUD

> We have adopted the concept of the social market economy, which will open new and wide vistas for individual initiative and will make market mechanisms the defining factor within a framework of the state's leadership of the development process, its management of economic activity and its preparation of a motivating organizational environment, while maintaining its role as guardian of the rights of the poorer sections of society. This implies the achievement of social justice, combating poverty and unemployment and enhancing social security networks.
>
> —Syrian president Bashar al-Asad, July 17, 2007.[1]

> The social market policy has failed and caused a disaster.
> —Mounir al-Hamash[2]

Since independence Syria has pursued forms of statist economic development whereby the state was positioned as the dominant economic actor within the country. Under the rule of Hafiz al-Asad, Ba'thist statism was underpinned by a model of social, economic, and political organization that was marshaled in support of state building rather than economic

---

1. "President al-Asad's Speech on His Re-election," *Syrian Arab News Agency*, July 17, 2007.

2. *Day Press News*, Dec. 15, 2009, accessed Sept. 3, 2010, http://www.dpnews.com /pages/detail.aspx?l=2&articleId=25201.

45

development. This statist model placed the corporatist logic of inclusion, stability, and state dependence ahead of economic development. As Raymond Hinnebusch rightly argues, this model eventually exhausted itself because it fostered "consumption at the expense of accumulation" (Hinnebusch 2009a, 17). The exhaustion of Ba'thist statism forced the regime to engage in a series of economic reforms in the late 1980s and throughout the 1990s, which were accelerated considerably after 2000 when Bashar al-Asad assumed power. In the decade 2000–2010, economic reforms aimed at introducing market relations into the economy while gradually rolling back the policies, institutions, and distributional patterns of decades of central planning. Despite being framed under the Ba'th Party's rather vague and ambiguous strategy of a "social market economy," these reforms failed to address many of the more pressing social demands in Syria. Furthermore, the reforms disrupted, and in some cases ruptured, the vertical relationships between state and society that made material gains, benefits, and welfare provision possible.

Throughout the world, central planning and public ownership have declined as models of accumulation and (re)distribution. Syria has not been immune from these trends. And while the country was spared external intervention by the International Financial Institutions (IFI) such as the World Bank and the International Monetary Fund, it nevertheless felt the pressure of external change. The changes wrought in Syria through the introduction of market policies led to the gradual deinstitutionalization of Ba'thism as both a political and an economic model, and as a cultural and belief system supportive of its institutions (see Hsu 2007). The story of the social market economy in Syria, as elsewhere in the formerly centrally planned economies, was one of the gradual retreat of the state from its active and hegemonic role in the economy and the simultaneous dismantling of corporatist institutions that linked it to different societal actors.

The social market economy strategy in Syria was thus not merely a set of policies and reforms that would have objective economic outcomes, as intended by their designers; rather they had wide-ranging social, political, and ideological implications.

The aim of this chapter is to provide an analysis and critique of the social market economy strategy, with an emphasis on the absence of the "social" in this strategy. I will begin with a discussion of what the social market economy entailed in the Syrian context. Here, I am interested in exposing some of the main themes emphasized by Syrian planners and in presenting a broad framework for understanding the logics, strategies, and goals of the social market economy. Second, I will discuss the social market economy as a public narrative and will demonstrate how a number of discursive shifts occurred that were indicative of the ways in which the social market economy was talked about, discussed, and debated within Syria. This section will also include some discussion of the main reforms pursued in the last decade, particularly since 2005. Finally, I conclude with a discussion of some of the impacts of social market policies. This section will consider how previous models of distribution and social mobility were disrupted and ruptured by the economic reforms. In this way, the decline of social welfare and provision was a structural problem generated by the emergent forms of resource distribution that privilege accumulation at the expense of the widening of the socioeconomic basis of wealth distribution. Here, structural shifts refer to the ways in which economic activity, distribution, and accumulation occur in an economy. In Syria, these structural shifts were not sufficiently oriented toward satisfying social goals, which called into question the "social" concern in social market economy policies. And thus, as I discuss very briefly in the conclusion, the demonstrations in Syria that began in 2011 were partially rooted in the socioeconomic dislocations wrought by economic policies pursued between 2000 and 2010.

What Is the Social Market Economy Strategy?

The transition of political authority that occurred when Bashar al-Asad took power on July 17, 2000, accelerated ongoing transformations in the country's political-economic development. Despite the lack of a comprehensive program or a public acknowledgment by officials, since the late 1980s the country had been moving toward a market economy through gradual, selective, and strategic economic liberalization. This process accelerated between 2000 and 2005 and further hastened in the second half of the decade. The first official acknowledgment of a shift toward a market economy was given in 2004 by then deputy prime minister Muhammad al-Hussein, who publicly claimed that the country's economy would begin to rely more on market mechanisms. In 2005 the Ba'th Party at its Tenth Regional Conference adopted the social market economy as a new economic strategy.

While Syria's political system remained restricted and subject to authoritarian control, there was considerable, and indeed critical, debate in the public over the economy, the government's economic policies, corruption, and other matters that had been in the very near past considered to be too sensitive for public discussion. The government's commitment to a new model of development through the adoption of the framework of a social market economy generated much of this discussion as academics, businesspeople, workers, students, and a broad range of societal actors debated the future direction of the economy. Two things in particular stand out from these debates: everyone agreed that the government had adopted a social market economy approach to planning and policy, and nobody knew what the social market economy approach actually was. The vagueness of the model and the absence of a coherent strategy suggested to many that it was merely a slogan. It was obvious that the social market economy model remained intentionally void of substantive policy direction and instead relied on a vaguely defined formula whereby the private sector was supposed to assume the reins of economic growth while the public sector maintained a role in the economy, and the government assumed the role of guarantor of social protections. In this formula, the private sector would become a partner and leader in the process of development.

The problem is that very few people understood what the content of the model actually was. What were the labor and employment policies? How were investment policies made? What was the future of monetary policy? Samir Seifan made it very clear that for this model to be successful, there had to be a division of labor between the different actors: government, public sector, private sector, cooperative sector, and so on. Clearly there was recognition of this necessity, but the division remained vague and open to constant interpretation. All that was really known was that social protections were not to be sacrificed on the altar of economic growth. To ensure this protection, the strategy required a strong, interventionist state. Seifan (2008a) mapped out the new role of the state in the social market economy, mainly to

- Promote competition and prevent monopolies;
- Establish the legal and institutional structure to expand the income base;
- Maintain a strong public sector;
- Adopt effective industrial and technological policies;
- Promote income (re)distribution;
- Enable effective tax collection;
- Establish a network of social guarantees;
- Strengthen unions; and
- Secure balance between growth and societal well-being.

The social market economy model was thus based on reconciling the market with social protections, which was to be achieved through a renewed interventionist role of the state. The state was (re)positioned as the guarantor of social stability and welfare, which was to be accomplished through the direction of market mechanisms toward social ends.

While this description perhaps established the goals of a social market, it still did not tell us what this new social market economy should look like in terms of the relationships between different societal actors and what economic outcomes could be expected from policy decisions. It also did not tell us how, for example, a network of social guarantees would be resourced. Indeed, the entire concept of a social market economy was so ill-defined that the government actually formed a committee to establish a definition. The basis of the confusion over the definition is clear: the terminology and phrasing conjured up different and sometimes contradictory meanings. What, for example, was the difference between a social market economy and a transition economy? How could the government cede economic (and hence distributive) authority to the market while still protecting social stability and social welfare? But perhaps the biggest reason behind the confusion was the fact that the government adopted it as a new approach without having a definition of it. This lack led to a great deal of conflict among government officials and nongovernment observers, who had their own visions and ideas of what the substance of a social market economy should be. In turn, this conflict produced divergent schools of thought within the government and led to internal battles over policy and economic planning. Perhaps the best examples of this divergence were the disputes between Abdallah al-Dardari and Taysir Raddawi. The latter took over as director of the State Planning Commission (SPC) from the former in 2007, and thereafter the two reportedly argued in public forums over substantive policy issues. In January 2010 Raddawi was dismissed as director of the SPC and replaced by up-to-then minister of economy Amer Husni Lutfi.[3]

Beyond the internal battles among decision-makers, the slogan of the social market economy produced other tensions and questions within Syria that were routinely debated: How to break from central planning? What degree of privatization should be pursued? How can social protections be guaranteed? I would like to suggest that these broader questions and debates about the social market economy were about the public–private sector balance in the economy, and that this balance between the two sectors was what framed policy and bureaucratic thinking within the social market economy framework. Indeed, resolving tensions in the public–private sector balance could potentially have contributed to resolving questions over the level of subsidies, domestic spending, taxation issues, the policy and institutional matrix of a market economy, and how to reach public goals through private means. While it must be acknowledged that the privatization of the public sector was not a real option in Syria, private entry into the economy through the attraction of foreign investment in hitherto publicly owned sectors, such as banking and insurance, began to reduce the role of public ownership in the economy. At the same time, economic production in the non-service, non-oil economy was overwhelmingly from the private sector. The public sector was hollowed out, handicapped by massive labor surpluses (Sukkar 2006),

3. On the very public split between Raddawi and al-Dardari, see *Khaleej Times*, Jan. 19, 2010.

over-bureaucratization, and inability to provide sufficient wages commensurate with the rising living costs.[4] It ceased to create new employment, with the government claiming that the burden of employment should mainly fall on the private sector. Seifan (2010b) is thus correct in claiming that Syria underwent de facto privatization after 2000 as the government shifted public sector responsibilities to the private sector. But this shift again brings up the key critical question about this new strategy: how can social ends be achieved through private means?

Abdallah al-Dardari stated that the "social" aspect of the strategy translated into policies focused on education, healthcare, and social security. These were to be realized through government investments in these three areas. In addition, the private sector and associative sector were to play supporting roles: "The government is aware of its primary responsibility as the main provider and regulator of social safety, while making all necessary efforts to involve other stakeholders, such as the private sector and civil society, in sharing the social responsibility."[5] The most obvious and important social issues were unemployment and poverty. The government's decision to cease all new public sector employment removed a major source of social mobility and economic stability for many Syrians. It is estimated that 25–30 percent of all Syrians were employed in the public sector, and it remained the primary sector in which young people aspired to work (Kabbani 2009). The private sector did not absorb enough university graduates, largely because 99.5 percent of private businesses had fewer than fifteen employees and were predominantly family-run (SAR 2009). Poverty was also a major socioeconomic problem in the country. This problem was particularly acute in the northeast regions of the country that had suffered from drought in recent years and the loss of their economic livelihoods as a result (Aita 2010a). It is estimated that

---

4. Despite this, most Syrians still desired public sector employment because of the strong benefits. Syrians in the private sector did not fare any better in regard to wages. As will be elaborated below, private sector salaries were high in areas such as banking, but this area only employed a small number of Syrians. Private sector workers in agriculture and industry continued to receive low wages commensurate with living costs.

5. "Q&A: Abdullah al-Dardari," *Syria Today*, Aug. 2010, no. 64.

close to 60 percent of the population in the northeast suffered from poverty (ibid).

While the government acknowledged the need to address these social issues, it was committed through the Tenth Five-Year Plan to fiscal "discipline" in regard to social spending. The plan called for the abolishment of expenditures that distorted prices and induced inefficiencies in the production cycle. This meant a dismantling of the direct and indirect subsidy system. Furthermore, the plan called for the reduction and restructuring of public sector enterprises, but not privatization. It also called for more "rational" spending and allocation of resources to targeted areas and sectors of the economy, rather than "blanket" subsidies. To replace these social support mechanisms, the government committed to creating a broad range of social institutions to serve the needs of the lower strata of society. It also, as suggested by al-Dardari's reference above, moved toward allowing private firms and NGOs to provide services.

There was an obvious contradiction between strategy and practice. Declining oil revenues forced the government to adopt fiscal measures that reduced the state's budgetary commitments in regard to public spending and investment. The budgetary restraints of declining oil revenues forced the state's withdrawal from public expenditures and targeted investment, raising doubts about whether the state had the capacity and resources to direct policy in the three key social areas identified by al-Dardari. Indeed, the government's diffusion of economic authority, paradoxically, led to its loss of control over the direct and indirect mechanisms that had ensured social protections in previous decades. The government rolled back subsidies, ceased public sector employment, and reduced its role in internal investment. The diffusion of economic authority from the public to the private sector actually served to absolve the state from its social obligations by transferring responsibility for welfare to the market.

In parallel, the transfer of authority from the public to the private sector undermined the strength of traditional corporatist actors, such as workers and peasants, and the linkages they had enjoyed with the regime and the state; as they lost power vis-à-vis the state apparatus, a new class was introduced into the corporatist framework, mainly the business class. The state's dependence on business and private interests to generate economic activity and assume some role in social stability and welfare was simultaneously born out of and produced by economic reforms. Therefore, the social market economy strategy, as a discourse and set of policy choices, was an attempt to alter the nature of the state's embeddedness in society relative to various social forces.

In the absence of clear definitions and strategies, what then can we reasonably conclude the social market economy framework and strategy actually entailed? First, it represented an attempt at rebalancing public–private sector authority, with the private sector assuming a greater role in economic development and social welfare provision. In this context, there was a dramatic rise in the number of charitable organizations responding to deteriorating social conditions and the withdrawal of the state from its welfare role. Second, it was a strategy based on introducing market mechanisms into the economy, and by doing so it aimed to consolidate the market as the main source of the (re)distribution of services and goods. Third, it reoriented the state's role in the economy from its traditionally hegemonic and central role to a more limited interventionist role. Fourth, policies undertaken within this framework disrupted the old corporatist models and introduced the business classes into the ruling bargain. This disruption reduced the authority of groups such as trade unions while increasing the role of private business interests in decision-making. The social market economy strategy can be understood as the culmination of at least two decades of regime-bourgeoisie reconciliation. Fifth, the public sector was to be preserved; privatization would occur not through the sale of public assets to private interests, but rather through the removal of barriers to private economic activity, such as the alleviation of ownership and investment requirements, and the breaking up of public sector monopolies throughout the economy. For example, prior to the first decade of the century, all banks were owned and operated by the public sector. Privatization in Syria maintained public ownership of these banks but allowed for private banks to be established in competition with them.

These five points are by no means exhaustive. As an ill-defined and vague strategy, the social market economy framework was always open to interpretation and constantly being developed by policy-makers. As suggested earlier, it was precisely this vagueness that made it difficult to discern what the strategy actually sought to accomplish. It is even fair to say that it was nothing more than a slogan, void of precise policy substance. Nevertheless, the idea of a social market economy strategy informed policy-making in this period, as well as the ways in which Syrians thought about the economy.

The Social Market Economy as a Public Narrative— Discursive Shifts and the Social Market Economy

The wholesale dismantling of the social, political, and economic institutions of the Syrian state could have completely delegitimized the Ba'thist tradition pursued since 1970, not to mention wreaking havoc on social stability. Thus economic problems and solutions had to be framed in such a way that could make them compatible in some meaningful way with the policies of the past. In other words, the policies and institutional arrangements of the 1970s–2010 could not be publicly abandoned or discredited, but rather readjusted to serve contemporary demands. This adjustment was achieved through the social market economy as a public narrative, which was published, disseminated, and discussed by a range of actors in Syria. As a public narrative, it was what allowed average Syrians, academics, bureaucrats, and businesspeople to make sense of the economic changes that were occurring in the country. In the context of economic transformation, big or small, people needed to make sense of what was happening around them, and these public narratives allowed people to do precisely that. They also helped people make sense of potentially new institutions that might arise in the process of economic transformation. But, more important, these public narratives did not contradict pre-2000 Ba'thist public narratives and slogans about the economy to avoid discrediting the perceived economic achievements of Ba'thist socialism since the 1970s. Thus narratives about the social market economy had to be articulated as an extension and continuity of previous economic policies, and not as a criticism of them. In this way, the social market economy strategy led to a number of discursive shifts in the way that the economy was talked about and acted upon in Syria. The following is a summary of the main discursive shifts.

The Market Has Been Accepted as the Primary
Mechanism for Resource and Wealth Distribution

This shift meant that the state would gradually withdraw from its hege-monic role in the economy. Henceforth, the Syrian economy was to oper-ate according to the logic of supply and demand, and thus reform would slowly dismantle the central planning system. Price liberalization allowed for the introduction of market pricing into the economy and the grad-ual fragmentation of the subsidy system and public sector monopolies. The rollback of state spending in internal investment and social welfare spending was justified as necessary because of the fiscal stress on the state budget and the decline of oil revenues that had sustained high levels of spending in the first place. At the same time tax evasion, and the reduction in tariff receipts owing to trade liberalization, reduced the state's extrac-tive capacities and budgetary revenues.

After 2000 there were considerable reductions in social security spend-ing through cutbacks to the pension system. Spending on healthcare and education had not risen in accordance with population growth. In this con-text, the government had embarked on the gradual privatization of schools, in particular universities and colleges, with the passing of Decree 36 (2001) that allowed for private sector investment in postsecondary education. While the privatization of healthcare and education was proceeding at a slow pace, the reduction and elimination of subsidies was rapid. Subsidies were removed on key foods as well as on gas and other energy sources. Price liberalization meant that products essential to everyday life, including heating oil and even basic foods such as potatoes, were increasingly unaf-fordable for most low-income families. Marketization impacted all facets of everyday Syrian life, from food prices to the provision of education services.

The Private Sector and Private Economic
Interests Are Partners in Development

Since 1986 the government had embarked on a gradual process of reform that opened up the space for increased private sector activity. The decline of oil revenues and stagnation in the public industrial sector meant that in the first decade of the 2000s the private sector contributed a greater percentage of annual gross domestic product than the public sector despite the latter's control over monopolies in key sectors of the economy, particularly hydrocarbons. In this economic climate, Seifan (2008a) argued that the policies produced by the social market economy model failed to address the effect of economic policies on the redistribution of wealth. The growth of the private sector—both in its actual size and relative to the public sector—was articulated as an end in itself, with very few coordinating mechanisms between government and the private sector.

The Main Goal of the Social Market Economy Is Economic Growth

This strategy was grounded in the neoliberal assumption that rapid economic growth would lead to an increase in living standards. Rapid economic growth, it was believed, should occur even at the expense of the equal distribution of wealth and social protections previously provided by the state. The Tenth Five-Year Plan set a goal of annual economic growth rates of 7 percent by 2010.

There Is a New National Partnership Between
the Public-Private-Nongovernmental Sectors

At the beginning of the decade, nongovernmental organizations barely existed in Syria and were confined largely to charitable organizations established and operated by religious institutions. By late in the decade, there were close to 1,500 legal NGOs in addition to these religious charitable organizations. The rapid growth of NGOs even led to the government's declaring the need to establish a "third national sector," and it proposed the creation of a new law to regulate and govern the NGO sector.

Economic Policy Should Concentrate on Attracting
Investment in Services, Banking, and Tourism

Economic growth was thought to be best achieved through the attraction of foreign investment and Syrian funds held outside of the country by nationals and expatriates. Economic policy was clearly aimed at the creation of economic opportunities that would facilitate inward capital flows to service sectors. This policy was consistent with what Adib Mayaleh, governor of the Central Bank, claimed to be the goal of economic reforms: "to move from an oil economy to one based on banking, services and tourism" (Raphaeli 2007, 41). However, most of the country's existing economic activity and production, especially in the private sector, was located in agriculture, textiles, and light industry, which was predominantly of a small-scale nature. Since 2000, barely 13 percent of all foreign and domestic investment was in manufacturing areas, while the rest was directed at services and tourism, the sectors that Mayaleh indicated should be the future sectors of growth for the Syrian economy. This discrepancy was particularly evident in Damascus, which witnessed the construction of multiple luxury hotels and shopping malls. The concentration of investment in these two sectors can be attributed to the nature of privatization in Syria, which was pursued according to a strategy whereby new economic opportunities are created for capital, while existing public sector institutions and enterprises remain under public ownership.

In the banking sector, Decree 28 (2001) opened banking to the participation of private citizens and non-Syrians. In 2002 the government created the Credit and Monetary Council (CMC) to oversee and direct monetary policy, while simultaneously working toward the unification of the exchange rates and the granting of greater Central Bank autonomy to direct monetary policy and to be responsive to monetary indicators. The banking sector was significantly expanded in 2007 when Decree 15 provided the licensing and regulations for the operation of microfinance institutions. By 2009 the government enacted further banking reforms, including increasing the minimum capital requirement to US$80–100 million in compliance with Basel II standards. Further liberalization occurred the next year when the government enacted Decree 3 (2010), which increased the foreign ownership ceiling of banks to 60 percent, thus making it possible for non-Syrians to have majority control of Syrian banks. While these reforms increased the role of the private sector banks in the total share of assets, credit distribution, and deposits and savings, the private banking sector was limited to regional banks from

Jordan, Lebanon, Kuwait, and Saudi Arabia. This limitation was owing to a number of diverse factors, including the targeting of Arab investment by Syrian authorities, the unwillingness of international banks to circumvent US sanctions against Syria, the small market size of the Syrian banking sector, and unstable property rights that discourage investments.

Similar developments occurred in the insurance sector, which, prior to reforms, was wholly operated by the public sector. In 2004 Decree 48 established the Insurance Act and the Insurance Supervisory Authority, while establishing legal private insurance firms. Prior to this time, Syrians purchased life insurance with Lebanese or Jordanian firms, while holding basic insurance for cars and homes with the Syrian public sector. The banking and services sectors were further liberalized with the creation of money and stock markets in 2005. In 2006, Decree 55, known as the Market Securities Act, formally created the Damascus Stock Exchange, which began operations in 2009. In line with the expansion of banking and services, the government issued a new companies law, No. 3 (2008), which created new business categories, including financing and leasing companies. Finally, in 2007, the Council of Ministers passed Decree 60 (2007) to approve and regulate the issuance of treasury bills and bonds. Taken together, these reforms significantly expanded the Syrian banking and services sectors. However, this expansion was entirely reliant on outside investment.

Trade Liberalization Is Necessary to Enhance Syria's Integration into the Global Economy and to Support Private Sector Development

The process of eliminating trade barriers was accelerated with the implementation of the Greater Arab Free Trade Area (GAFTA) and bilateral agreements with neighbors such as Turkey and Iran (Abboud 2010). Trade liberalization was considered to be a means of encouraging competition and the enhancement of domestic production capacities. Decades of central planning had stunted the competitiveness of the domestic industrial sector through the guarantee of domestic markets and protection from foreign competition. Because of this, there was a concern among Syrian businesses that increased competition through trade liberalization would result in loss of markets and possibly bankruptcy and closures. Nevertheless, trade liberalization was defended by the government as supporting the competitiveness of domestic industry as well as expanding consumer choice through the elimination of trade barriers. Indeed, one of the main justifications for economic reform was drawn directly from global neoliberal discourses about the need to be "competitive" and to have "efficient" industry with an export capacity. Adapting the country to globalization was thought best achieved through trade liberalization.

Syrians Should Adopt a Culture of Consumption,
Economic Freedom, and Individual Responsibility

"Social responsibility" was considered one of the cornerstones of the social market economy. The language saturating government plans and documents stressed the need to have an engaged, participatory, and above all responsible citizenry that acted as stakeholders in the reform process. This expectation amounted to an emphasis on self-reliance and independence from the state. Abdallah al-Dardari stated that this meant "the establishment of an economic system in which economic activities were fashioned in such a way so as to allow people to take care of themselves."[6]. Elias Nejmeh (2003) defined the social market economy as a formula that gave "individuals, businessmen, and all active members of the private sector the freedom to produce and the flexibility to carry out economic activities, while guaranteeing the rights of workers, work factors, and social rights." The new economic freedoms afforded to producers and consumers were seen as an outcome of a rollback of state functions within the economy.

These discursive shifts that informed public narratives about the economy were important in shaping how economic problems and solutions were framed, by both policy-makers and citizens. While the social market economy strategy did not offer a particular policy path or set of prescriptions, these narratives about the economy underpinned the many reforms

---

6. "Q&A with Abdullah Al-Dardari, Deputy Prime Minister for Economic Affairs," *Syria Today*, Dec. 2009.

discussed above. Beyond merely the policy implications of these discursive shifts lie the structural impacts generated by the policies pursued in this framework. Thus these policies were not adopted in a vacuum, and they also considerably shifted the ways in which economic activity, distribution, and accumulation occurred in Syria. It is precisely because of these structural shifts that social welfare and social provisions were threatened. The structural mechanisms that existed prior to these reforms, which largely satisfied social needs, including the specific corporatist model of development, the institutions of social mobility, and government extraction and distribution patterns, were all considerably adjusted and transformed during the last decade.

The Impact of Social Market Policies

Clearly social and economic life changed considerably for average Syrians in the ten years after Bashar al-Asad took power. The values, expectations, and capacities of different societal actors were transformed. And while the social market economy strategy officially adopted in 2005 ostensibly aimed at improving living standards and maintaining high levels of social protections, much of the evidence in the last decade suggests that market policies actually exacerbated social problems. Unemployment remained extremely high, wages remained well below the rising costs of living, and price volatility created economic uncertainty for hundreds of thousands, if not millions, of average Syrians. Social market policies did not, thus, prove successful because the structural shifts that were engendered by economic policy did not sufficiently direct resources toward the achievement of social ends.

The Ba'thist model of development had considerable structural flaws, which were alluded to at the beginning of this chapter. These problems were numerous and indeed necessitated some sort of structural transformation to spur economic activity within the economy. However, the post-2000 reforms did not necessarily address these structural flaws. Instead, they disrupted the traditional Ba'thist institutions of social stratification without creating new, more effective ones. In particular, the institutions of social mobility, including redistributive policies and guaranteed public sector employment, were disrupted if not entirely destroyed, and this impact was most felt by poor urban classes as well as by rural communities. In the 1960s and 1970s poverty began to decrease in Syria as an outcome of state policies to redistribute land to peasants and the welfare to the poor, and through the creation of new institutions that provided them social benefits and protections. Redistributive policies in the form of nationalizations and taxes on luxury products allowed the state to guarantee the provision of free education, healthcare, services, and subsidies, which significantly improved the standard of living for peasants and the poor. During this period, even when rural people migrated to cities, they could typically find employment in the public sector. These policies provided peasants and the poor with the capacity and institutional support for social mobility.

However, starting in the 1980s and accelerating in the last decade, the state began to reduce its support of rural communities as well as of the agricultural sector. The removal of subsidies on agricultural inputs, especially fuel, oil, seeds, and fertilizers, caused the decline of agriculture's contribution to the national economy and considerable economic and social stress in rural communities, in particular those in the northeastern governorates. The government's increasing focus on the nonagricultural sectors of the economy meant the continued neglect of agricultural communities, especially in the northeastern provinces. Not surprisingly, this neglect led to considerable migration to Aleppo and Damascus, and has placed considerable stresses on the service systems in these two cities. A generation ago, rural migrants might have been assured of some sort of employment in the city, and, at the very least, access to healthcare, education, and other services. This assurance was no longer necessarily the case in the first decade of the 2000s. Most rural migrants ended up living in slums on the outskirts of the cities, and Mahmoud Abdel Fadil estimates that more than 32 percent of the Syrian population lived in some sort of slum village (Fadil 2004, 150).

The adverse impacts of policies on social mobility were also revealed in growing wealth gaps between rural and urban classes. High birth rates in rural areas meant that more people were searching for fewer jobs. As the public sector ceased and contracted employment, the logic was that the private sector would assume responsibility for providing employment to the growing population. While the private sector grew considerably in the 1990–2010 period, it proved to be very weak in providing sufficient employment opportunities for Syrians. Meanwhile, wage gaps grew considerably. Senior managerial salaries in the private sector, particularly in banks and other financial institutions, were extremely high compared to average salaries and even to those salaries of public sector managers. Despite these high salaries and new jobs in services, there was little benefit for the majority of Syrians. It is estimated that around six million Syrians lived below the poverty line, and millions more in conditions of economic uncertainty (Seifan 2010b). Thus, while economic policy indeed created a high-wage-earning managerial class, this class remained very small. The income base of the rest of Syrian society did not correspondingly expand, meaning that the middle class's ability to save and consume progressively dwindled.

To be sure, it was not only the emerging (but small) managerial classes or those businesspeople with privileged connections to the state that reaped the benefits of economic reform. The private sector as a whole benefitted from policies that liberalized economic activity. Yet we should not conflate the growth of the private sector's contribution to overall national production with the achievements of social goods. Clearly the image of the bourgeoisie and capitalist classes changed in Syria during the last decade: no longer was this class the "historical enemy" of the regime, nation, and state, but rather an active partner in national economic development. Indeed, many of the individuals and networks of this class emerged during 2000 to 2010 as prominent public figures. The gradual introduction of the bourgeoisie into the ruling bargain fundamentally changed the nature of Ba'thist corporatism. The social contract of the 1960s and 1970s linked societal actors to the state, while peripheralizing the bourgeoisie and capitalist class. The contemporary social contract reversed this relationship. Structural economic transformation led to the retreat of the state and the abandonment of its linkages to the former corporatized groups.

To be sure, this rupture was not complete, but equally alternative institutions to satisfy the material needs of the formerly corporatized actors were not established. For example, there was no private sector labor law, public sector wages were not increased commensurate to rising living costs, and rural communities continued to suffer from a combination of drought conditions and the policy neglect of the central government. The failure to materially appease the former corporatized actors led to dissatisfaction among large sectors of society and a subsequent, gradual delegitimization of Ba'thist authority.

A final impact of social market economy policies similarly concerns the question of authority. In 2000 Syria's charitable organizations were confined to religious orders, and NGOs were effectively not allowed to operate in the country. By 2010 the NGO presence had proliferated and the state had begun to actively encourage their activities. The reasons behind the toleration of these groups was clear: the withdrawal of the state from its direct role in the economy required some sort of authority(ies) to serve as a proxy and provide services to communities. This need created a tense and paradoxical situation for the state authorities. On the one hand, NGOs and religious orders provided a necessary public good, but on the other hand, they were emerging as alternative sites of authority, a process that undermined state legitimacy and control over society (Pierret and Selvik 2009).

The persistence of negative socioeconomic patterns amid reform is not merely an accident of policy or poor decision-making, but is a function of the new model of development that privileged accumulation at the expense of equal distribution. The impacts discussed here reflected these structural shifts that policy created. The introduction of the bourgeoisie into the ruling coalition meant the elimination of the material basis, and the ideological and political grounding, for the maintenance of social welfare. The state was forced to transform and diffuse economic authority to markets, private actors, and nongovernmental actors. In doing so, officials made the assumption that the market would solve the economic crises and stagnation facing the country. This process was not decided overnight, nor was it completed by 2011, as there existed great resistance to it within Syria. In any case, the gradual opening up to the private sector ignored the reality that individuals and private actors are profit-seeking and do not consider public goals or social responsibility as an end. The dismantling of distribution networks that fulfilled public goals was not, therefore, replaced by market mechanisms.

Conclusion

Authoritarian populist states often attempt to govern according to slogans. Contemporary Syria witnessed its fair share of Ba'thist slogans reflecting the state's political, economic, and cultural expectations. In this way, the social market economy strategy was another slogan, or, more accurately, a public narrative, that not only communicated a set of values, beliefs, and expectations to the public at large, but also informed policy and decision-making. This chapter has attempted to present the broad outline of what a social market economy meant in the Syrian context. Although there was no established definition agreed upon by policy-makers or observers, this new strategy ostensibly entailed a commitment to both the market and social protections. I have argued in this chapter that the shifts toward the market accelerated faster than social protections. Thus economic policy during the first decade of Bashar al-Asad's rule did not sufficiently address many of the pressing socioeconomic problems experienced by most Syrians. The "social" in the social market economy was quite peripheral. The absence of social benefits flowing from these policies was caused by economic policies that neglected resource distribution for social ends.

It is not surprising then that when Syrian demonstrations began in 2011, economic grievances were at the core of protestors' demands. Protestors not only took aim at the Ba'th Party's repressive security apparatus, but at the economic conditions that had led to deteriorating standards of living and that were the outcome of the economic policies of the 2000–2010 period. This period, defined largely by a marketization of the national economy, led to weaker distribution of social resources; a decreased role of the state in providing resources such as employment and subsidies; a growing concentration of wealth into the urban, upper classes; and a slow, gradual depopulation of the rural areas, which were hit hardest by a combination of drought and poor economic policy. These economic patterns, which existed prior to 2000 but were exaggerated in the decade after, reflected the weaknesses of the social market economy model. As I have argued in this chapter, this social market economy model was premised on the delinking of the state from the economy, while trying to maintain social protections through market mechanisms. Although this marketization of the economy was not the primary cause of the massive demonstrations witnessed in Syria in 2011, it certainly contributed to protestor grievances against the state and the ruling regime.

4

Nationalism and Reform under Bashar al-Asad

Reading the "Legitimacy" of the Syrian Regime

AURORA SOTTIMANO

Since the early days of what is now known as the "Arab Spring," scholars and policy-makers have approached popular protests and the reactions of the regimes in terms of "legitimacy." They have generally considered popular demands to be "legitimate" so long as they can be inscribed within a call for democracy. By and large, international actors have denounced the violent repression of peaceful demonstrations as an unacceptable practice, and whenever Western powers have taken a clear-cut stand about an uprising in any Arab state, they have described it as a "loss of legitimacy" by the respective regime involved. For their part, authoritarian regimes have not shied away from using riot police, armies, and militias against protesters. They have justified these actions as a necessary reaction to foreign-instigated attempts to disrupt internal stability, while they themselves stage pro-regime demonstrations ostensibly to support their own legitimacy. As for the protesters, it seems obvious from their call for *isqat al-nizam* (the fall of the regime) that they themselves have little doubt that their leaders lack legitimacy—a deficiency that led to the revolt in the first place. In Syria, the uneven unfolding of local dynamics has further complicated the picture. A clear development in the priorities of the protestors—from urging the government to implement its reformist agenda without further delay to overt demands for an end to the regime—has failed so far to gather the support of the majority of the population, despite the fact that the uprising has spread throughout Syria. By their very silence, a Syrian "silent majority" seems to send the disquieting message that the regime continues to enjoy a certain "legitimacy." Opposition groups, painfully aware of their initial lack of organization both within Syria and without, as well as their difficulty in achieving recognition abroad, were unable to assert a unified leadership of the revolution—a situation that points to another possible "legitimacy" problem.

The meaning of "legitimacy" in the Syrian context is at best opaque. It appears to be an evaluative concept embracing a variety of issues—shared ideological positions, representative institutions, legality and accountability mechanisms, cultural values, and customary loyalties—each and all of which can play a role in justifying and maintaining effective political authority.[1] Analysts who speak of a progressive "erosion" of legitimacy that parallels the growing use of violence on the part of the Syrian regime seem merely to equate legitimacy with "popular support" while implicitly endorsing a dualist analytical framework that places legitimacy in opposition to violence and repression.

Most scholars of Syria point to the ideological legacy of the Baʿth Party—a mixture of Arab nationalism and populism—as the legitimating backbone of the regime, although they offer little explanation for both the enduring impact of a largely discredited party ideology and for the ahistorical character of such a notion of legitimacy. Only a few weeks before the beginning of the Syrian uprising, President Bashar al-Asad famously predicted that Syria would avoid the popular unrest seen elsewhere in the Arab world because of the fact that its foreign policy was more aligned with the popular will than were the pro-American stances of Tunisia and Egypt.[2] Other scholars point to the economic opening of Syria under President Bashar al-Asad and his popularity as a young, Westernized, and approachable reformer as part of his personal legitimacy. Nevertheless

1. On legitimacy, see Lipset (1960) and Beetham (1991).

2. Asad interview with the *Wall Street Journal*, Jan. 31, 2011. His statement appeared to be borne out on Feb. 5, 2011, when a Syrian "Day of Rage," organized via the Internet to mimic similar successful protests in Egypt and elsewhere, drew only a handful of demonstrators.

there is little question that the Syrian uprising stemmed from the popular frustration not only with a despotic regime that curbed civil and political liberties, but also with continued impoverishment of large strata of the Syrian population. This was a result of the broken policies of the regime, which brought dismal economic performance and unjust economic reforms.[3] These factors helped to perpetuate, rather than renovate, an enduring economic and political order that was corrupt, inefficient, and despotic (Seifan 2010a).

This is not to say that legitimacy is an altogether irrelevant issue, for several reasons. First are the assertions of Syrian leaders themselves that they alone possess the mandate to defend both population and state against the chaos engendered by radical Islamic groups supported by foreign elements. Second is the remarkable caution displayed by Western powers in withdrawing the legitimacy credit from a corrupt Syrian elite already subjected to sanctions—thus the fanfare given to the American declaration that "Asad has lost his legitimacy in the eyes of his people," when it finally came in mid-July 2011 after a mob attack on the US embassy in Damascus orchestrated by the Syrian government itself. Finally, there is the importance scholars place upon this concept as they continue to weigh the remaining political capital held by Bashar al-Asad after more than two years of turmoil that left more than 100,000 Syrian citizens dead. All these factors suggest that both Syrian and foreign actors view legitimacy—however each understands it—as indeed playing a central role in the maintenance and transformation of power relations.

The purpose of this chapter is to cast a closer look at the alleged legitimacy of the Bashar al-Asad regime as expressed by its nationalist foreign policy and its domestic reformist agenda. Specifically I will look at the ways in which *claims* to legitimacy act to uphold the domestic and regional political agendas of the Syrian regime, maintain its authority,

---

3. The uprising erupted in Derʻa, an agricultural center in the impoverished Hawran region, in mid-March 2011. The arrest and torture of schoolchildren, held responsible for writing graffiti imitating antiregime slogans that appeared in Tunisia and Egypt, sparked popular anger and demonstrations (see ICG 2011).

and guarantee its survival. I am concerned with the mechanisms that make people obey, comply, or show allegiance to authoritarian rulers, even if they are brutal, inefficient, or incompetent. My focus is on the imbrications of legitimacy and domination, that is, the way in which patterns of authoritarian state-society relations are established, justified, and adapted to changing circumstances; in sum, how people are drawn into the sphere of power. Such an analysis, I believe, will help us to understand the magnitude of current events in Syria and will contribute to a reflection about how the movement away from authoritarianism can be achieved and sustained.

The Syrian Nationalist Legacy

In the Syrian context,[4] there is a scholarly consensus that postindependence governments in the Arab world relied on a broadly speaking nationalist legitimacy flowing from their participation in the struggle for independence, a widely shared ideology of Arab nationalism, and a growing public sector that created the semblance of a middle class and delivered basic services unevenly to the countryside.[5] Born in a tense regional climate that included the founding of both Israel and the Arab-Israeli conflict, Syria played a prominent regional role throughout most of its history as a leader of the confrontation front against Israel and a vigorous opponent of American plans for regional domination. The 1973 "victory" over Israel and the ability of the regime to keep Syria largely immune from the wars and foreign invasions that plagued the region while it continued to embody Arab steadfastness against those who assailed Syrian, Palestinian, and Arab rights are historical achievements of Ba'thist Syria for which Syrian policy-makers claim credit. Under the rule of President Hafiz al-Asad, Syria, "the country of steadfastness" (*bilad al-sumud*), paid its dues

4. This section is based on research done in 2010 for the University of Amsterdam and HIVOS (International Humanist Institute for Cooperation with Developing Countries).

5. Anthony Shadid, "Assad's Cousin Says Syria Will Fight Protests till 'the End',," Yalibnan.com, May 10, 2011.

through economic sacrifice, political isolation, and domestic militarization. Yet Syria was able to retain a remarkable degree of independence
from foreign encroachment while maintaining internal stability, regime
longevity, and ideological consistency in its foreign policy.[6]

There is little doubt that Syrians strongly hold Arab nationalist sentiments and support regime policies that favor the Palestine cause and
seek to regain the Golan Heights, lost in the June 1967 war and partially
regained after the conflict of 1973.[7] Palestine has become a veritable symbol of injustice and foreign domination, to the extent that the constellation of issues and values around it—liberation, patriotism, commitment
to struggle, a just and comprehensive regional peace—are woven into the
very notion of politics in Syria. Given the turbulent political history of
Syria and the Middle East, and the persistent state of tension fueled by
both old and new conflicts, it is understandable that nationalist sentiments remain very much alive. Also there is little surprise that, in the
face of actual or potential external aggression, the Syrian people rallied
behind a regime that successfully steered Syria through a series of regional
and international crises, from the Cold War to the American occupation
of Iraq, hence the general consensus among Syrian scholars that Syrian
foreign policy remained the main source of the legitimacy of the Syrian
regimes (see for example Seale 1988 and Hinnebusch 1990).

Nevertheless it would be naïve to credit the regime's successful grip on
power solely to a community of sentiment between Syrian leaders and citizens on regional issues. Genuine popular backing for the nationalist line
of Syrian foreign policy notwithstanding, such a policy has carried the
heavy baggage of social discipline and authoritarianism. By conveniently
blurring the distinction between party, state, regime, and polity—all
united in an epochal struggle against the archenemy Israel—any criticism

6. The legitimacy of Hafiz al Asad's regime was largely based on the relative success
of the 1973 war (Hinnebusch 2001, chap. 7; Dawisha 1978).

7. Although public opinion polls are lacking, interviews and informal discussions
with Syrian officials, activists, intellectuals, and ordinary citizens conducted by this
author during the years 1985–87, 1998, and 2010 support this view (see also Hinnebusch
1995; Gelvin 1997; Perthes 2004; and Sottimano 2009).

of the ruling establishment and the leading party was made tantamount to sabotage of the state and its mission while it undermined the moral foundations of the nation and betrayed Syrian identity. In sum, nationalism in Syria was a political dogma, a critical element of Syrian identity, and a pillar of the Baʿthist state-society pact.

Moreover, the Syrian regime took credit for the internal stability that Syria enjoyed throughout the Asad years and presented itself as the guarantor of social cohesion. The peaceful coexistence of a multiethnic and multireligious society was undeniably a remarkable achievement, especially in the conflict-prone Middle East, so often plagued by sectarian clashes. Yet this much praised Syrian "stability" rested on the denial of internal cleavages, whether based on ideology, religion, ethnicity, or class. Such rejection was combined with the suppression of dissident and even discordant voices, which might "weaken nationalist sentiment."[8] The sway of the Baʿth Party over every public expression pertaining to culture and politics, combined with a militarization of social relations and capped by a virtual carte blanche given the authorities to guard their power monopoly while keeping all social groups distant from the sites of power—these were the key elements of the formula for Syrian "stability."

Up to 2011, Syrian popular opinion apparently endorsed this equation. Despite mounting criticism of the harsh conditions of domestic repression, of official corruption, and of national underdevelopment, the Syrian public appeared to accept that support for the nationalist leadership and the ruling system was a safer option than risking the uncertainty of change, which might lead to the dismemberment of the state along ethnic and sectarian lines. Swallowed up in an all-encompassing ideology of entrenched nationalism, Syrian communities managed to maintain jealously their identities and social traditions divorced from a public and political sphere under the hegemony of the Baʿth Party in the name of its exclusive nationalist mission.

The corollary of this paradigm was the implicit acceptance that political authority is a strong power, which "the masses" have entrusted with

8. This is the common charge levied against antiregime activists in Syrian courts.

the means of supervising society, while it inculcates the "right" attitudes and eradicates any deviation from the given dogma. This was the thrust of the Syrian governmental paradigm: that political power was more effective the more it is "above" society. Thus stronger power and harsher rule, rather than the search for a mediated solution, were the official response to any problem (al-Haj Saleh 2011). The price of the unmistakable Syrian stability after the inception of the "corrective movement" in 1970 was a security regime and a one-party system; a quasi–civil war in the 1980s; and a decline in participation at all levels, particularly manifest in the crushing of the dignity and freedom of citizens. In its later phase, Syrian authoritarianism became "a cold, paternal authoritarianism, disinterested in any form of peoplehood, and governed openly by an avowed marriage of business and state elites" (Bamyeh 2011).

Syrian Nationalism: From *Sumud* to *Muqawama*

There is little doubt that this governmental paradigm also applied to Bashar's Syria. His claim to legitimate succession to the Syrian presidency was "contingent on faithfulness to the standard of national honor defended by his father, namely the full recovery of the Golan Heights from Israel without being seen to abandon the demand for Palestinian national rights" (Hinnebusch 2009b, 14). The power of these legitimating arguments—and their array of implicit social disciplining mechanisms—was put to the test shortly after Bashar's accession to power.

The US-led "war on terror" as well as the Anglo-American invasion and occupation of Iraq reinforced nationalist sentiments among Syrians, froze any prospect for peace negotiations, and made any collaboration with Western agencies more difficult, all the more so because the Asad regime feared this association would open a door for foreign intervention.[9] The war awakened Kurdish opposition, but the Kurdish *intifada* in

9. Author's interviews with Syrian journalists, activists, and intellectuals, Damascus, Mar. 2010.

Syria played into the hands of the regime, which accused Kurds of seces-
sionism and of favoring US intervention. At that time, Syrian activists
were pressing for democratic reform and human rights in the civil society
fora that had earlier animated the Damascus Spring, but the fragmentation of Iraq and the chaos that ensued made "democracy" appear to be a
sinister irony.[10]

Moreover, the regime portrayed mounting international pressure
on Syria as part of a broader American-backed conspiracy, casting it as
a stark choice between stability—that is, Asadian rule—versus chaos, as
was amply demonstrated in neighboring Iraq. Hence "a strident nationalist discourse that equates patriotism with loyalty to the regime . . . and
the cult of the ruler" (al-Haj Saleh 2011) helped President Bashar al-Asad
to weather a series of tempests, not the least of which was the "low-hang-
ing fruit" argument for regime change that circulated during the second
Bush administration. Israeli and American military provocations that
challenged Syrian sovereignty—Israeli air strikes on Syrian soil, targeted
assassinations of Syria-based Hezbollah activists, and incidents with US
forces on the Iraqi border—as well as stands taken by the regime on behalf
of still popular Arab causes, generated solidarity between regime and people and even strengthened Syrians' feeling of a special stature in standing
up to imperialism (Hinnebusch 2009b).

The victory of Hezbollah in the 2006 Lebanon war marked a turning point in both Syrian regional policy and popular sentiment, which
led to the emergence of what has been called "a resisting Middle East"
(Hroub 2009). The war demonstrated the weakness of the Israeli military
machine: this revelation changed perceptions of the regional strategic balance of forces and helped to erase Arab feelings of inferiority.[11] As many
Syrians put it, "in Lebanon we won."[12] With the victory of Hezbollah,

10. Ibid.

11. Author's interviews with Syrian journalists, activists, and intellectuals, Damascus, March 2010.

12. Author's interview with Imad Fawzi al-Shuaibi (director of Data & Strategic
Studies Centre, Damascus), Mar. 13, 2010.

"the Arabs have found their leader, a hero who can challenge Israel."[13] On the wave of such popular enthusiasm, the Syrian elite embraced the "resistance front" with Hezbollah, Hamas, and Iran, a front that stood for Arab nationalist and Islamic resistance to Israel and America. In August 2006 President Bashar al-Asad set forth the prospect of a new Middle East "whose essence is resistance," and which enjoyed the enthusiastic support of Arab public opinion.[14]

The adoption of the rhetoric of resistance by Syrian leaders was both a tribute to the victory of Hezbollah and a praise for the Palestinian resistance and the Iraqi resistance fighters, who had disrupted the easy democratization plans propounded by the Americans, and therefore probably saved Syria from becoming the next destination of "regime change." Crucially, Syrian leaders presented the victories of the Lebanese resistance as a vindication of Syrian *sumud* (steadfastness) in the face of Israeli and US efforts—portrayed as remnants of colonialism in the Middle East—to steal Arab land and resources. The establishment of strong historical and ideological links between steadfastness (sumud)—the pillar of Syrian political mobilization under Hafiz al-Asad—and resistance (*muqawama*) should not be seen as a mere justification for the burial of traditional Ba'thist Pan-Arab unity aspirations and the embrace of religious Shi'a forces by the secular Syrian leadership. Rather, it was part of a defensive strategy of the Syrian regime when faced with the rise of a non-state actor seeking to wrest leadership of the "resistance front" and, in the process, to popularize the potentially subversive practices of counter-power.

The concept of muqawama, as promoted by Hezbollah, is linked to the Shi'a political culture of ideological purity and moral rejection of injustice, whose object is another world order under the true spirit of Islam.[15] It is also a powerful call to rebellion and to uncompromising opposition against an "unjust" status quo. Moreover, it is a celebration of defiance,

13. Marwan Kabalan interviewed by Darren Foster, "Syria's Delicate Balancing Act," *World Dispatches*, Sept. 22, 2006.

14. President Bashar al-Asad speaking at the Syrian Journalists' Union on Aug. 15, 2006, and at the Arab Parties Conference, Nov. 11, 2009; see SANA, Nov. 12, 2009.

15. On Shi'a political history and culture, see Nasr 2006 and Saad-Ghorayeb 2002.

heroism, and martyrdom against any oppressive force, coupled with a faith in the ability of individuals to withstand injustice through constant armed combat and a spirit of sacrifice (Noe 2007, 173–74 and 222–23; and Ajemian 2008). Implicit in this new resistance culture is a celebration of the guerrilla fighter and a preference for close relations with the masses "on the street." Part of the appeal of the resistance was that it placed itself in a steadfast opposition to futile compromise and negotiations; to the crumbling Arab system; and to the treasonous inertia on the part of Arab leaders. This rise of non-state actors, who were successful in confronting the enemy and closer to popular concerns and sensibilities, was a worrying scenario for Arab governments whose central concerns were regime survival and control of mass mobilization.[16] The popularity and success of religio-military movements in Lebanon, Palestine, and Iraq increased the danger that such movements would become a model of political deployment for the embittered masses.

By establishing a link between muqawama and sumud—which is both a pillar of Syrian nationalism and a sovereign state-building strategy— Syrian leaders turned the people's right to rebel against "unjust" authorities and the admission that the leaders of *bilad al-sumud* had failed to reach a military or a diplomatic solution of the Israeli challenge into elements strengthening Syrian nationalist discourse. The turn from sumud to muqawama reinforced the nationalist credentials and legitimacy of the Asad regime. The enormous Arab nationalist prestige garnered by Hezbollah in the victorious war benefited its Syrian ally by validating its long-cultivated image as the only Arab country that had not abandoned the Palestinians for peace with Israel, and one that would never give up its national rights and pride.

By stressing the fact that "there is a national consensus on the centrality played by the role of resistance" (*al-Thawra*, Apr. 5, 2010), Syrian state media alluded to fears about the radicalization of public opinion

---

16. As an opposition figure put it, "they spend more on repressing us than fighting Zionism." Author's interview with film director and activist Omar Amiralay, Damascus, Mar. 17, 2010.

rather than celebrations of it. This disquiet demonstrated that the goal of the regime was to enframe popular anger and discontent within the "national" discourse, that is, under the umbrella of the state, and to restrict any potentially seditious meanings. Despite its acclamation of Hezbollah's victory over the historic enemy, it thus becomes clear why Damascus has viewed the rise of Islamic—especially Shi'a—forces in the region with some apprehension.

Three years later, the Gaza war, and the wave of popular furor that this aggression unleashed, marked both a deep crisis and the summit of President Asad's popularity. The ferocity of the Israeli attack on Gaza; the collusion of Western powers with Israeli "genocidal" plans; the failure of Arab states to do more than issue criticism of Israel despite the carnage of civilians trapped in a strip of land with neither escape nor help—all this shocked the Syrian people. The Gaza assault exposed the Arab system as merely "the operating network of empty and declarative élite diplomacy that long allowed Arab regimes to pretend that their regular summit meetings and collective statements amount to anything" (Hroub 2009). With Egypt "reduced to the role of Israeli postman,"[17] and no Syrian military support for "brother" Lebanon, this sorry spectacle of the failure of the Arab state system drove the Arab street into paroxysms of fury while the Israeli military machine was ravaging Gaza. There was a palpable fear on the part of Arab leaders that the situation might soon get out of control, and for the first time since the Iranian revolution there appeared the specter of a mass uprising of unprecedented proportions, one that would target not only "imperialist enemies" but also the inept and corrupt Arab leaders.[18]

Yet at the same time, Syrians rallied behind President Asad, who accused Israel of perpetrating a Palestinian genocide that "will generate

17. Author's interview with Imad Fawzi al-Shuaibi, Damascus, Mar. 13, 2010.

18. Author's interviews with Syrian activists, Damascus, March 2010. King Abdullah II of Jordan pointed to the danger of a new wave of violence, for which "the whole world will pay the price," during his talks with US Vice President Joe Biden on Mar. 11, 2010. See www.jordanembassyus.org.

generations of Arabs imbued with hatred for Israel."[19] By doing so, he voiced the amorphous cry of rage, and differentiated himself from the attitudes of treasonous inertia that emanated from other Arab leaders. Thus Asad rescued the nationalist mission of Syria and its people, while he reinforced his own political stature in Syria and in the Arab world. These goals explain the vehemence of his attack on Arab leaders, and why, in the aftermath of the Gaza war, posters depicting the Hezbollah leader Hassan Nasrallah alongside Asad were left to fade on the walls of Syrian towns.[20] Meanwhile, Syria consolidated its relationship with Turkey, which was also highly critical of Israel at the time, and vigorously launched a strategy for the reorganization of the regional system that would bring Syria, Iran, and Turkey into a "Tripartite Front."[21] In short, Bashar al-Asad had seized the banner of muqawama from the hands of "an Arab Muslim resistance addressing the conscience, honor and rights of the Arabs"[22]—forces that were undeniably popular, but ultimately uncontrollable.

By brandishing this standard, the Asad regime achieved a number of objectives. On the domestic level, it gave due recognition and a voice to public anger at regional conflicts while framing this anger within a state-centered nationalist rhetoric and finding common ground with Muslim activists. Regionally, it refashioned the historical role of Syria as confrontational state and regained the leadership of resistance forces that were dangerously slipping away from state control. By doing so, it stifled antiregime discontent while reinforcing state dominance over a

19. See *al-Ba'th*, Jan. 17, 2009; *Tishreen*, Feb. 5, 2009; and President Asad's speech at the Doha summit on Gaza, Jan. 16, 2009, accessed May 9, 2009, www.sana.sy/eng/22/2009 /01/16/pr-283519.htm.

20. Author's interviews, Damascus and Nebk, Mar. 2010.

21. From the middle of 2009, Bashar's vision of the Four Seas (actually five: Mediterranean, Black Sea, Red Sea, Arab Gulf, and Caspian Sea) has become a pillar of Syrian foreign policy. This strategy was designed to put Israel back into its natural position of a small state, while Syria would become the core of this new world order. Author's interviews with Imad Fawzi al-Shuaibi, Mar. 13, 2010, and Samir al-Taqi (director of the Orient Centre for International Studies, Damascus), Mar. 15, 2010.

22. See "The Conscience of the Arab Resistance," *al-Thawra*, Apr. 5, 2010.

turbulent social space. Finally, by brandishing the muqawama banner before Israel and international powers while demanding to be recognized as a key player in any regional peace settlement, the Asad regime gave a signal that unless Syrian interests were taken into consideration, "this is what you will get."[23] At the same time, Syrian leaders suggested that only a strong regime in Damascus would be able to deliver both domestic and regional stability when confronted by the intransigence of the Syrian and Arab masses. Furthermore, its strong connection with both emerging regional powers and resistance groups made Syria the pivotal interlocutor in any regional settlement.

The Syrian Social Market Economy: A Guarantor of Regime Power

As well as acting as a guarantor of the stability and regional status that Syria enjoyed under the late President Hafiz, Bashar al-Asad presented himself as a young and approachable modernizer, who led a decade of gradual market liberalization, giving Syrians access to the Internet, mobile phones, and satellite television (Lesch 2005). In this way he sought to strengthen his own legitimacy as the heir and continuator of the Asad dynasty. Western as well as Syrian media affirmed his claims by cultivating this image of a well-meaning reformer who was constrained by the need to safeguard Syria's strategic interests in a hostile world. Bashar's role in initiating economic reform is beyond dispute.[24] Yet a decade of liberalization produced meager economic results and raised more questions about the peculiarities of Syria's reform path and the links between economic reform, social engagement, and authoritarian rule.

On balance, reform policies seemed to follow the line laid down by the late president Hafiz al-Asad: politically cautious, with the aim of generating goodwill in the business community without openly antagonizing the regime's traditional constituency. Indeed, the reform process was launched under the slogan "change within continuity" with neither

---

23. Author's interviews with Syrian journalists and activists, Damascus, Mar. 2010.
24. On Bashar's economic reform, see Seifan 2010a and Perthes 2004.

a clear strategy nor a proper economic reform plan. In 2005 a Ba'th Party congress was convened with great fanfare under the slogan of "development, renewal, and reform" (*tatwir, tahdith wa islah*) amid rumors that it would make "courageous decisions" about Syria's future.[25] During the Ba'th Party congress, it was announced that Syria would adopt a "social market economy." Yet details about how the government perceived the actual dynamics of the social market economy were conspicuously absent in the Tenth Five-Year Plan, which was presented to the party congress as the key instrument with which to guide economic reform.[26] In 2007, after acknowledging that "there has been a lot of talk about the term social market," President Bashar bluntly stated that "we ourselves decide which term to use and what meaning to give it."[27]

Nevertheless, despite the ambiguity, the slogan of a social market economy became a leitmotiv in Syrian official and media language (Seifan 2008b). The message of policy-makers to the Syrian public was clear enough: the green light for the "free market" was not an absolute commitment because the government intended to maintain welfare policies alongside its adoption of a potentially socially disruptive, but inevitable, economic reform. Thus sections of Syrian society with a stake in the maintenance of subsidies and free public services were reassured by the "social" part in the phrase "social market economy," while businessmen and reformers saw the promotion of the social market economy as the formal declaration of Syria's entry into the global market—though gradually—and with certain precautionary "social" measures, which were justified by the difficulties of "the transition" (Selvik 2009).

The "transition" narrative implied that the reform process would bring with it difficulties and hardship, which were unavoidable but temporary,

25. Ba'th MP Ahmad Suleiman in *Tishreen*, May 24, 2005.

26. "*The 10th Five-Year Plan, Chapter One: The Five-Year Plan Approach*," accessed Oct. 18, 2008, http://www.planning.gov.sy/SD08/msf/Syrian_Economy.pdf.

27. Bashar stated that "nobody can impose on us a term or any other thing we must abide by." Bashar al-Asad's speech to Parliament 2007, accessed July 7 2014, http://www.presidentassad.net/index.php?option=com_content&view=article&id=260:president-assad-2007-inauguration-speech&catid=86&Itemid=474.

thus quietly suggesting that such difficulties would have no direct relationship with official economic goals and policies. Moreover, all Syrian
economic actors accepted that there was no alternative to market-oriented
reform. The combination of the transition and the "there is no alternative" arguments conveniently preempted potential criticism of the social
market economy strategy and made any discussion of it almost redun-
dant. As a result, critical issues such as the social effects of the reform,
the redistribution of losses and gains, and the mechanisms needed for
implementation and accountability were hardly broached. Framed in a
grand narrative of "continuity" with the Ba'thist socialist/populist legacy
and based on opaque notions of "the social" and "the market," the Syrian
debate over economic reform merely reflected existing ambiguities and
brought about the political polarization of Syrian policy. By marketing
its professed social commitment as "continuity," and some of the "social
gains" of the Ba'thist revolution as "redlines," the Syrian government was
clearly reassuring its historic, Ba'thist constituency that it would continue
to consider their interests.

Nonetheless, certain new initiatives not only ran counter to Ba'thist
policies from the days of socialist-populism, but also seemed to make non-
sense of the social commitment professed by the regime. These included
such acts as the abolition of fuel and food subsidies, and the introduction in 2010 of a highly controversial new labor law eradicating what was
described as "overprotection" granted to workers by previous legislation,
even though the labor movement remained very weak in the private sector and had been state-controlled in the public sector.[28] Moreover, with
no policies to address the widening gap between rich and poor, the com-
mencement of the de facto privatization of public industries,[29] and the proposed introduction of a VAT tax while income tax was decreased—all are

28. Yet the passing of the new labor law took several years of heated discussions in
parliament, chambers of commerce, and unions. Author's interviews with Simon Bojsen-
Moeller (EU economy and trade attaché, Damascus); and Nabil Sukkar (director of the
Syrian Consulting Bureau, Damascus), Mar. 11 and 17, 2010.

29. The public sector is frozen—neither reformed nor privatized-according to Samir
Seifan (author's interview, Damascus, Mar. 2010; and Seifan 2010a). Yet some public

further indications that the regime has made a mockery of its professed concern for the welfare of the masses.[30] Indeed, because social policies and Ba'thist redlines have appeared to be inextricably linked, critics of the reform were easily identified as those sections of Syrian society—including public workers, unions, and bureaucrats—who were the beneficiaries of subsidies, public employment, and other social policy measures. As a result, free marketeers blamed them as the culprits responsible for Syria's economic stagnation. With unions, leftist groups, and grassroots social movements already silenced or co-opted by the regime of Hafiz al-Asad, it was hardly surprising that such critics of the reform were labeled "the new reactionaries."[31]

On the other hand, advocates of reform who blamed the Ba'th Party—especially its disgraced old guard and other regime clients—for both the status quo and the snail's pace of reform, were often themselves corrupt businessmen and officials on the outer fringes of the regime with vested interests in the opportunities offered them to enlarge their own "networks of privilege,"[32] rather than liberals supporting market autonomy from state interference. With both Westernized pro-reform enthusiasts and diehard Ba'thists discredited in the eyes of the public, many disillusioned Syrian citizens did not give government reformers any credibility, but believed they merely sought to reinforce the power and wealth of the few who were already close to the upper echelons of power.

In the social market economy, Syrian leaders surely saw a "defensible issue," however contradictory their policies might seem (Seifan 2010a). It is precisely the elusiveness of the concept of the social market economy as practiced in Syria, a quality that the Syrian press has freely

---

sector manufactures have been de facto privatized: author's interviews with SEBC senior consultants, Damascus, Mar. 15 and 22, 2010.

30. Some of these measures were frozen or reversed in spring and summer 2011 to pacify protesters.

31. Author's interview with Bassel Kaghadou (senior adviser, German Technical Cooperation (GTZ) Programme Support to the Syrian economic reform), Damascus, Mar. 24, 2010.

32. On the Syrian "networks of privilege," see Haddad 2007.

acknowledged,[33] that allowed observers to see it at one and the same time as an attempt on the part of the leadership to counterbalance opposing ideological currents inside the state apparatus while reassuring worried citizens about the adoption of free market policies. Moreover, a social market economy that was all things to all people displayed the government's good intentions toward international agencies, which had been pushing Syria toward the market economy, while it enhanced the public image of President Bashar and his technocrats as legitimate agents of modernity.

Besides, the social market economy conveniently satisfied a number of other objectives by serving as a political slogan within the discourse of power-holders, rather than as an economic model or a social policy program.[34] First, in accordance with the Syrian political culture of statism, the Syrian social market model made the state a central player in governing the economy rather than an instrument of a predefined, rule-based strategy. The limits of market encroachment on the social, that is, what qualifies for state intervention—or does not—and the general rules of economic interaction do not originate in the economic model, but are part and parcel of the sphere of governmental "autonomy." In other words, the Syrian social market economy is based on the assumption that economic policy-making is a matter of sovereignty. Thus it is a state prerogative to define the content, the limits, the reach, and the modalities of its economic action. By claiming a right to autonomy in deciding matters related to "the social market"—from its definition to its implementation—the Syrian government was also claiming immunity from any criticism of its policies on economic grounds.

Second, by being the judge and arbiter of market correctness, the Syrian state posed also as the only possible guarantor of the equity of the economy. What was "right" and suitable for the time, for the country, and

33. Struggling to find a definition of the concept, a Syrian journalist noted its ability "to contain the economic status of each and every economic system." Nihad Roumieh in *Syria Times*, Aug. 11, 2005. This total flexibility is not only "its most advantageous feature," but all that remains of the model.

34. Samir Seifan, Yasin al-Haj Saleh, and Nabil Sukkar explicitly agreed on this point (author's interviews, Damascus, Mar. 11–17, 2010).

for the people were judgments the Syrian state itself claimed it was entitled to make within the limiting and enabling framework of its self-imposed "continuity." Thus the Syrian social market economy signifier re-posited the centrality, autonomy, and power of the state as preconditions for its operation. In this view, a strong state, independent of social parties and above market mechanisms, was essential for the higher state authority to realize the imperatives that it takes upon itself. Thus only if the state arrogates to itself a wide latitude and relative autonomy could it guarantee protection and privileges to its citizens.

Finally, despite the wording of the Tenth Five-Year Plan, which listed the vital forces in the Syrian polity as "state, private sector and civil society organizations," it was clear that these three were not on the same level of importance. In Ba'th historiography, the state was the patron of the "struggling masses"—workers and peasants—and a watchdog over business activity; with the new reform process, *al-jamahir* (the masses) gradually disappeared, while business and entrepreneurship were praised and welcomed. With the adoption of the social market economy, the state became the sole patron of all economic parties: both those who sought protection from the market in the form of social policies guaranteeing benefits, subsidies, and public services and those who sought benefits through market regulation as well as tax holidays, incentives, and protection from competition. By allowing diverse parties to emphasize either the "social" or the "market" component of the signifier, and by postulating the autonomy of the state from both social classes and market as a precondition for the Syrian market to function, the social market economy presented the state as the one and only interlocutor for each and all economic groupings. In so doing, the stage was set for Syrian domestic politics to be at best restricted to a series of bilateral interactions between the state and each part of society in isolation from other social forces. Within this framework, political practices were bound to remain fragmented, dependent on the center, and aimed at capturing the attention and receiving the benevolence of the authorities.

If there was "continuity" in Syrian domestic policies, it was not with Ba'thist populism, but rather with the modus operandi that underpinned Syria domestic governance, which remained in crucial ways the old one—*pace* Bashar's pose of modernizer.[35] Even before the introduction of a minimum of structures and institutions to allow for the functioning of market mechanisms, the Syrian leadership had already set the preconditions that enabled it to recast the "rules of the game" between authority and polity. For them, political authority had, first, to act as supervisor and arbiter of social actors and market rules in order to guarantee the rationality, equity, and independence of the Syrian reform project; and, second, above all it needed to ensure that the reform process would not endanger the strategic balance of power that underpinned the Syrian political system.

Conclusion: The Syrian Uprising and an Uncertain New Legitimacy

In this chapter I have dissected the Asad regime's claim to legitimacy while analyzing it from within the political discourse of which it is a part. Even a cursory examination of the two main legitimating credentials of Bashar al-Asad—namely, his nationalist and his reformist missions—shows that they carry with them an array of implicit norms and commitments that shape the Syrian state-society relationship in such a way as to draw non-state actors into the spheres of power. Hence the focus of this study is not on the legal validity or the moral justification for the then existing political institutions—as the notion of legitimacy suggests—but rather on those mechanisms of power and strategies of government that elicit discipline and compliance with *dicta* of the authorities.

The twin nationalist and modernist-reformist discourses of the regime served for roughly a decade as the ideational component of the regime's domestic and foreign policies. With the outbreak of popular antigovernment revolts in many Arab states during 2011, the Ba'thist state-society pact began to break down. Speaking to the *Wall Street Journal* on January 31, 2011, a fortnight after the flight into exile of Tunisian President Ben

---

35. On Syrian domestic governance see Salwa Ismail, "'Authoritarian Civilities' and Syria's Stalled Political Transition," paper presented at the American Political Science Association annual meeting, Philadelphia, 2006.

Ali and in the midst of the eruption of the Egyptian revolution, President Asad still claimed that his own regime was secure because his anti-American and anti-Israel stances gave him credit with the Syrian people. The regime responded to demonstrations, staged by angry citizens demanding an end to the abuse of power by the ubiquitous security services and asking for reform, by following the old script: President Asad denounced a "conspiracy" of foreign and Islamist extremists in the most strident nationalist language, one that equated patriotism with loyalty to the regime. To this day, the regime continues this brutal response.

Nevertheless, by using the argument of a "conspiracy plot" to delegitimize the demands of protesters and justify deadly repression of a popular uprising, the regime squandered its nationalist credentials in the eyes of a significant portion of the population. Most Syrians were well aware that the regime was inflicting more damage on the country and its society than were its foreign enemies. Hence "the fig leaf has fallen."[36] Two months into the uprising, Rami Makhlouf's blunt statement to the American press that Syria is an essential pillar of the regional status quo, and specifically that the security and stability of Israel are actually tied to the stability of the Asad regime, merely confirmed to many the hypocrisy of a nationalist and rejectionist regime, which spends more resources in repressing its own citizens than in fighting the country's archenemy.[37]

After the onset of the Syrian uprising, the personal image of Bashar al-Asad sharply deteriorated. The infamous speech that he delivered to the Syrian parliament after several weeks of demonstrations had left dozens of protesters dead in the streets, and the disgraceful display of a sycophantic personality cult that accompanied it certainly dashed the expectations of those who had counted on Bashar to live up to his vaunted image. Moreover, even those who gave credit to Bashar and his policy of *gradual* reform

---

36. "The regime is actually begging Israel and other states to secure its existence so as to secure their interests": see the interview with Burhan Ghalioun, "The Syrian People Want Unity, Freedom, and a Civilian State," *Qantara.de*, Aug. 16, 2011.

37. Rami Makhlouf interview with the *New York Times*, May 10, 2011. He also declared that the Asad family would fight to the end in a struggle that would bring turmoil and even war to the entire Middle East.

as the best strategy to preserve social cohesion during the transition could hardly fail to notice that, after only a few weeks of popular unrest, he introduced in a matter of days many of those reforms that he had been promising since his investiture in 2000, and that had been on the agenda of the Ba'th Party since at least 2005. Nor could they fail to notice that the regime quickly introduced countermoves nullifying such reforms.[38]

The change in the rebels' slogans, from calls for regime reform to calls for regime fall, showed unequivocally that many Syrians believed neither in Bashar's will nor in his ability to deliver reform, nor that it is even possible to reform the system. Bashar as an enlightened modernizer was the latest incarnation of the Ba'thist social pact. Yet it was this very pact that Syrians now vociferously denounced because the Ba'th and their president no longer embodied what the Arab revolutions had shown them to be the new standards of modernity and progress.

Two years into the uprising, a growing number of Syrians saw their president as "an emperor who wears no clothes." His authority rested on a naked violence that belied his nationalist and reformist credentials, while his regime closed ranks and increasingly shrank into a narrow circle of power, thus further exposing the fraudulent nature of that much-celebrated legitimating narrative that is "wider than itself." Nevertheless, it was still hard to assess how many Syrians truly wished to support the revolution. Many ordinary citizens still seemed to sit on the fence, unwilling to face the risks of an uncertain future. The militarization of the Syrian uprising revived fears of foreign encroachments and conspiracies, which fed off the deep-seated nationalist sentiments of Syrians and echoed the nationalist posture of the regime.

Confronted with the task of explaining the continued deadlock, observers resorted once again to the notion of legitimacy. The "legitimacy because no alternative" argument they invoked to explain the attitude of the Syrian "silent majority" was exposed as inadequate as an analytical criterion because it downplayed practices of discipline and normalization

---

38. For instance, "antiterrorism" legislation promptly replaced the scrapped emergency law.

that shored up the regime and enforced compliance without necessarily producing legitimacy. Yet this argument does hint at the persistent grip of power mechanisms on Syrian citizens, which operate by curbing their ability to imagine different solutions, even when legality, representation, and morality have shown themselves to be merely veneer. This chapter has examined some of these mechanisms while arguing that the notion of legitimacy is misleading because it obscures processes of power, consent, and acquiescence. The reasons why the "silent majority" remains silent are to be found in the power of ingrained habits, of unspoken norms and authoritarian practices that have colonized society while they instill fear, demand compliance and "acting as if," and command conformity with "politically correct" behaviors.[39] Mesmerized by the mapping of those various cleavages they see within Syrian society—ethnic, religious, class, and ideological—analysts have ignored the fact that Syrians have been instead united by the common experience of a pervasive authoritarian rule that has molded society for decades. Indeed fear, cynicism, depoliticization, and compliance with authoritarian power are practices that cut across all sections of Syrian society and explain such passive attitudes.

Thus the Asad regime does not anymore rely on any value-laden notion of legitimacy. Its hopes for continued existence rest on the grudging compliance of state employees frightened by an uncertain future and loss of their comfortable sinecures; on the survival instinct of praetorian units who dread the revenge of those whom they have oppressed for so long; on some members of religious minorities who fear the advent of Islamic rule; and on the support of that section of the business community whose wealth stems from its proximity to the regime.[40] The regime had banked on its perception of the political immaturity of the Syrian people, the apathy of the "silent majority," and the inability of activists to mobilize a critical mass to overthrow it. Yet during the past two years, the revolutionaries have nullified these presumptions. This revolt might

39. On "acting as if" in Syria, see Wedeen 1999.
40. Harling and Malley, "How the Syrian Regime Is Ensuring Its Demise," *Al-Arabiya*, July 2, 2011.

not bring about regime change, but it is certainly changing Syrian political culture.[41]

The regime has indeed acknowledged that the revolutionaries have some legitimate demands, but has yet to recognize any legitimate interlocutors. The premise of course is that the regime alone has a monopoly on power and offers this dialogue to its subjects out of the goodness of its heart. Yet real dialogue and a new Syria can only be based on a new notion of society, a new notion of authority, a new notion of political accountability and legitimacy, and a new political modus operandi. Unfortunately, Syrian leaders continue to cling to their outmoded power paradigm, apparently unaware that what they are defending is no longer the *status quo*, but the *status quo ante*.

41. Rami Nakhle interview with Deborah Amos, "Syrian Activist in Hiding Presses Mission from Abroad," *National Public Radio*, Apr. 22, 2011.

PART TWO

Reconstructing the Regime's Social Base

5

Contesting Authoritarianism

Opposition Activism under Bashar al-Asad, 2000–2010

NAJIB GHADBIAN

The Syrian uprising of 2011 was not, by any means, the first opposition movement under Bashar al-Asad. Dissident activism during his first decade cycled through rises and declines, articulating several enduring demands but ultimately failing to bring about the desired changes.

We may divide oppositional activity into three pre-uprising phases. Phase one was the Damascus Spring, during Bashar al-Asad's first year (2000–2001). Expectations had climbed when the young president, during his inaugural speech, described a need for reform. Syrians pressing for the expansion of civil society openly held meetings for the first time in years. Less than a year after Bashar's succession, this "Spring" was nipped in the bud. The Syrian dissident movement revived again between 2003 and 2007 when the regime was under mounting external pressure. In October 2005, opposition groups issued the "Damascus Declaration for Democratic National Change," calling for a "comprehensive and complete democratic transformation" of Syria. No document since the beginning of Ba'th rule in 1963 had received endorsement from so many different political forces, including leftists, nationalists, Kurdish parties, intellectuals, artists, and the Muslim Brotherhood. Parallel to this development, in 2006 exiled Syrian opposition leaders created the National Salvation Front (NSF), a coalition to bring democratic regime change in Syria. The Front included former Syrian vice president Abdul Halim Khaddam; the Muslim Brotherhood; smaller Kurdish, liberal, and communist parties; and independents.

The last phase (2008–10) saw government crackdown on the opposition when even elected MPs were arrested, paralleled by international rehabilitation of the regime. Until the start of the 2011 uprising, dissidents continued their struggle, albeit under more difficult conditions, with opposition figures paying a mounting price for challenging the status quo.

This chapter outlines dissident activities in Bashar's first decade, then analyzes their relative failure to achieve change in a domestic and international context stacked against them. In 2010 the question was whether the neo-Asad regime was ripe for reform and movement toward a more representational political system; however, the violent repression following the 2011 uprising answered this question negatively in the strongest possible terms.

Opposition Activism under Bashar Before the Uprising

Phase One: Damascus Spring (2000–2001)

With the death of Asad senior, most Syrians felt that a new era had begun, and Bashar's inaugural speech raised expectations for genuine reform. Demands for change came from two quarters: dissent inside Syria and exiled opposition movements, particularly the Muslim Brotherhood (abbreviated hereafter as MB).

Ninety-nine prominent intellectuals in Syria issued, on September 27, 2000, an open letter calling for an end to martial law, in effect since 1963. The "Manifesto of the 99" called for releasing political prisoners, allowing exiled Syrians to return, and granting freedom of expression and of the press.[1] Next, a wider group calling itself "Friends of Civil Society" circulated a petition that came to be known as "Manifesto of the Thousand," reiterating demands of the ninety-nine and adding a call for political pluralism. A figure in this movement, independent parliamentarian Riyad Seif, formed a new party, "Movement for Social Peace," endorsing the

---

1. *Al-Hayat*, Sept. 27, 2000, 1; and for an English copy of the statement, see George 2003, appendix 1.

principles of free market and democracy.[2] The Damascus Spring witnessed a proliferation of literary salons and civic forums, discussing human rights and prospects for reform, held in private homes of Syrian citizens. A second source of demands for further openness came from the outlawed MB. The themes advanced by the Brothers during this period were similar to those in the statements of the ninety-nine intellectuals and the Friends of Civil Society; the MB notably expressed commitment to democracy and peaceful change, plus requesting legal status inside the country for their party (Ghadbian 2001, 636–37).

The Syrian government took two positive steps in this phase. On November 16, 2000, the government released six hundred political prisoners. In early 2001, it authorized Syria's first privately owned newspaper in four decades (however suspending it in 2003). Eager readers snapped up the first 75,000-copy edition of al-Dumari (The Lamplighter; Ghadbian 2001, 637).

By February 2001 members of the regime, including Bashar, began to backpedal, warning dissidents of consequences.[3] Dissidents pressed on. On April 16, 2001, the Civil Society Committees behind the Manifesto of the Thousand published a new "Social Pact," presenting criteria for equal citizenship and listing democracy as a condition for economic reform, as much a priority as the liberation of occupied land. Democracy, they asserted, included "transparency, political and media pluralism, civil society, rule of law, separation of powers, and free elections under independent monitoring."[4] Shortly thereafter, the MB issued a pact committing themselves to working through democratic means and denouncing the use of violence.[5]

The crackdown came when a Damascene Spring figure pushed the envelope. Independent Member of Parliament Mamoun al-Homsi began a

2. For a detailed discussion of the rise of the civil society movement, see George 2003, chap. 2.

3. "Muqabalah Ma' Al-Ra'is Bashar Al-Asad" (Interview with President Bashar al-Asad), Al-Sharq al-Awsat (London), Feb. 8, 2001, 1.

4. "Toward a New National Societal Pact in Syria," Al-Hayat, Apr. 16, 2001, 4. An English translation of the document is available in George 2003, appendix 3.

5. "A Proposal for an Honorable National Pact for Political Action." It was issued on May 4, 2001.

hunger strike in his Damascus office to protest what he called the arbitrary practices of the authorities and the government's campaign to defame him. He circulated a statement demanding the rule of law, independence of the judiciary, curtailment of the *mukhabarat*, and the formation of a human rights committee in parliament. Homsi was arrested and charged with evading taxes, undermining the constitution, and defaming the state.[6] Nine other leaders of the Damascus Spring were then arrested and sentenced to prison terms from two and one-half to ten years.[7] Other activists came under surveillance and harassment.

Early analysis of the crackdown on the Damascus Spring focused on the dynamics of the transition from old to new Asad regime. Analysts not willing to give up faith in Bashar as a closet reformer blamed the regime's hard-liners who perceived the aggressive criticism of the dissenters as threatening. When Bashar joined the old guard in criticizing oppositional activities, he revealed that his mentality was that of in-house regime reformers bred in the womb of authoritarian structures (Ghadbian 2001, 638).

Phase Two: Second Resurgence (2003–2007)

The Syrian dissident movement was reinvigorated by several events between 2003 and 2007. Energized by the fall of Iraq's Ba'thist regime after US intervention, Syrian dissidents mobilized. On May 17, 2003, more than 250 activists and unionists, including some Ba'thists, petitioned Asad for the release of political prisoners, the end of martial law, and a reduced role for security agencies, all to forestall American pressure against Syria (Ghadbian 2006, 167). On March 8, 2004, anniversary of the 1963 Ba'th coup, human rights activists and dissidents demonstrated in front of the Syrian parliament for an end to emergency laws. Security forces detained ninety-nine participants. The US State Department protested the

6. Ibrahim al-Hamidi, "Na'ib Souri Yudhrib ʿAn Attaʿam" (A Syrian Parliamentarian Stages a Hunger Strike), *al-Hayat*, Aug. 7, 2001, 1, 6.

7. The ten leaders of the "Damascus Spring" were Mamoun al-Homsi, Riyad Seif, Riyad al-Turk, Kamal al-Labwani, Walid al-Bounni, Aref Dalila, Habib Saleh, Hassan Sadoun, Habib Isa, and Fawaz Tello.

detention for a couple of hours of one of its embassy officials, who was observing the demonstration. Days later, following a soccer match, police tried to suppress Kurdish demonstrators in the northern city of Qamishli; an estimated twenty-four people were killed, and hundreds of Kurdish Syrians were arrested (ibid., 169–70). Then came the assassination of former Lebanese prime minister Rafiq al-Hariri, on February 14, 2005. The ensuing Lebanese protest movement, or "Cedar Revolution," demanded withdrawal of Syrian troops from Lebanon. Syrian activists petitioned the Syrian president to withdraw from Lebanon, to save the historic relationship between the two countries.

The MB issued a new platform in this phase, "Political Project for Syria's Future." While affirming that Islam remained a religious and civilizational frame of reference for the Syrian people, rather than demanding an Islamic state, the document calls for "a modern state" (al-dawla al-haditha), defining this as a contractual state that respects international conventions for human rights, institutionalizes the separation of powers, transfers power through free and fair elections, and exhibits pluralism.[8] This development facilitated coalition-building among the MB and secular opposition groups in Syria. On April 4, 2005, the MB issued a request for a national conference with the goals of lifting martial law, resolving pending human rights cases, and preparing a new constitution that ends the monopoly of power by one party. This call was echoed by activists inside the "Committees of Civil Society" in Syria, which demanded the inclusion of the MB in any initiative for serious national dialogue. One month later in Damascus, Ali al-Abdulla, board member of the Atasi Forum, the only civil society forum remaining from the days of Damascus Spring, read a statement from exiled MB leader Ali al-Bayanouni reiterating the MB's renunciation of violence and endorsement of the modern democratic state (Ghadbian 2006, 330). Four days later, security forces arrested Abdulla and closed down the Atasi Forum.

8. The document is available at the Brotherhood website, accessed June 5, 2011, http://www.ikhwansyria.com/index.php?option=com_content&task=view&id=35&Itemid=137.

Activists inside and outside Syria articulated five demands to the Congress of the Ba'th Party on June 6, 2005: (1) lifting the martial law, (2) releasing political prisoners, (3) allowing the free formation of political parties, (4) amending the constitution to end the Ba'th monopoly, and (5) conducting free and fair elections in which all political forces compete. The answer from the Ba'th congress was a negative.[9] While there was a long discussion of expanding political participation, the long awaited law to expand allowed political parties was not issued. The only unusual event at the congress was the resignation of Vice President Khaddam.[10]

Shortly after the Ba'th Party congress, dissidents concluded that Bashar was not serious about reform, and raised the ante. On October 16, 2005, opposition groups issued the "Damascus Declaration for Democratic National Change," calling for a "comprehensive and complete democratic transformation" in Syria from the mukhabarat state to a civilian/democratic state. The Declaration reiterated early opposition demands, including repeal of martial law, release of all political prisoners, and return of political exiles. The Declaration asserted the role of Islam as a "cultural and civilizational" frame of reference for all Syrians, Muslims and non-Muslims alike, and affirmed Kurdish cultural and political rights.[11] No other document since the beginning of Ba'th rule in 1963 received as much endorsement from so many different political forces, including leftists, nationalists, Kurdish parties, artists, and Muslim Brothers.[12]

9. See "The Final Statement of the Tenth Congress of the Baath Party: 6–9 June 2005," as appendix in Ghadbian 2006, 484–90.

10. There were rumors that Khaddam was going to be relieved of his positions anyway. Khaddam claimed that his long and critical speech was very well received by the majority of the delegates. Interview by the author, Paris, Apr. 7, 2008.

11. For an English copy of the declaration, see http://www.nidaasyria.org/en/home, accessed July 7, 2010.

12. For an early example of the endorsement of the document, see the special edition of *al-Mawqif al-Dimokrati* (The Democratic Position), which was the official publication of the National Democratic Gathering, an alliance of five secular parties; the most important among them are the Arab Socialist Union and the Communist Party-Political Bureau. The issue is dated mid-November 2005.

The last development of 2005 was former Vice President Khaddam's announcing his defection on al-Arabiya TV station on December 30, from his house in Paris. He supported the findings of the UN Independent Investigation Commission's Detlev Mehlis Report, which implicated Syrian and Lebanese intelligence officers in the Hariri assassination.[13] On March 17, 2006, Khaddam formed an umbrella opposition group, the Syrian National Salvation Front (NSF), with the MB and some leftist, liberal, Kurdish, and independent dissidents. The NSF charter reiterated the Damascus Declaration, calling for a democratic state to replace the "authoritarian and corrupt" regime of Bashar al-Asad.[14]

The regime continued to respond with repression throughout 2005–8. One of ten Damascus Spring leaders, Kamal al-Labwani, who had spent four years in prison under Bashar, was arrested in November 2005 and sentenced to twelve years in prison. Another group of activists was detained in May 2006 for having signed the Damascus-Beirut Declaration demanding normal and equal relations between Syria and Lebanon. Among them Michel Kilo was sentenced to three years for weakening national morale. Syrian authorities dismissed most signatories of the Declaration from their government posts (SHRC 2008, 4–6).

On December 11–12, 2007, members of the Damascus Declaration held a conference attended by 163 activists from all over Syria. They elected a national council headed by Fida al-Hourani, daughter of erstwhile Ba'th leader Akram al-Hourani, and a secretariat headed by Riyad Seif.[15]

Phase Three: Repression and Retreat (2008–2010)

Intelligence agencies launched a campaign of arrests against the members of the council and the secretariat. Twenty-three Declaration-elected

13. A transcript of the interview was available one week later on http://www.alara biya.net, accessed Apr. 17, 2006.

14. The charter of the NSF and other statements are available at http://www.save syria.org, accessed Jan. 7, 2009.

15. A list of the elected leadership is available at http://www.nidaasyria.org/ar/coun cil, accessed Dec. 15, 2008.

members were arrested by early 2008. Twelve were sentenced to two and one-half years in prison for weakening national morale (SHRC 2009, 8–10). Other regime human rights violations in 2008 included execution of an unknown number of inmates in the Sednaya prison, continued arrest and torture of Islamists and Kurdish activists, harassment of civil society institutions and charitable organizations, and heavy censorship over the press and the Internet.[16]

Dissident activity outside Syria weakened when the MB suspended its opposition to Syria during the Israeli attack on Gaza in January 2009, a move that took other opposition groups by surprise.[17] When members of the NSF publically criticized the Brotherhood's move, the MB withdrew from the NSF. This retreat damaged dissent by the Syrian opposition inside and outside the country throughout 2010, and was accompanied by a feeling of self-confidence by the Syrian regime and by its continued emergence out of regional and international isolation.

In sum, several themes emerge from this review of dissident activism in the first decade of Bashar's rule. First, opposition demands were consistent and, over time, more effectively articulated. The enduring and unifying cause among Syrian dissidents during that time was the demand for improved human rights, a constant theme from the Manifesto of 99 in 2000 to the demonstrations of Syrian activists in several European and American capitals on April 17, 2010, protesting international silence on human rights violations in Syria. Human rights organizations in Syria, none of them permitted by the government, became "more communications savvy, feeding a constant flow of information to international nongovernmental organizations, thereby deterring the most egregious abuses" (Pace and Landis 2009). Another salient theme in dissident discourse during 2000–2010 was that political reform was essential for the economic and administrative reform advocated by the regime. Last, the

16. See reports by SHRC, Human Rights Watch, and the State Department's 2009 Human Rights Report.

17. The MB statement is available at http://www.thisissyria.net/2009/01/07/syria today/01.html, accessed Jan. 12, 2010.

dissident approach to political reform advocated change from within, emphasized peaceful means, and subscribed to gradualism in bringing about change. In the first five years, some dissidents still perceived Bashar as a closet reformer. This perception changed following the Ba'th convention in June 2005 when the regime refused all demands of the opposition. While the opposition failed to articulate a detailed program for political change, all versions and phases of Syrian dissidence demanded that martial law must end. All agreed that the Ba'th Party monopoly on power must end. All endorsed a multiparty system. In short, the vision was one of a more pluralistic and more representative polity—a demand that would remain central during the Syrian uprising from 2011 onward.

A second significant feature of opposition activism was the coalescing of alliances across ideological, sectarian, and domestic-dissent-versus-exiled-dissent divides. Two primary examples were the Damascus Declaration for Democratic Change and the National Salvation Front. Noteworthy here was the inclusion of two very different oppositional elements, the Kurdish movements and the MB, in these two recent coalitions. The MB's return to mainstream oppositional activism was made possible by its endorsement of the modern democratic state instead of the Islamic state, as well as by the fact that the MB was perceived by other opposition groups as having a measure of sympathy from the Sunni portion of Syria's population. Meanwhile, acknowledgment by other opposition groups of the plight Kurds suffered in Syria made it possible for various Kurdish dissident groups to support these alliances.

These alliances formed because leading opposition groups knew how little power they had separately, compared to the power the regime wielded. They formed because dissidents wanted to counter the regime's claim that there was no viable alternative, should the Ba'th hold on power be loosened, except an even less attractive Islamic extremism or unbearable chaos of the sort that destroyed day-to-day life in Iraq after the US invasion. While dissident activism accomplished much during the first decade of Bashar's rule, the fact remained that the Syrian opposition movement during the 2000–2010 period failed to effect consequential reform or to create a mass movement capable of bringing about change. Why?

Explaining the Limits of the Opposition
Movement During 2000–2010

A mix of three factors explains the limited success of Syrian opposition during the first decade of Bashar al-Asad's rule. First, the sustained efforts of the Syrian regime to upgrade itself and to cap autonomous development of civil society, through repression and intimidation, were effective. The nature of the opposition and its available resources, or lack thereof, is a second factor. Third, the contest between regime and opposition unfolded in a regional and international environment not conducive to democratic change or to formation of a sustained civil society movement in Syria.

Authoritarian Upgrading

The principal determinant of political opportunity for any opposition movement was the regime. The Syrian regime consolidated its power on the heels of the Damascus Spring in a manner similar to what Steven Heydemann terms "authoritarian upgrading," which involves reconfiguring authoritarian governance to enable mastery of changing societal, political, and economic conditions. Five features identified by Heydemann as characterizing authoritarian upgrading include appropriating civil society; managing political contestation; capturing the benefits of selective economic reforms; controlling new communication technologies; and diversifying international connections (Heydemann 2007). Each of these features describes Syrian regime responses to opposition between 2000 and 2010.

Four features characterized the regime that Bashar inherited from his father, Hafiz al-Asad. First, it was a one-party system dominated by the Ba'th Party, balancing formal institutions such as the People's Council (parliament) alongside informal military-security institutions dominated by Asad's 'Alawite community. Second, the structure of the Ba'thist political economy, often described as "populist authoritarianism," favored public sector employees, peasants, and selected private sector entrepreneurs. Third, the security apparatus of the regime never hesitated to employ repression against domestic opponents. Finally, Asad senior prioritized foreign policy over domestic issues such as the economy, and was known for masterful manipulation of the international environment. While Bashar initially expressed preference for domestic politics over foreign policy, he later followed the model of his father.

Political reform was never a priority for Bashar. Rather, the new president focused on modernizing the economy and the administrative system, giving hope that gradual limited political liberalization could arise. Syrian regime officials spoke of pursuing the "Chinese model" of reform. To them, this meant improving living standards and using that improvement to legitimize the regime. The result was, to quote the title of Alan George's book about Syria, that Bashar achieved *Neither Bread nor Freedom*.

Under Bashar, political change took the initial form of replacing with a younger generation many of the old officials in both formal and informal regime structures.[18] Other formal political processes during Bashar's first decade included the two legislative elections in 2003 and 2007, followed by a presidential referendum. By all accounts, these elections were controlled by the regime. In 2003 the Ba'th Party and its allies in the National Progressive Front were allocated 167 seats; so-called "independent" candidates won the remaining 83 seats. The government introduced cosmetic changes to the electoral process prior to the 2007 election, including caps on campaign spending (at around US$58,000), transparent election boxes, and civil servants to monitor polling stations. In practice, these changes neither enhanced the fairness and freedom of the process nor convinced more people to take part in the all-too-familiar ritual. Official results released on April 26, 2007, showed that the National Progressive Front won 169 seats, while independents won the other 81 seats, two seats fewer than in the previous election. Official turnout was 56.12 percent of 11.96 million eligible voters; thirty female candidates were elected, exactly as many as in 2003 (table 5.1).

18. By one estimate, three-quarters of the top sixty political, administrative, and military officials were replaced in Bashar's first two years (Perthes 2004, 9). Observers speculated that newly appointed technocrats, in particular, could lead the country into a new direction (see, for example, Leverett 2005, 74–79).

Table 5.1
Official Results of the 2007 Parliamentary Election

Party	Seats
National Progressive Front (Total)	169
Arab Socialist Ba'th Party	134 (out of the 169)
Arab Socialist Union	8
Socialist Unionists	6
Communist Party of Syria (Wissal Farha Bakdash faction)	5
Democratic Socialist Unionist	4
Arab Socialist Movement	3
Communist Party of Syria (Yusuf Faisal faction)	3
National Vow Movement	3
Syrian Social Nationalist Party	2
Arabic Democratic Unionist	1
Independents	81
Total	250

Source: Figures reported by the Ministry of Interior and posted by the *Syrian Arab News Agency* (SANA), accessed May 2009, http://sana.sy/index_ara.html.

However, for the first time in the history of the Ba'th, an independent civil-society group, Tharwa Community, monitored elections and provided taped and written reports. Tharwa reports indicated that those who boycotted the elections did so because of a conscious decision, rather than out of apathy. This boycott led to the lowest reported turnout in Syrian parliamentary history, less than 4.5 percent.[19]

In preparation for the presidential referendum, the regime mobilized to avoid the embarrassing turnout figures of the 2007 parliamentary elections. Bureaucrats organized spectacles called "*'urs dimuqrati*"

19. See "Monitoring the Syrian Legislative Elections," Tharwa Community, accessed Sept. 6, 2007, http://tharwacommunity.typepad.com/syrianelector_english/2007/04/the _syrian_auth.html.

Table 5.2
Results of the 2007 Syrian Presidential Referendum

Referendum	Votes	%
Yes	11,199,445	97.62
No	19,653	0.17
Invalid	253,059	2.21
Total (turnout 95.86%)	11,472,157	100.0

Source: *Syrian Arab News Agency* (SANA).

(democratic wedding), forced celebrations in which people expressed loyalty and jubilation in front of media. Security agencies tightened monitoring of polling stations. Nonetheless, human rights and international media noted widespread violations of the very rules set by the regime. For instance, there was no privacy at the polling stations, security agents were observing how people were voting, people were not required to show their ID cards, the "yes" section was already circled for the convenience of the voters, and children were allowed to cast votes.[20] Official results provided by the minister of interior gave Bashar 97.62 percent of the vote (table 5.2).

The Syrian regime's dealings with the opposition exhibited both continuity and innovation. Innovative tactics used to repress the opposition included: (1) refusal to license the new civil society forums and human rights organizations; (2) penetrating oppositional assemblies; (3) banning certain activists from travel while allowing travel for a few others to create suspicion that the latter were collaborating with the regime; (4) ordering activists to report to heads of intelligence agencies; (5) defaming the reputation of activists and spreading rumors about their collaboration with the mukhabarat; and (6) shifting the redline on activists. An example of a new tactic for restricting political assemblies, before they were totally

20. See the final report from Tharwa Community, "The Syrian Presidential Referendum 2007: Fear, Lies, and Deception," accessed Sept. 10, 2007, http://tharwacommunity.typepad.com/syrianelector_english/2007/05/the_syrian_pres.html.

banned in 2005, was that meetings were allowed on condition that conveners secured a permit from the security apparatus fifteen days before said meeting and provided the name of the lecturer, a copy of the lecture, a list of names of participants, the host's name, and the location and time of the meeting (Wikas 2007, 12).

Continuity with the old Asad regime was apparent in the regime's steady program of arrests, prolonged detention, recurrent torture, and long prison sentences. Yet repression became different under Bashar. No longer did prisoners languish for decades without trial or even acknowledgment that they were imprisoned. The neo-Asad regime used the legal system for show trials of activist-dissidents. During the first Bashar decade, activists were sentenced to prison terms ranging from two and one-half years—given to the Damascus Declaration council members—to twelve years in the case of Kamal al-Labwani. Typical charges were "weakening national morale" (violating Article 285 of the Syrian constitution), "inciting sectarian strife" (Article 307), and "conveying false news that could debilitate the morale of the nation" (Article 278). Two cases of excessive repression particularly reminded Syrians of the willingness of the mukhabarat to exercise brutality, one the kidnapping and murder of shaykh Mohammad Mashuq Khaznawi, a Kurdish Islamic scholar, in May 2005; the other was the killing of unknown numbers of inmates in the Sednaya prison on the 4th of July 2008.[21]

In its first two years, the regime was slow-witted about the satellite TV age, while oppositional figures adroitly used this new medium. Eventually, the regime caught up and pursued a multipronged approach to proliferating TV channels, including increased visibility of regime's apologists in the programming, restrictive new rules for granting media permission to open offices in Damascus, intimidation against "unfriendly" broadcasters such as some of the Lebanese stations, and blatantly jamming the two stations launched by the opposition from Europe. The modus operandi for the Internet was to restrict access and to punish violators. Domains such

---

21. See reports by SHRC, Human Rights Watch, and the State Department's 2009 Human Rights Report.

as Facebook and YouTube were banned and more than 244 other websites were blocked by the end of 2009 (SHRC 2010, 38).[22]

New economic policies reforming the private sector benefited a small number of individuals inside the ruling circle, particularly Rami Makhlouf, Bashar's maternal cousin. Rami controlled an important state bank, the Real Estate Bank, and owned newly created free-trade zones throughout the country as well as the largest share in Syria's leading cellular telephone service provider, Syriatel. It was generally believed that the Makhlouf family, the richest family in Syria, managed the wealth of Bashar, in return for a cut. Makhlouf's net worth multiplied and "the extent of the Makhluf's empire . . . [was] impressive, both in its wealth and in the family's ability to leverage political ties for personal gains" (Leverett 2005, 84).

The Nature of the Opposition and Its Resources

The Syrian opposition that survived the "Great Repression"[23] of the mid-1980s was by 2000 made up of sympathizers with the exiled MB; the National Democratic Gathering, comprised of communists, Ba'thists, and Nasserites who refused to join the National Progressive Front; leftist and secular intellectuals and artists, some of whom were freed from prison in the late 1990s; and a few human rights activists. These survived the first Asad regime by keeping their activism extremely secretive and limited. After massive defeat of the MB opposition in the mid-1980s, all these dissenting elements concluded that toppling the regime by violent means would backfire[24] and that a democratic system was the only viable alternative to the authoritarian Ba'thist regime.[25] Thus, when power was

22. The ban was lifted in early 2011.

23. This expression is borrowed from Middle East Watch 1991.

24. Thus dissidents in some ways predicted the regime's brutal backlash toward the 2011 Syrian uprising, which was met with violent repression even in its initial, nonviolent phase. This repression increased exponentially after the arming of the opposition, with regime killings spiking from hundreds per month to thousands.

25. For a good analysis of the Syrian opposition in the early 1990s, see Lobmeyer 1994.

transferred from father to son, intellectuals, artists, and former activists used the brief window of opportunity to begin shaping new avenues for political participation. This context produced the Damascus Spring, Friends of Civil Society, and the Damascus Declaration, plus renewed activism by Syrian opposition abroad.[26]

Activists in the first few years took advantage of the new global media to help articulate their objectives and to form wider alliances. A website that became a forum for the exchange of ideas among Syrian activists was "thisissyria.net," managed from London by the Levant Institute.[27] Other media that gave the Syrian opposition a place to express their views included the Lebanese daily *al-Nahar*[28] and the al-Jazeera satellite TV station. As significant as these venues were for Syrian dissidents, the margin allowed by even these media was limited, and the Syrian regime quickly became adept at fighting back in kind. As relations between Bashar and the emir of Qatar improved in the second half of the decade, the margin provided by al-Jazeera became more restricted. By 2009 Syrian dissidents in Brussels and London launched two satellite TV stations, Zanoubia and Barada, sponsored by NSF and sympathizers with the Damascus Declaration respectively. Both channels closed after financial and technical difficulties, including being jammed by the Syrian regime.

In addition to limited resources, factors familiar to any opposition movement emerging out of decades of oppressive rule pertained to Syria's dissidents, including internal disagreements. Mistrust circulated among activists inside Syria owing to the lack of ordinary means of communication and assembly. Syrian dissidents were—and remain—fragmented by regional interests, sectarian splits, and personal animosities (Lust-Okar 2006, 6). Of the political parties in the Democratic National Gathering,

26. Interestingly these opposition activities did not directly produce the 2011 Syrian uprising, which erupted in the rural areas of Der'a.

27. This institute is run by individuals close to the MB.

28. It is noteworthy that the editor of *al-Nahar*, Ghassan Tuwaini, and journalist Samir al-Qasir, both of whom were sympathetic to the Syrian opposition, were murdered in the wave of assassination that targeted Lebanese critics of the Syrian regime in the aftermath of the Hariri assassination.

the Communist Party–Political Bureau, headed by Riyad al-Turk, which transformed itself into the Democratic People's Party, had the potential of becoming an inclusive modern political party. There was an obvious Islamic revival under Bashar, but it was unclear how much it would translate into a political Islamic movement or support for the old MB (see, for example, Pierret 2009). In sum, while opposition groups tried to take advantage of new media and to form wider coalitions overcoming internal disagreement, the scarcity of internal resources, narrow access to the media, and regional, sectarian, and ideological divisions all hampered its ability to create mass constituencies capable of pressuring the regime to bring about the desired reform.

Regional and International Environment

Syrian dissidents had to combat the old/new Asad regime in a regional context that, prior to the recent Arab Spring, was not conducive to democratization. During the first decade of Bashar's rule there were three distinct periods in the regime's regional and international standing.[29] The honeymoon phase overlapped with the Damascus Spring; there were high expectations of the new Asad, and international goodwill.

Then the second Palestinian intifada intensified and the United States invaded Iraq; the regime used these to deflect Syrian public attention from democratic reform, in a manner reminiscent of Nasser's famous motto "no voice is higher than the voice of the battle." During the second phase, opposition discourse wavered between condemning the US occupation of Iraq and calling for the Syrian regime to clean its own house by democratic reform. The regime response was a massive propaganda campaign equating dissident demands with support for the hawkish US-Zionist agenda in the region and its veiled threat to Syrian sovereignty. Syria was being targeted because of its staunch Arab nationalist stance in Iraq, Palestine, and Lebanon went the regime narrative. Activists who signed the

29. For a similar analysis, see chapter 11, Carsten Wieland's contribution to this volume.

Beirut-Damascus Declaration were accused of treasonously abetting the anti-Syria camp in Lebanon, tantamount to being in league with American-Zionist designs to bring Iraq-like anarchy to Syria.

Several factors led to the third phase, that of international rehabilitation of the Syrian regime from 2007 onward. First, the regime believed that it had dodged a bullet in the form of an international tribunal for the Hariri assassination. Second, the regime was emboldened by the failure of Israel to disarm Hezbollah. At the end of that 2006 Israeli assault, Bashar gave his defiant speech in which he pronounced the leaders of the moderate Arab countries "half-men." Third, the failure of Bush's democracy project in Iraq strengthened the status quo in the region. Finally, Israel's war on Gaza in 2008 redirected pressure away from the Syrian regime and enhanced its nationalist and Islamist credentials for its support of Hamas. The regime renewed its rhetoric about confronting Israel and the United States, which served well to stave off internal demands for democratization. By the end of 2007, the regime gave critical support to stabilizing Iraq and to creating a viable new government in Lebanon. This indispensability caused the international community to give up on isolating Syria, a warming trend that continued until the regime's violent repression of the 2011 uprising.

The 2011 Uprising and the Opposition

Syrians followed the Tunisian and Egyptian revolutions with interest and, with the help of new social media and satellite TV stations, with considerable ease. They could easily compare their own conditions to those of their contemporaries and felt that they, too, deserved dignity and freedom.

By refusing to allow for any meaningful and gradual reform, the regime missed the window of opportunity in which it could potentially have placated the demonstrators. For instance, in an interview with the *Wall Street Journal* following the demonstration in Tunisia and Egypt, Bashar acknowledged the need for reform. In the interview he stated, "If you didn't see the need for reform before what happened in Egypt and Tunisia, it's too late to do any reform." But when he was pressed about his vision, he sounded convinced of his country's immunity to such unrest, and promised to initiate new municipal elections, grant more power to NGOs, and introduce a new media law. Finally, he stated clearly that his country needed more time to build institutions and improve education before he could open Syria's political system.[30]

Even with the government's unwillingness to stay true to its promises of reform, the revolution needed a spark. In early February Suhair al-Atassi organized a candle vigil for the Egyptian revolution, and a bigger demonstration took place in front of the Libyan embassy on February 22, 2011, in order to protest Gaddafi's crackdown on the Libyan people. These demonstrations were also occasions that allowed the somewhat elitist opposition movement to connect with the people. The most important spark to the Syria revolution, however, occurred on March 18, when the people of Dar'a marched for the release of fifteen boys who had been arrested and tortured by the Syrian authorities for allegedly painting slogans calling for the downfall of the regime. During these demonstrations, security forces used tear gas and eventually opened fire on peaceful demonstrators, killing five people. Despite this brutal attempt by security forces to deter demonstrators, these demonstrations marked the crucial point at which the barrier of fear of speaking out against the government was broken among the people.

Initially, these demonstrations were not for regime change; rather, their demands were local and reformist in nature. For instance, in Dar'a, the demands of demonstrators were for the release of the young children and for an end to local political corruption by replacing the head of the local security forces and the governor. Security forces' brutal response to these demands, coupled with the lack of responsiveness on the part of the regime to calls for reform, led to an increase in the scope and intensity of protestors' demands. Their chants soon became "The people demand the downfall of the regime." The protest movement's sights shifted from basic, local reforms, then, to the overthrow of the regime.

30. Jay Solomon and Bill Spindle, "Syria Strongman: Time for Reform," *Wall Street Journal*, Jan. 30, 2011, accessed Feb. 5, 2011, http://online.wsj.com/article/SB10001424052 748704832704576114340735033236.html?mod=WSJ_World_LEFTSecondNews.

The government's two-prong strategy to deal with the protest movement was to continue to repress protests by killing and arresting protestors and to offer simultaneously too-little-too-late piecemeal concessions that the government not only did not follow through on but negated by action in complete contradiction to such promises. For instance, on April 21, the regime lifted the state of emergency—a long awaited demand of the opposition—and abolished the state security court. The day after this declaration, however, government forces slaughtered 110 demonstrators, resulting in one of the deadliest days in the Syrian revolution up to that date. It became clear to the Syrian people that the Syrian regime could not be reformed.

Conclusion and Prospects

Despite repressive conditions, Syrian dissidents managed to hold steady during 2000–2010. When the regime arrested dissidents inside Syria, including Fida al-Hourani and Riyad Seif, those outside the country stepped into the gap. By 2010 the picture for political dissent in Syria was bleak. Bashar survived—an achievement by itself—for more than ten years. What is more, the recoil of the Hariri murder tribunal, Israel's attack on Lebanon in 2006 and Gaza in 2008–9, and above all the melancholic failure of the democracy project of the United States in Iraq restored regime self-assurance; European as well as Arab leaders recommended relations with Syria after years of diplomatic boycott (Witson 2010).

Even though the regime attempted to silence its opposition by putting them behind bars,[31] it was bestowing on them more credibility and publicity. By the end of 2010, the regime's refusal to make any concession was

31. While most imprisoned Damascus Declaration figures were freed after serving their full sentences by summer 2010, new activists were facing trial or sentenced. Haytham al-Maleh, veteran human rights activist, was sentenced for three years in jail, while another activist, Muhannad al-Hassani, has been jailed since 2007. "Syria Jails Leading Rights Lawyer," *BBC News*, June 23, 2010, accessed July 3, 2010, http://news.bbc.co.uk/2/hi/world/middle_east/10396760.stm. Both were eventually freed in the spring of 2011.

providing dissidents with the necessary ammunition to continue their struggle. The deposit of ammunition included a young population yearning for better opportunities, an increased Islamic resurgence among the Sunni population, mounting sectarian and ethnic tensions, and an inefficient economy and outdated bureaucracy with epidemic corruption (ICG 2009). By closing door after door on the demands of its opposition, the Asad regime increased the possibility of far less desirable changes, of the sort that may not spare the regime itself. Thus poor socioeconomic conditions, lack of political opportunities, and lack of government response to such conditions paved the way for the protest movement of 2011.

Even though the previously existing opposition did not start or plan the revolution, its activism and the programs it organized had an impact on the youth who were initiating the revolution. Some of the leading figures of the opposition such as Suhair al-Atassi, Razan Zaytouneh, Walid al-Bounni, and Haytham al-Maleh became symbols of the revolution and were crucial in coordinating the resistance activities of local youth. The opposition's role inside and outside of Syria was primarily to spread messages and YouTube videos, provide direction, lend political support, provide media commentary, and present a unified vision of the revolution. At least in the beginning of the uprising, the majority of opposition groups agreed on a vision of comprehensive democratic transformation of the current regime, and the establishment of a civil, modern, democratic state—as was stated in the Damascus Declaration. Leaders of the opposition formulated a strategy based on four principles: First, to keep demonstrations and protests peaceful; second, to emphasize national unity by demonstrating that this revolution was cross-sectarian and cross-ethnic and by insisting that all components of Syrian society—including Kurdish, Christian, and 'Alawite minorities—were represented; third, to preserve the territorial integrity of the country; and fourth, to reject foreign military intervention. Unfortunately, because of the brutal repression of the Syrian uprising by the regime, many of these stands were subsequently endangered.

In conclusion, all of the work of the opposition during the first decade of Bashar's reign finally came to be translated into a real grassroots movement. It became a mass movement that, at least initially, was guided by this activism and the hard work and the sacrifices of the members of the opposition both inside and outside. Thereby, the youth movement had the opportunity to benefit from the experience and leadership of the opposition activism of the men and women who had contested Bashar's authoritarianism for more than a decade and who had pushed for replacing it with a more democratic order, a prospect that seemed plausible, at least in the first months following March 15, 2011.

6

The Co-optation of Foreign-Educated Syrians

Between Legitimizing Strategy and Domestic Reforms

TINA ZINTL

Bashar al-Asad's first decade in power was characterized by exceptionally high risks and pressures, both politically and economically. Not fully in the saddle, he was faced with a myriad of new regional crises like the US invasion of Iraq in 2003 and the Hariri murder in Lebanon in 2005, all in addition to inherited conundrums such as the continued Israeli occupation of the Golan Heights and the Palestinian Question. Rapid population growth, rural-urban migration, and dwindling oil resources aggravated existing economic problems. Under these circumstances, sustaining authoritarian rule was a challenge, even before the start of the Syrian uprising, and even more so because the political system was tailor-made not to Bashar but to his father, Hafiz al-Asad. In order to establish his grip on power and to confront accusations by the old guard that he was too young and too inexperienced to follow in his father's footsteps, the young ruler had to create a loyal group of followers and, most important, to forge his own image.

With the purpose of setting himself apart and establishing new trust in—or at least respect for—his rule, the president used his first decade in power for nurturing an image as a modernizer. He tried to achieve this end by pushing ahead "modern" domestic policies and by bringing in competent experts from outside the regime. He thus mounted a campaign promoting foreign-trained technocrats and their supposedly efficacious skills and state-of-the-art policy solutions acquired from training in the West. *The present chapter investigates to what extent these foreign-educated Syrians influenced policy reforms during Bashar al-Asad's first ten years in power, and to what extent their involvement had an effect on the domestic balance of power.*[1] Consequently, it also helps to assess the damage done to the regime's legitimacy when this strategy of modernizing authoritarianism was revoked with the crackdown on popular demonstrations from spring 2011 onward, which the regime blamed on a "foreign conspiracy."[2]

Several publications described the air of expectation surrounding Bashar al-Asad's ascent to power and the short-lived nature of both the so-called Damascus Spring in 2000–2001 and the Damascus Declaration in 2005.[3] Most problematic for the regime, these initiatives were, to some extent, linked to foreign-educated returnees or to the Syrian diaspora, that is, exactly the pool of people that it also needed as economic experts and technical modernizers. Taking foreign-educated persons "on board" thus entailed a risk for regime stability: knowledge and skills transfer often go in conjunction with value and norms transfer. Likewise, the uprising in spring 2011, with a sizable role played by Syrian expatriates via social networking sites like Facebook, exemplified and accentuated this risk. However, throughout this first decade, co-opting active and well-connected foreign-educated personalities also translated into wider support for the regime. The paradox was that al-Asad needed to engage those foreign-educated modernizers who were powerful enough to push through wanted reforms against regime hard-liners, but at the same time weak enough to

1. This chapter is based on fieldwork for my PhD research in Syria, March to May 2010, for which I thankfully received a Russell Trust Award from the University of St. Andrews. Some information stems from another fieldwork stay in March and April 2011. All interviews were coded by date and—where several interviews were conducted on this day—a Roman number, to provide confidentiality. I would like to express my gratitude to my eighty-five respondents without whom this study would not have been possible.

2. See Bashar al-Asad's speech on March 30, 2011 (English text on *Syria Comment*, 2011, accessed May 2, 2011, www.joshualandis.com).

3. See Ghadbian's contribution in this volume (chap. 5), as well as George 2003 (on the Damascus Spring) and Pace and Landis 2009 (on the developments in 2005).

refrain from unwanted reforms. As the present chapter shows, this paradox was solved through the co-optation of loyal returnees and through opening up particular incentives channeling their influence into "wanted" fields. In addition, returnees to a different degree had to cope with difficulties of readaptation to the Syrian context,[4] enabling the regime to follow a new version of divide-and-rule politics.

The chapter is divided into two main parts that take a closer look at these persons and at their assumed political clout: In a first step, recruitment patterns developing toward a perceived "meritocracy" will be analyzed (asking *who* benefited from this kind of politics). In a second step, reform policies and processes, which to a considerable degree were engineered by Western-trained individuals, will be identified to enable discussion as to whether or not they bear a discernible "Western import" trademark (asking *what difference* these persons' inclusion made for taken reforms). Finally, a brief conclusion will be drawn.

The Recruitment of Foreign-Educated Technocrats?

With certain reservations in the field of political reforms, foreign-educated persons constitute an apt pool of staff capable of furthering modernizing reforms in an authoritarian regime such as the Syrian one. Most crucial for this modernizing is their expert knowledge and skills acquired abroad, including their foreign language skills, with English as the biggest asset. Through their meritocratic credentials they help to attach credibility to the reform process and to legitimize the regime internationally as well as at home—in Syrian public opinion Western degrees in particular enjoy an extraordinarily high reputation. One interviewee exemplified this perception: "A [Syrian] farmer cannot even convince himself that he knows the best solution" (interview 05.04.2010II) but rather trusts in foreign expertise. Furthermore, foreign-educated people have a vast network of international contacts, which, to some extent, could be useful for the regime

---

4. On the issue of readaptation after returning to one's native country, see, for example, Adler 1981 and Szkudlarek 2010.

when, for instance, between 2008 and 2010 it tried to "get back on stage" after years of international ostracism.

But how successful was the regime in winning over persons with these highly desirable characteristics? Before giving an account of some of the most important successes and failures in recruiting foreign-educated persons during the decade, I will draw the readers' attention to two restraining factors and to the strategies used by the regime.

The first constraint, as already implied in the introduction, was the continuing hostility of regime hard-liners to the reform process. Enforcing policy reforms against an old guard was obviously a risky job;[5] consequently, incentives to co-opt foreign-educated experts needed to be rather high, both in remuneration and in responsibilities and scope for making decisions. Additionally, even before the so-called Arab Spring began, Syrian politicians did not enjoy a favorable public image, which also drove up potential nominees' "price."

The second constraint concerned availability. While there was a large number of Syrians holding foreign university degrees, it was difficult for the regime to recruit the ones it deemed most appropriate for supporting the reform process. This difficulty was linked to these persons' diverging willingness to return to Syria and in their different stances toward the regime. Graduates of universities in the former Eastern Bloc mostly returned and were more inclined to work for the government: a majority of them had received a government scholarship for their studies and thus were obliged by contract to return for a set number of years or otherwise to pay a high penalty.[6] Syrian migrants to Western countries, namely those most needed for liberalizing reforms, mostly financed their studies themselves and hence were free to return or stay abroad. Syria therefore had a disadvantage in comparison to other authoritarian states like Egypt

---

5. The terms "old guard" and "young guard" have been criticized as an oversimplification because they seem to imply a generational divide, while, of course, young people can belong to the old guard as to their political outlook and vice versa. My usage of the terms therefore refers only to their stance toward modernizing politics.

6. Especially in the 1980s there were large delegations of university staff and ministry employees studying abroad. See SAR/MoHE n.d. for statistics.

or China, which had a tradition of sending government-funded students to Western universities. A third group—persons educated at universities in other Arab countries, mostly in Lebanon or sometimes in Egypt—had mostly returned because their migration from the outset was planned for a short time.[7] During 2000–2010, a considerable share of all three groups did not return to Syria but went to the Gulf countries, which had more favorable labor markets and market regulations for small businesses. Unfortunately, there are no reliable statistics on this topic, and even estimations on the number of Syrian expatriates are extremely divergent (partly owing to different definitions regarding how far back in generation they are considered expatriates). The then Syrian Ministry of Expatriates (MoEX, see next paragraph) followed a rather comprehensive definition, estimating between twelve and fifteen million expatriates.[8] In order to gain more comprehensive statistics, MoEX tried during its brief existence to establish a database of foreign-educated Syrians and their qualifications, but this effort did not have tangible results.

Shortly after Bashar al-Asad took power, permission to establish an NGO called "Network of Syrian Scientists, Technologists, and Innovators Abroad" (NOSSTIA) was quickly given. After 2001, it organized a number of highly specialized workshops and conferences, but, according to interviewees, never was very active because of its members' alternative commitments (interview 22.03.2010I) and internal quarrels (interview 12.04.2011).

Furthermore, in 2002, the Ministry of Expatriate Affairs was founded and assigned to high-profile UK-educated Dr. Bouthaina Shaaban as its first minister. It staged two expatriate conferences, in 2004 and 2007, and

7. Most interviewees did not consider this group to be foreign-educated. However, I argue that they are, at least to some extent, especially since most of them graduated from universities with Western curricula like AUB and AUC. Of course, their exposure to a foreign culture was lower than for the other groups, but there are always degrees of exposure owing to different durations of staying abroad, studying only versus also working, etc.

8. See MoEX, last accessed Sept. 2010, http://ministryofexpatriates.gov.sy/cweb/MO EX_ENG/Activities_en/Expatriat_studies.htm.

reached out to Syrian expatriates in Western countries as well as, later, to descendants of Syrian emigrants to Latin America. However, situated at the far end of Damascus's suburb of Dummar and understaffed,[9] the ministry never had much stature: It steadily lost clout after Bouthaina Sha-aban left in 2008 to become presidential advisor for political and information affairs; Flynt Leverett (2005, 103) even implies that MoEX had been created to accommodate Shaaban, who had not gotten the post of minister for foreign affairs, allowing her to promote Syria abroad in a different capacity. Finally, in the cabinet reshuffle of April 2011, MoEX was merged with the Ministry of Foreign Affairs (Legislative Decree 50 as printed by *al-Ba'th* newspaper, 15.04.2011).

In comparison to these institutional attempts to reach out to foreign-educated Syrians, more individualized, personal co-optation strategies were more important for identifying potential reformers since this method allowed hand-picking suitable individuals for "wanted" reforms. The personalized nature of the recruitment scheme can best be illustrated by the significance that was attached to two foreign-trained members of the regime: Abdallah al-Dardari and First Lady Asma al-Asad, who were promoted as the archetypal modernizers.

Abdallah al-Dardari was *the* architect of economic reforms in Syria during 2000–2010. He stepped onto the political scene when appointed as head of the State Planning Commission in 2003, and his so-called Economic Team was talk of the town until its dissolution and al-Dardari's dismissal in the 2011 cabinet reshuffle mentioned above.[10] Up to that point, he had been the symbol for the reform process, drafting the Tenth Five-Year Plan in 2005 and winning over regime hard-liners, as recounted by an entrepreneur:

9. It had only seventy-nine employees in 2009 (SAR/CBS 2009, 72). Perhaps this was the case because the new ministry did not suffer from the same red-tapism and over-staffing as long-established ministries and because its main responsibility—"mediating" between expatriates and other Syrian ministries—required only a small number of staff.

10. For example, Obaida Hamad, "Reshuffling the Deck. Syria Has a New Economic Team," *Syria Today*, Mar. 2010, 16f.

[Take] for example the Minister of Finance [Romanian-educated Mohammad al-Hussein]: for the first two years of the plan, he was opposing the plan . . . after two years, he understood that the president is accepting this plan and that he is supporting this person and his plan, so he had no other choice: either he resigns or he comes back to this person. (Interview 05.04.2010IV)

Al-Dardari's foreign education—a BA in economics from Richmond University in London and an MA in International Relations from the University of Southern California (Zorob 2006)—was not so much played up and, in fact, several interviewees cast doubt on the authenticity of these degrees. His clout was rather that of a practitioner with international working experience with *al-Hayat* in London and at the United Nations Human Development Program (UNDP). Although his economic team consisted mainly of non-foreign-educated persons, several interviewees argued that it gradually "internationalized" its linkages: "The core team around Dardari was not foreign-educated and [after its re-structuring of 2010] still is not foreign-educated but . . . [it] is more capable than before because these people dealt all the time with World Bank, IMF, and the Syrian consultants that had studied or worked abroad" (interview 07.04.2010). Two former members of the economic team went abroad later for further education (interviews 31.03.2010, 20.05.2010). Al-Dardari was seen as a gateway to the world and as a model for foreign-trained Syrians; likewise, sidelining him in 2011 also marked the end of an era.

First Lady Asma al-Asad was the female hero in the same story.[11] Born in England to cardiologist Fawaz Akhraz, founding member and co-chairman of the British Syrian Society, she grew up and studied computer science in London before working as an investment banker for JP Morgan: "The president got married to an English woman, basically" (interview 07.04.2010). After she came to Syria in 2000, she quickly became the pretty

---

11. This title possibly was contested by Bouthaina Shaaban, who, however, could not play on the newcomer image since she had already been in politics pre-2000 as translator and consultant for the late president Hafiz al-Asad.

and charismatic face next to Bashar and a symbol of the "modern" developmental state, creating an image of herself similar to the one of Queen Rania of Jordan.[12] The president's marriage with a non-'Alawite, non-Damascene woman not only broadened the regime's base,[13] but her activist stance and commitment to social projects also won her many admirers. Yet some criticized her initiatives' monopolizing and elitist tendencies: "She's trying very well, but . . . there is a certain negative side in what she is doing, which is a bit of a snobbist benevolence" (interview 18.03.2010); "It's like killing a mosquito with a canon" (interview 05.04.2010II). At the same time, the organizations she helped to fund, like the Syrian Trust for Development, also acted as a measure against brain drain and attracted several highly skilled expatriates back, who praised the international professional standards on all levels from job description to remuneration (for example, interviews 05.04.2010I, 06.04.2010). However, after the regime's U-turn in 2011, it went quiet around her and her initiatives: while, as the First Lady, she could not be dismissed like al-Dardari, there were rumors in May 2011 that she had returned to London and in November 2012 that she had attempted to leave the country.[14]

A third figure who, on a smaller scale, acted as "the ideal modernizer" was US-educated and former World Bank economist Nabil al-Sukkar. Heading Syria's oldest economic consultancy, the Syrian Consulting Bureau (SCB, founded in 1991), he was the prototype of the foreign-educated economic consultant. He was proud to say that several newer consultant agencies were run by former foreign-educated trainees in his bureau (interviews 12.05.2010, 09.05.2010II).

These three persons represented areas—economics and finance, philanthropic activities, and economic consultancy—that, as the next section will show, between 2000 and 2011 drew heavily on foreign-educated Syrian experts. Other areas that gave preference to recruitment of returnees

12. Like Queen Rania, and contrary to Syrian custom, Asma uses her husband's last name more than her maiden name, somewhat underlining her Western outlook.

13. The Akhraz family is Sunni and from Homs.

14. Nabila Ramdani, "Is Asma Assad in London?" *The Telegraph*, May 10, 2011.

with foreign degrees were international organizations operating in Syria, Syrian private universities, and, to a smaller extent, private publishing houses.

Many foreign-educated returnees worked with international organizations, for example, UNDP, with bilateral development agencies, or with the former EU-project Syrian Enterprise and Business Centre, that only since 2006 has been fully Syrian-owned (SEBC; founded in 1996, the acronym formerly stood for Syrian-European Business Centre). Returnees' familiarity with different working environments, the Syrian and the Western one(s), was key to their success: in most cases, they were fluent in both languages and aware of distinct mentalities and "ways of getting things done." However, foreign-educated Syrians were indeed so well suited for cooperating with foreign institutions that there was the danger of their driving out other Syrians, who may have been more representative or suitable to the job.[15]

Private universities and, to a lesser extent, private media also recruited foreign-educated returnees. It is little surprising that private universities, where teaching is often in English, depended on staff with international degrees and offered them higher salaries than locally educated staff (interview 18.3.2010II). It is more surprising, however, that many foreign-educated interviewees taught at a private university *in addition* to having a relatively well-paid job or even a successful business.[16] This multiple employment strategy was attractive because, in addition to providing the opportunity to pass on knowledge and experience acquired while studying abroad, private universities were excellent networking places for the foreign-educated. Several interviewees pointed out that teaching there had been the ideal first point of contact after their return to Syria and had put

15. Foreign-educated staff thus belonged to the "cocktail civil society" as Salam Kawakibi called foreign institutions' key contacts; "an easily accessible category of people . . . [who however expressed] an attitude [that] excludes those people who are truly representative of civil society" (2009, 243f).

16. While multiple employment has traditionally been widespread in Syria because of the meager salaries, the need for extra income was not the main reason for those interviewees who continued teaching at private universities.

them in touch with their later employer or business partner (for example, interview 18.03.2010II).

Yet, as already implied, recruitment of foreign-educated persons was no one-way street: Even before 2011, several foreign-trained high-level politicians had had to leave office before they could make a real impact, for instance Isam al-Zaim (minister of industry 2000–2003), Nibras al-Fadil (presidential advisor 2004–5), and Ghassan al-Rifai (minister of economics and trade 2001–4).[17] As with other returnees further down the hierarchy, their failure was often blamed on their inability to sufficiently readapt to the Syrian work environment: "If you are *only* foreign-educated and you don't know how the country operates, you get surprised, and you spend your tenure in government discovering how things are done . . . They brought in, for example, Ghassan al-Rifai [who is a] brilliant guy, but he spent his two years in government discovering how the ministry operates. Because it was too alien for him" (interview 04.04.2010II). These dismissals fed into the collective memory of foreign observers and foreign-educated reformers alike; many of my respondents recounted and related to these cases (for example, interviews 18.03.2010I, 23.03.2010, 04.05.2010II). The dismissals thus affected the confidence of potential successors to the positions, lowering their expectations of "what can be done" as well as reducing their general willingness to serve in such risky jobs, a downward spiral that was further accelerated in 2011. However, these early dismissals also served to downwardly adjust international and domestic audiences' expectations of Syria's modernization: Bashar al-Asad could present himself as "the good guy" attempting to bring about reforms but being obstructed by the old guard, who did not accept his foreign-educated appointees in office. Yet, even after the 2005 Ba'th Party Congress, when old guardists were weakened—for details see Hinnebusch's contribution in chapter 2 of this volume—there was no renewed wave of recruitment bringing foreign-educated reformers into cabinet positions. Instead, returnees' influence

17. Foreign-educated persons were even particularly well suited to being fired from high positions: once they fell out of favor or were scapegoated for misfired reforms, they often had practicable exit options abroad.

was welcomed more in the private sector, in NGOs, or in international organizations, namely, working as high-achieving professionals without a political mandate. Thus they gradually became important actors in Syria's turning toward private sector activities (see below).

In general, recruitment was kept rather flexible and confined to individuals, and did not target foreign-educated persons as such. This flexibility ensured that reformers were handpicked and that reform processes could not spill over into sensitive, security-relevant areas.[18] One consultant stated in regard to foreign-educated persons in past cabinets: "[This strategy] is not clear, it's not organized. In one phase, this idea was in mind . . . they invited experts from outside as a part of executive administration. Just some persons here or there, they were not organized in a kind of an institution or in a forum"(interview 23.03.2010II). Owing to the challenging process of readaptation to the Syrian "system," there were few bright and shiny success stories of foreign-educated Syrians: Several experienced a "reverse culture shock" (for example, interview 23.03.2010I) that they had not anticipated in contrast to the culture shock when going abroad. Others complained that locally educated colleagues saw them as "arrogant" since they "always know better" and "threaten" to take the positions of senior colleagues (interviews 23.03.2010I, 01.06.2007). Sometimes they became highly frustrated and retreated into private life or remigrated.

This problem of reintegration was reduced or circumvented by recruiting foreign-educated but locally well-established persons, often Western-trained children of the existing business and political elites.[19]

---

18. This assumption is corroborated by the perceived ambiguity of international contacts: Even pre-2011, several interviewees stressed that international contacts could be a burden rather than an asset if the regime felt it could not control or supervise them (for example, interview 18.03.2010I). Furthermore, these contacts were not difficult to establish for other, non-foreign-educated members of the existing business elite (interviews 05.05.2010, 18.05.2010I).

19. In all contexts, the causality between higher education and class background is two-way: On the one hand, higher education helps in upward mobility; on the other hand, persons with a privileged social background have the means to finance higher education and more frequently acquire postgraduate degrees.

Foreign-educated offspring of crony capitalists—for whom studying at a Lebanese, North American, or British university was very common[20]— were more likely to permanently return to Syria because their parents, who mostly were the ones covering the costs for their children's studies abroad, asked them to come home or needed them for the family business. Furthermore, the family business provided know-how, capital, and—most important—local contacts for venturing into new businesses, starting a club or an NGO, and last but not least exerting influence on reforms.

Hence new recruitment criteria did not necessarily induce the rise of new modernizing agents because older criteria remained valid and a degree at a foreign university was simply added to them. Children of the old guard were given a tool, namely, international education, to wipe their slate clean and transform themselves into "new guard" reformers, simultaneously increasing the probability of their being entrusted with shaping domestic reforms. Therefore, this co-optation strategy, instead of broadening the regime's base, in many cases narrowed it further: Persons from well-connected, often wealthy families loyal to the regime (old criteria) were given more opportunities for success if they were also foreign-educated (new criterion). Thus, while international education often merely disguised old clientalist relationships and left the same people in charge of reform decisions, their international degree sometimes made a difference on the direction and content of reforms. This influence on reforms will be discussed in the following section.

Influence on Reforms and on Policy-making Procedures

It has been demonstrated that, between 2000 and 2010, foreign-educated individuals were, although selectively, "in demand" by the Syrian regime and worked in several areas vital for domestic reforms. In the following,

---

20. This tradition also applied to attending prestigious private secondary schools in Damascus, for example, the French or the American school, which were often seen as an important precondition for individuals' later careers like tertiary education pursued abroad (interviews 18.03.2010I, 27.03.2010, 01.04.2010I, 01.04.2010II).

it shall become clearer how (un)successful these people were in influencing reforms and in what way they did. Would these reforms have come about, and in a similar form, without the involvement of foreign-educated returnees? This section also sheds light on whether these "agents of change" shaped and implemented only those reforms for which they were commissioned or whether they also demanded and became active in additional, more far-reaching reform projects.

Syrian domestic reforms during 2000–2010 served a double logic of regime maintenance: first, to secure power and legitimacy through progress and modernization, and second, to provide al-Asad junior with a new image and track record setting him apart from his father. These goals were achieved, in particular, in the field of economy and finance but also in higher education, the media and information technology, and—maybe most peculiarly—through NGOs that were regime-controlled or regime-sponsored in so-called government-organized NGOs (GO-NGOs). Foreign-educated Syrians were most engaged in economic reforms and philanthropic activities, that is, those dynamic policy fields symbolized respectively by Abdallah al-Dardari and Asma al-Asad.[21] For example, several business-related NGOs were established at the initiative of foreign-educated Syrians, such as the Syrian Business Council (SBC) in 2007, the Syrian Young Entrepreneurs Association (SYEA) in 2004, and, in the same year, the Junior Chamber International Damascus (JCI) as a local branch of an international NGO.[22] SBC, a rather exclusive club of the Syrian business elite, aimed at furthering cooperation between its members and at lobbying governmental and international institutions; in a way it served to "institutionalize" clientalism by influencing economic reforms indirectly and hardly noticeable to the outside observer. SYEA and JCI, on the other hand, were devoted to helping young business startups through capacity-building trainings, thus having a target group,

21. For more detailed information on foreign-educated Syrians' influence on either the economic or the associative field, see also Zintl 2013 and Zintl 2012, respectively.

22. The foreign-educated initiators were also heavily overrepresented in these organizations' boards. Most were from business families allegedly on good terms with the regime.

goals, and working methods similar to those of the SHABAB project of the Syria Trust for Development, which was established in 2005. These initiatives were engaged in very limited advocacy. However, another NGO established in 2005, BASMA,[23] concerned with children suffering from cancer, saw itself "not only [as] a charity but also [as] a pressure group" (interview 21.05.2010). The UK-educated initiator added that she had seen in England that NGOs can also function as lobbies while "here many people thought it can only be a charity" (ibid.). In contrast, groups specifically designed for foreign-trained Syrians like NOSSTIA or associations for graduates from particular countries did not engage in advocacy work,[24] let alone enter the political scene. They organized expert conferences or academic lecture series, thus rather functioning as academic or social clubs and sometimes as first point of contact for recent returnees.

Several economic consultants, predominately graduates of US universities, played a substantive role in formulating reforms through policy recommendations and feasibility studies. For example, they were commissioned to draft several chapters of the Tenth Five-Year Plan (FYP) (interviews 23.03.2010II, 27.03.2010, 30.03.2010, 05.05.2010, 09.05.2010II, 12.05.2010). Equally, two lawyers, educated in the UK and in France, reported they had been very involved in the legal side of several economic reforms (interviews 09.05.2010I, 09.05.2010III). Often, recommendations by foreign-educated professionals were sought on an informal and personal level: for example, one US-educated person had been invited to comment on the draft law allowing the establishment of private banks. Several of his recommendations were taken on board (interview 25.03.2010). Thus these consultants contributed to policy formulation only at the request of the Syrian government, which outsourced to freelancers wherever a reform required particular expert knowledge.

23. BASMA is not part of the Syria Trust for Development but is supported by the First Lady personally.

24. For instance, Syrian Society of US Graduates (SSUSG), Syrian Association of the Soviet and Russian Higher Education Institutions' Alumni, and Syrian Graduates of German Universities (SADU).

Returnees with US university degrees or with working experience in the United States were most frequently engaged; a second tier was formed by persons with degrees from the United Kingdom (especially degrees in finance), from France (especially legal studies), and from Germany (especially technical fields of study). It thus seems that neoliberal interpretations with the United States as the preferred model, and with it US-educated advisors, got the upper hand.[25] The specific background of the advisors also reflects the fact that Syria was moving toward a free market economy or even toward *ra's-maliyat al-mutawahisha* ("wild capitalism," interview 12.05.2010) and not toward a "social market economy" as announced by the Tenth FYP.[26] Sometimes this neoliberal tendency was counterbalanced by other trends as in the case of a consultancy led by an US-educated repatriate who explained, "I have employees who are pro-command system, I have employees who are liberal, you know, very pro-market system . . . and when we write our report I always want to show both points of view . . . how are both systems going to impact on [the client's] business?" (interview 27.03.2010). However, this balancing was not as strong as could be expected in a country led by—at least on paper—a socialist party[27] and proud of never having accepted a conditioned structural adjustment program by the World Bank or International Monetary Fund: in quarrels on the direction of change, neoliberal voices had the last word.[28]

25. Encouraging private sector philanthropists instead of establishing a sustainable social welfare system also pointed in this direction.

26. See Seifan 2010a, 28, or Abboud's chapter 3 in this volume.

27. Some persons who openly opposed the neoliberal pathway to reforms were recruited, like the above-mentioned former minister of finance or economic consultant Samir Seifan, who has an Eastern German degree and vast international working experience. Seifan argues for a social market economy with a place for cooperative ownership, like cooperative stock companies, trade unions' ownership, or local municipalities' ownership (Seifan 2010a, 42–48).

28. See, for instance, the dismissal of the head of the State Planning Commission, French-educated Taysir al-Raddawi, in January 2010. Reportedly he was sacked because of his Keynesian public critique of the Tenth FYP as well as, allegedly, an ongoing personal quarrel with Abdallah al-Dardari (All4Syria, *Important: The Dismissal of the President of the State Planning Commission. Days after he criticized the centralization of the*

In addition to economic and financial reforms as well as mainly development-oriented or business-related NGOs, there were two sectors with notable though more dispersed involvement by foreign-educated returnees: higher education and the media.[29] In both fields, the groundbreaking change was that in 2001 private entities gained permission to enter these fields.[30] And in both fields, foreign-educated Syrians were well represented among those who grasped the new opportunity and successfully established private institutions.[31] Syrians with foreign degrees constituted a major source of personnel for these new entities, and thus helped shape them from within.

For instance, the two best-known and prestigious private universities, al-Kalamoon University and Arab International University (AIU, formerly Arab European University) employed large numbers of foreign-educated returnees. AIU was established by German-educated Abdulghani Maa Bared, former president of Damascus University. Al-Kalamoon was, just like Syrian Wadi University near Homs, an endeavor by local businessmen but drew heavily on returnee lecturers and on cooperation with, respectively, British and German universities. Yet subjects taught concentrated on natural sciences, technology, or management so that the knowledge transfer from abroad was largely confined to concrete technical and professional fields.

In regard to media, English-language monthlies *Syria Today* (owned by Canadian-educated business tycoon Abdulghani Attar) and *Forward*

---

wealth in a few cases, Jan. 13, 2010, (corroborated by interviews), http://all4syria.info /content/view/19985/75/, last accessed 5/9/2010.

29. These policy fields are important for regime stability and legitimization since they deal with socializing the next generation or, respectively, with shaping public opinion.

30. Legislative Decree 36 allowed private universities, and Legislative Decree 50 permitted private magazines and newspapers.

31. In state-owned universities, foreign-educated persons were also grossly overrepresented: most professors received their PhD in Eastern Europe financed by a government scholarship. For instance, in 2004–5, between half of the faculty staff (at Damascus University) to about three-quarters (at Ba'th University Homs) were Eastern-educated (see Zintl 2009, appendix). There were few Western-educated staff members, and these were the ones particularly attracted to private universities.

Magazine (by Lebanese-educated entrepreneur Abdulsalam Haykal) were cases in point. Both employed a foreign-educated chief editor, just as the English daily *baladna English* did, which was launched in October 2009 as the first of its kind after the closure of state-owned *Syria Times* in summer 2008. Several of the contributors were foreign-educated too. Yet the influence of these publications on reforms or discussions about reforms was limited since English was not understood by a wider audience in Syria. They rather aimed at transmitting a positive image about Syria to foreign diplomats and, especially in the case of *Forward Magazine*, to Syrian expatriates. They did not establish themselves as mouthpieces for foreign-educated Syrians and both were discontinued after the start of the uprising.

Foreign-educated persons' influence exercised through existing channels for policy formulation—however weak in Syria—like the parliament and the chambers of commerce and industry was more sporadic and anecdotal. While Rateb al-Shallah, holding degrees from Oxford and Berkeley, definitely had a massive impact as long-standing president of the Federation of the Syrian Chambers of Commerce, other business(wo)men involved with the chambers stressed that foreign education was the exception rather than the rule (interviews 01.04.2010, 05.04.2010, 05.04.2010III). Yet, also in these institutions, the regime seemed to be willing to promote foreign-educated persons' influence, not least because attracting foreign investment was key to economic reforms' success: those board members of the chambers who were foreign-educated or spoke foreign languages had reportedly not been elected but appointed by the president (interview 12.05.2010).

Indeed, visible political influence by foreign-educated Syrians remained within the set limits of the regime's "wanted" foreign and domestic policy reforms.[32] Interviews indicated that most initiators of

---

32. Despite the realignment with Western powers and particularly with Turkey between 2004 and 2010, foreign-trained persons' influence in the Ministry for Foreign Affairs remained rather low (interview 22.03.2010II). Exceptions are ambassadors such as 'Imad Mustafa and Sami al-Khiyami, who, however, were appointed to the United States and the United Kingdom, respectively, rather to protect them by removing them from

"real" NGOs—however sparse and mostly concerned with issues like domestic violence, not directly affecting or even questioning the regime's dominance—were not foreign-educated. Moreover, although seeking intercultural dialogue and exchange of experiences, such NGOs were cautious about accepting foreign support, particularly funding (interviews 23.03.2010III, 04.05.2010III, 18.05.2010).

There was a delicate balance between returnees' readaptation to Syria and their innovative influence. While trying to blend in with their new milieu, returnees often did not apply what they had learned abroad, as one US-educated returnee criticized: "Some people said, 'How about throwing away our education?' and became like the rest of the people in this country. So they just left their education behind. . . . They found their education is a heavy load, so they threw this load [aside]" (interview 26.04.2011). Readaptation came to play a paradoxical role because returnees needed to be readapted enough to acquire and retain a position of influence, yet not readapted "too much" in order to have an innovative impact on their work or on politics. In conclusion, foreign-educated individuals' main channels of influence were rather indirect (with the exception of foreign-educated ministers, whose difficulties to assert themselves in their position were outlined above). They influenced reforms as independent advisors on an ad hoc basis or by establishing NGOs as possible pressure groups. Or they worked for foreign institutions, so that a Syrian ministry that was the cooperation partner with such institutions took the relevant decisions about whether to pass and implement policy suggestions. Thus the main tendency was to establish parallel structures that circumvented surviving old structures. With the help of incentives such as higher salaries or more challenging responsibilities, which were made available to highly skilled returnees in these sectors, this practice provided the opportunity to monitor and filter foreign-educated persons' political influence and to protectively situate them outside the old guard's strongholds.

---

regime hard-liners' reach than to grant them more influence (interview 18.03.2010). Yet it was difficult to gain data since this ministry has been hardly accessible for researchers.

Conclusions: A Decade of Transnationalizing
Authoritarianism and Entrenched Clientalism

Between 2000 and 2010, the Syrian regime increasingly recruited foreign-educated persons, but this recruitment was largely confined to revocable, temporary positions and to limited policy areas, albeit some of these pivotal for modernization. Moreover, the recruitment of foreign-educated Syrians remained subject to the domestic power balance: those who benefited from the reforms, especially children of the business elite, provided most of these foreign-trained technocrats. Apparently, the pool of Western-educated Syrians was large enough for the regime to enlist only those whose loyalty it could take for granted. This favoritism created a quasi-monopoly of what could be called "mate modernizers"—analogous to the term "crony capitalists"[33]—and it also redefined the old deal of "loyalty versus patronage": By assisting the state, through their philanthropic activities, in its social responsibilities (for example, education, training, and to a smaller extent health and poverty alleviation), businessmen could in exchange protect their privileges. Foreign-educated returnees could especially take advantage of this arrangement, because they had suitable skills and contacts to offer, but at the same time their knowledge transfer was hampered by pressures to readapt to the "Syrian way of doing things"; it should be added that these readaptation pressures often were, too, less restrictive for returnees from well-known families on good terms with the regime.

The finding that the established crony bourgeoisie's offspring had the biggest impact also among the foreign-educated returnees may be disillusioning, but these people's inherited elite status also helped to add considerable authority to planned reforms, pushing them through against hard-liners in the ruling elite. Thus domestic reforms in the 2000–2010 period tended to be better informed by technical expertise than they were

33. While economic reforms can particularly be distorted toward maximum profits for crony capitalists, reform processes in general can cater to the specific interests of one part of society only (the "mate modernizers") and secure the continued participation and influence of these few in policy-making.

ten years earlier, but the social background of people providing this expertise was still largely the same. The inclusion of foreign-educated nationals
underlined that growth and performance were prioritized over equality
and social mobility.

Regarding policy fields, foreign-educated people's activities concentrated on areas of reform that were already set by the authoritarian state,
particularly where figures like Asma al-Asad and Abdallah al-Dardari led
by example. Thus, as long as they remained within these areas, foreign-
educated returnees were, to some extent, safeguarded by the hands-on
image and immunity of the foreign-educated presidential couple and by
the high esteem for foreign degrees in Syrian society at large. Toward the
latter half of the decade, foreign-educated individuals mostly helped with
implementing adopted reforms rather than pressuring for or formulating
new ones; thus, with the regime's pushing for more active private and associative sectors, they were more involved with the practical than with the
political aspects of policy changes. Returnees abstained from bringing up
additional, so far "unwanted" reforms because they were busy fighting over
the direction of "wanted reforms," too concerned about falling out of favor
with the regime, too heterogeneous and atomized for concerted action,
and, most important, debilitated by accusations of not having readapted
sufficiently (the negative repercussions of these accusations became particularly visible from spring 2011 onward, when the regime's rally cry against
"foreign conspirators" led to a heightened suspicion of returnees as possible foreign spies). These factors and returnees' indirect channels of influence—through their own business or as employees in newly established
organizations such as GO-NGOs, private banks, private universities, or
international organizations—made it easier for the state to retain control.

In conclusion, the authoritarian strategy of co-opting individuals
with foreign degrees did, in spite of setbacks, work remarkably well during Bashar al-Asad's first decade in power. In spite of this success, Bashar's
legitimizing and modernizing strategy was largely discarded in 2011,
when popular protests were officially blamed on foreign interference. How
foreign-educated Syrians will react to the new situation and what political
role they will play after the civil war has ended remain to be seen.

7

"To Promote Volunteerism among School Children"

Volunteer Campaigns and Social Stratification in Contemporary Syria

MANDY TERC

In the decade after Bashar al-Asad assumed the Syrian presidency from his father, economic liberalization became both the primary symbol for and source of change in this strongly authoritarian Arab state. As the transition from a socialist, state-run economy to a market-oriented "social market economy" took place, much attention was devoted to analyzing the somewhat opaque relationship between the social and the market.[1] What is clear, however, is that the process of economic liberalization begun in the 1990s opened new possibilities for a small class of elite Syrians in the new millennium (Perthes 1995). Through the consumption of newly imported luxury goods, adoption of newly widespread English usage, and employment in newly permitted private business sectors such as banking and insurance, a newly visible elite class utilized economic changes to establish itself as a salient and influential social group of the new economic order. In addition to moneymaking ventures, new elites embraced participation in newly available, albeit limited civic actions.

This chapter examines how the seemingly benign areas into which these Syrian elites poured much of their energy—entrepreneurship and

---

1. See Samer Abboud's contribution (chapter 3) in this volume.

volunteerism—actually created, ossified, and rendered visible social hierarchies and divisions. Other scholars have argued for "the salience of professional associations in the Arab world as an institutional lens to conceptualize change in authoritarian state-society relations," and these associations also carry a relevance to issues of social mobility and class production (Salloukh and Moore 2007, 71). This chapter will further illustrate the utility of this approach.

One of the most popular by-products of Syria's economic changes was the nongovernmental entrepreneurial organizations for young professionals that attracted upwardly mobile Syrians by the hundreds. The most prominent organizations were the Junior Chamber International (JCI) and the Syrian Young Entrepreneur's Association (SYEA). They brought together disparate branches of elite families: children of the most prominent families, private school students, employees at private companies, and ambitious university graduates hoping for entrance into more prestigious social and economic circles. Despite an official focus on entrepreneurship, they offered their members structured entrance into this new elite and provided an entire social world for active members, with almost-nightly meetings, weekend retreats, social outings, and public volunteering campaigns. They also relied on a distinctive interactional style, based on the repeated incorporation of key English words and phrases into Arabic conversation, to distinguish themselves and communicate their elite status. It is also important to note that "entrepreneurial organization" does not necessarily refer to business activities but instead to an embrace of entrepreneurship as the organizing principle behind young Syrians' professional ambitions and ideas about developing Syrian society at large.

Entrepreneurship Associations

SYEA was the first entrepreneurial organization to begin activities in Syria. Its founders represented the children of the wealthiest businessmen, those most closely connected to and benefiting from the regime. In 2004 it opened with great fanfare at an elaborate kickoff ceremony. Even First Lady Asma al-Asad attended the celebration, demonstrating both the founders' prominence and close connections to the regime and the regime's support of the fledgling organization. The cozy relationship between SYEA and the government did not escape the notice of other Syrians, and SYEA was viewed as compliant with the regime. One young woman, herself from a prominent family with several members who possessed very close ties to the regime, noted that "SYEA has a strong backing from the government. Asma al-Asad was at the opening, and she was backing them. To be honest, people in SYEA are bigger, richer than in JCI [Junior Chamber International]." While SYEA's entrepreneurial bent placed it firmly within the new elite's practices, its organization and perceived intimacy with regime figures made it seem to be more a continuation of an entrenched system of nepotism and corruption than an innovative new organization. Still, its emphasis on making young Syrians "job creators, rather than job seekers" and on "create[ing] a new economic environment based on a modern entrepreneurial concept" (SYEA 2010) placed it firmly within the new elite's values and emphasis on evolving, if not changing, the status quo of employment and entrepreneurship activities in Syria.

The organization relied on "sponsorship" relationships as the core of its activities. The founders, wealthy children of wealthier parents and businesspeople in their own right, positioned themselves as more knowledgeable than those who could benefit from SYEA's educational programs and competitions for funding. From the beginning, the organization viewed its primary mission as "endeavour[ing] to deepen the culture of entrepreneurship among young Syrians, encouraging them and providing them with the necessary information and experience to launch and continue projects, in addition to financing entrepreneurial activities. Since its launch in 2004, SYEA has become one of the foremost authorities on entrepreneurship in Syria" (SYEA 2010). SYEA is depicted both by its membership and by most Syrians as more nationally rather than globally focused, more interested in business rather than civic activities or volunteer work, and more accepting of the social status quo. Its leadership retained their posts indefinitely, allowing prominent members to remain entrenched in influential positions. At the same time, however, one of its largest projects was the "Eastern Entrepreneurs" contest in which young people from three of the poorest rural districts in Syria competed for seed money for their business plans.[2]

In parallel, another group of equally prominent young Syrians established the first JCI chapter in Damascus. Like SYEA's founders, many of them were educated abroad and inherited family companies that conducted business globally. Many of them had spent significant amounts of time studying and working abroad, in the United States, Canada, England, and Lebanon. When they returned to Syria, as several of them explained to me in separate interviews, they wanted to bring the professionalism, creativity, and skill training they encountered abroad to their home country. They also felt that Bashar al-Asad's economic opening and protechnology stance provided them the right historical moment to introduce a new type of civic organization in Syria, where prior to this point the government had permitted virtually no civil society associations to operate. Through the International Chamber of Commerce (ICC), which already had an outlet in Syria, this group learned of the opportunity to establish a related group for a younger generation. Unlike SYEA, JCI was a local chapter of a global organization that operated under the auspices of its international parent group and had to adopt its practices, maintain its standards, and communicate with its central administration.[3] After applying for and receiving official recognition from the Syrian government, JCI Syria began operating in August 2004.[4]

2. Eastern here refers to Eastern Syria. The three districts are Deir ez-Zor, Hassaka, and Raqqa.

3. The first JCI chapter began in 1915 in Saint Louis, Missouri, and by 1944 was established in eight countries. The organization now boasts "200,000 members in 5,000 communities and more than 100 countries around the world" (JCI, "Junior Chamber International," 2011, www.jci.cc).

4. Like its parent organization ICC, JCI was registered and operated under the auspices of the Ministry of Economy. This affiliation was uncommon for NGOs, which generally were required to register with the Ministry of Labor and Social Affairs. It was widely believed that registering under the more forward-thinking Ministry of Economy allowed them more latitude to operate. However, one JCI founder dismissed this idea, stating, "As long as you're official in Syria, you're fine."

After its initial installation in Damascus, the organization spread to other Syrian cities, such as Aleppo, Homs, Lattakia, and Deir ez-Zor in the country's easternmost region, counting several thousand members across Syria. The organization formed four subcommittees—business area, community area, individual area, and international area—that were assigned a chairperson and held weekly meetings. Each area was responsible for creating and executing its own programming. The diverse results included a monthly business lecture series, a business networking event, a children's volunteering fair, lessons in business French, hosting of a conference on Syria for JCI members from around the globe, and even monthly karaoke nights. To join JCI, applicants completed a short written application, attended an orientation session, and then completed a probation period during which they had to attend weekly meetings and officially join a committee and subcommittee. After that probation period, they became full members without any other requirements. In order to maintain active membership, they had to attend a certain number of hours of JCI activities per year. There were no interviews or requirements beyond attendance and an age between eighteen and forty. The formal application process focused more on encouraging attendance and participation than on screening potential members.

Active participation in JCI was a time-consuming proposition. Each area held a weekly meeting that lasted up to two hours. In addition, it offered an almost weekly schedule of additional activities, planning sessions, volunteer opportunities, and social outings. Although members were not required to attend more than one area meeting per week, a surprising number of them regularly attended several meetings per week. Daylong weekend retreats, overnight conferences, and even international trips to regional or worldwide JCI events took place quarterly. After most meetings, that concluded around seven or eight in the evening, a group of members typically decamped to a nearby café to smoke water pipes, sip coffee, gossip, and plan additional activities. All these activities came in addition to the full-time jobs that most members held. The sheer volume of activities offered by JCI and the time members invested in them meant that JCI had the potential to completely dominate and restructure even the daily lives of its members. Yet most members reported genuinely enjoying every aspect of their involvement in JCI, from the satisfaction of the organization's accomplishments to the genuine friendships they developed with other members. In fact, JCI's most substantial potential impact was how it promised to reorganize and reorient the lives of its members. JCI's activities impacted all realms of a young person's life: their social lives, their professional development, and even their attitudes about achievement, ambition, social change, democracy, and fairness. It provided new styles and venues for social interaction, even new ideas about how one could and should forge social connections. Under the guise of business events, JCI proposed a somewhat radical idea for Syria: that social relationships and hierarchies could be engineered through JCI's activities, rather than occur through proximity or familial relationships.

Although the political climate in Syria did not permit radical political change, volunteer work on social issues with no obvious political ramifications burgeoned in the first decade of the 2000s, particularly in the context of these entrepreneurship organizations (Pierret and Selvik 2009). Whether designed to benefit rural families, orphans, poor college students, or children with cancer, volunteer campaigns were elaborate, sustained efforts that identified a population in need, created a long-term strategy for involvement, and implemented a program for intervention over an extended time period. They also, during the course of their existence, established new social categories: the giver and the recipient, the privileged and the needy, the benefactor and the beneficiary. I contend that volunteer campaigns, though well intentioned, often served as moments of sorting Syrians into a new social hierarchy that placed urban economic elites at its apex, ambitious English-speaking middle-class college graduates rising toward the top, and rural residents or poor migrants to the cities at the bottom.

Volunteerism versus Charity Work

From the entrepreneurship organizations such as JCI and SYEA to the local United Nations agencies to the Syrian First Lady's expansive Syrian Trust for Development,[5] an emphasis on volunteerism (*al-tataw'u*) pervaded Syria's limited scene of nongovernmental associations during 2000–2010. The phrase "culture of volunteerism" surfaced again and again, whether in conversations, JCI activities, or the numerous advertising materials distributed around Damascus during the course of my research. Local conceptions of volunteerism in certain Syrian contexts arose partly from their contrast with their supposed predecessor, "charity work" (*al-'amal al-khayri*). The comparison between the two concepts posited a teleological relationship in which Syrians under the archaic system in place before the last decade performed unplanned, nonstrategic acts of goodness (distributing food, donating clothing, or sponsoring medical treatments were examples used to describe charity work). Often, these sorts of charitable acts involving redistribution of wealth and resources were dominated by religious organizations, whether Muslim or Christian (Pierret and Selvik 2009). Syrians who became socially and linguistically engaged with international networks of NGOs, skill-building resources, and educational institutions saw themselves, by contrast, as advocating long-term, large-scale, well-planned interventions into societal problems. When using the term "volunteerism" in conversation, Syrians most often paired it with the paraphrased proverb that instead of giving the poor a fish, it is preferable to teach them how to fish so that they may feed themselves in the future. Just as these young Syrians invested heavily in their own skill sets and enthusiastically signed up for training sessions of all kinds, they advocated providing similar opportunities for those they deemed to be in need.

One example of a charity that adopted the tenets of volunteerism was Basma (its name means smile in English). Basma raised money and mobilized a corps of volunteers to provide support and treatment for children with cancer and their families. According to its own promotional

---

5. The peculiar position of the First Lady's charity has been described as a GO-NGO, or government-organized nongovernmental organization. Although it is officially nongovernmental, the First Lady's proximity or possible influence in the regime rendered the Trust partially governmental.

materials, it provided "psychological and moral support to the children and their parents during the treatment period, as well as financial support. BASMA seeks also to provide medical support to the children's cancer units in Syria in order to upgrade the medical services rendered to children."[6]

Its mandate to support and fund children receiving cancer treatment might have placed it well within the realm of traditional Syrian "charity work"; many organizations, from Islamic awqaf[7] to government-run associations, offered such straightforward interventions in causes with no possible political undertones, such as paying for medical treatment, providing entertainment for orphans, or feeding the poor on holidays. Such actions on the behalf of others were typically limited in scope and time, low in visibility, and without any comprehensive implications for how class relations were configured currently. However, it was Basma's comprehensive approach to creating a sustained fund-raising drive that demonstrated how much the concept of volunteerism aligned with other arenas in which elites distinguished themselves from nonelites, including upscale consumption and public displays of luxurious leisure.

In February 2009 Basma launched its campaign entitled "28 days of giving for children with cancer." To publicize the campaign, in which prominent and prestigious businesses were persuaded to donate portions of their profit on a certain day to Basma, Basma saturated wealthy neighborhoods of Damascus with a bright, graphic calendar that described the particular business making donations for each day. For instance, on February 12, the pricey Italian coffee chain Segafredo would donate all its profits to Basma. On the 24th, the CD store Eido would donate 25 percent of any purchases to Basma. The businesses included in the calendar were among the venues in which new elites consumed, socialized, and displayed their cohesion as a distinct social group. The calendar was

---

6. Basma, "Basma-Syria: Battling to Smile Again," 2010, http://www.basma-syria.org/.

7. Awqaf are an Islamic institution that "consisted of an object which was endowed to specific pious purpose for eternity" (van Leeuwen 1999, 11). They required property owners to turn over their property to a trustee who would utilize the asset for a charitable purpose, often to support mosques or to distribute alms.

printed on paper placemats in upscale cafes and restaurants, published as an advertisement in society magazines, and placed on billboards and posters in Damascus's upscale neighborhoods. Basma situated itself in the Syrian discourse of volunteerism by stressing its long-term strategies and its commitment to "improving social conditions of children with cancer in Syria." That Basma structured its purpose as a stated goal—to improve social conditions—followed by concrete, long-term actions to meet that goal demonstrated how the discourse and philosophy of volunteerism as an improvement over charity work functioned within Basma and among Syrian elites more generally.

The remainder of this chapter considers two volunteer events planned and implemented by JCI in late 2008 and early 2009 in order to further illuminate these issues. The first event, a children's fair staffed by local high school students, reflected how the very structuring of volunteering campaigns took into account a complicated calculus of class relations. Utilizing social and linguistic clues, the event instructed participants at every level about where they stood socially and the appropriate behavior they should exhibit to demonstrate their social position. The second event, an afternoon of fund-raising for Gazan children following the Israeli military campaign in early 2009, demonstrated how social and linguistic clues also differentiated elite reactions to regional events from nonelite responses. In addition, social and linguistic rules governing interactions at these events further communicated class nuances. In a new era of Syrian economic liberalization and civic possibilities, social hierarchies were shifting and reconfiguring (Hinnebusch 2008), but they remained as trenchant and powerful as ever.

JCI Children's Fair

JCI's Children's Fair was an annual event, and the one that took place in 2008 was the third consecutive fair JCI had held. Run by the community committee of JCI—the subgroup responsible for JCI's volunteer campaigns—the fair required months of advance planning and necessitated the labor of most JCI members. The first issue at stake in the fair was the joint participation of government school and private school students in

the creation and execution of the fair. This issue surfaced at an early planning meeting during which their respective competence at participation
was assessed and debated with a great deal of concern. In a hierarchy that
was reflected widely in both JCI and larger society, private school students
were assumed to be adept at participation in civic affairs and knowledgeable about the social norms demanded in such a situation. Foreign-
language private schools flourished during the economic liberalization
of the decade and quickly became important sites for younger members
of the new elite and their children. In them, students not only acquired
the linguistic skills of the elite, but they also learned the necessary social
comportment to gain acceptance in venues such as JCI and volunteer campaigns.[8] Public school students, in contrast, prompted concern from JCI
members about their capability to perform the role expected because they
would not have received comparable socialization. The perceived performance gap between government and private school students was a preoc-
cupation of JCI members, as illustrated in a meeting a week before the fair.

The discussion unfolded in the typical conversational style that reinforced the global sophistication of JCI and other new economic elites: a
dizzying and highly structured blending of fluent and idiomatic Arabic
and English. One member later summarized the issue with the government school students this way: "There are six public schools. There is nothing under control." She then included this as among the pressing "tasks
belonging to us." Another member then interjected her added concern
about the difficulties posed by incorporating government school students
into the fair, namely, that public school students were unlikely to understand how to participate in the event appropriately and thus required
additional supervision and support from JCI members. Finally, the meeting concluded with the meeting's chairperson reminding the members
to be aware of the difficulties posed by the government schoolchildren.

8. Although younger Syrian elites enrolled in these new private schools, they were
not available to Syrian elites in their twenties and thirties who attended high school in the
1990s, before such schools opened. Therefore these schools do not have the same social
significance to JCI members as they do to a younger generation.

She declared that government school students would need extra help producing decorations and extra time to assemble said decorations properly. She also explained that, unlike the arrangement with private schools that would use their funds to purchase their supplies, JCI would purchase supplies for the government schools.

Moments after these discussions, an elegantly dressed and impeccably groomed woman, sporting an immense diamond wedding ring, entered the room. She seemed slightly older than most of the members, perhaps in her late thirties or early forties. Indeed, she clearly recognized many of the members, as she waved silent hellos and mouthed greetings to several people. The community area chairperson introduced her as a representative from the Syrian Association for Autism (al-jam'iyya al-suriyya li-tawahud). When she began speaking, she framed her comments as those of a concerned mother of a son with autism. She spoke about the importance of such fairs for children like her son, afflicted with autism, and the need for autistic children to feel the caring and interest of their society.[9] At one point, she paused as tears filled her eyes although they never fell. Her emphasis on how the fair would bring joy and comfort to autistic children added an additional dimension to the fair's purpose.

After the meeting, one member clarified to me that the aim of the children's fair was to "promote volunteerism among school children." The fair's main purpose was to educate students from both the public and the private schools on the benefits of volunteerism, although it was assumed that the public students would need more assistance in this process. The autistic children and other disadvantaged or special needs youth would of course also benefit from a fun and enjoyable children's fair, but their participation mainly served to provide the opportunity, venue, and recipients for the "culture of volunteerism" that the fair was intended to spread and encourage.

The fair took place during the Friday and Saturday of a warm and sunny October weekend in a sporting arena in a peripheral Damascus

---

9. In Syria, special needs students do not attend mainstream schools. Instead, they are sent to government-run institutes or special venues.

neighborhood. Booths spread over several basketball courts, forming a tidy tent city of cheerful stations awash in colorful signs and bright decorations, offering face-painting, baked goods, and carnival games. American pop music, from Beyonce to 50 Cent, played through loudspeakers. Approximately fifty JCI members, recognizable by their gray JCI polo shirts emblazoned with JCI's English logo, supervised the event. They monitored a check-in counter, manned a booth selling JCI paraphernalia, circulated through the crowds, and hovered over the booths. Throughout the day, a stream of children entered the fair. Most of the attendees came via an affiliation with a charitable group, some of which contained no specific socioeconomic class affiliation such as the society for autism and others with direct class connotations such as organizations for orphaned children or disadvantaged rural youth. JCI members partnered with the NGOs' own chaperones to guide the children through the fair and entice them with the games and activities that overwhelmed them at first. Their friendly smiles and enthusiastic encouragement to try the games succeeded in welcoming the initially shy attendees. By the end of the day, the grounds were filled with smiling six-year-olds with painted faces munching on cookies.

As welcoming as JCI members were to the children from NGOs, behind the scenes they were more concerned with the performance of the government school students. The public school booths were interspersed with the booths of the private schools, and many more JCI members hovered around the former than the latter. They would not have found space in any case as the private school booths were crowded with fashionable teenagers of both genders enthusiastically welcoming the children and as many equally affluent-seeming teachers and parents. Their decorations featured huge, artistically drawn murals of children playing, sporting equipment, or intentionally cheerful imagery such as yellow suns and fluffy clouds. The government schools' booths followed similar themes but their decorations lacked the crispness of the drawing and the brightness of the colors. Their workforce differed too; no parents or teachers led the group, and their student bodies were one gender, usually female. Rather than wandering about the grounds in mixed groups chatting loudly, the government school students clustered among themselves and stayed in the confines of their own booths. The private Damascus Community School, better known by its nickname "the American school," which represented the apex of knowledge and ability in these moments of volunteerism, had the most professional decorations and games with signs done by computer. The International School of Choueifat, another expensive and prestigious private school, featured childlike cartoon characters playing baseball on their signage. Baseball is not available anywhere in Syria, and the images of mitts and bats likely meant little to the disadvantaged youth who had probably never even heard of the sport.

Disparate clothing choices also marked the differences between the three groups. The JCI members (many of whom had attended private schools or completed their university studies abroad) and private school students wore the latest Western fashions: tight-fitting skinny jeans, sunglasses with designer logos, and T-shirts with their school or JCI logos printed in English. The government school students also sported jeans and T-shirts, but many of their female students wore the Islamic veil, and their clothing was generally loose-fitting and covered their ankles and wrists. Their accessories were locally made and less expensive than the imported Italian brands, but the girls particularly sported colorful necklaces and bracelets in current styles. Finally, the children and parents of the partnering charity NGOs wore polyester dress pants and button-down shirts for the men and flowing skirts and elaborately ruffled blouses for the women and girls. It was obvious that they had come dressed in their best clothing for the occasion, and their sartorial choices did not reflect the latest European trends but seemed dated by several decades. Their attire clashed with the enforced casualness and trendiness of the entire event and signaled their lack of familiarity with the dictates of attending a casual fair for children.

Linguistically there were marked differences as well. Although the fair was officially bilingual, with the school names printed in Arabic and English on the booths that JCI provided, English titles and catchphrases dominated the booths' decorations. The private and prestigious Pakistani School posted the phrase "Welcome, our guests" on its booth. As per its typical branding, JCI hung professionally printed blue plastic tarps with its English logo and slogan all over the fairgrounds. Although it printed the Arabic translation of its formal name, Junior Chamber International, on its booth, its English logo and English materials far outnumbered the small amounts of Arabic. For an event that was at some level meant to attract disadvantaged Syrians, the heavy use of English seemed strangely opaque. Yet when one considers that JCI was promoting what it considered a new culture of volunteerism based on global standards and convened through a global organization, its insistent use of English becomes less perplexing even if it was no less exclusionary. The fair was about inculcating lower classes in the new ways of the new elite, and English usage was the unifying element in all the orientations, interactions, and principles of this elite. Without its English branding and framework, the fair and JCI's sponsorship of it would have lost its clear affiliation with the new elite.

As JCI members continually stressed to each other and to me during the course of running the children's fair, events like this one were not a common occurrence in Syria. NGOs and the potential civic actions that they undertook were a very recent development in Syrian society. A children's fair—convened by a nongovernmental, secular entity—was exotic for Syrians outside the upper classes. The bewilderment on their faces and their inability to dress like those sponsoring the event revealed their lack of familiarity with the concept. JCI members kept repeating that "this was only the fourth ever such fair" and there "just isn't anything else like this in Syria." This emphasis on the fair's newness and exceptional nature reinforced JCI's position as the arbiter of all that was current and progressive in Syria and reminded those attending or even participating that they needed to learn the corresponding new norms of behavior.

In between these extremes of assertive elites and their beneficiaries, the government school students navigated their own position both in the event and possibly in society at large. Like the JCI members and private school students, they were hosting the event. They were not recipients of its charity. They were expected to engage the NGO children, to use their assumed position of relative privilege to provide the entertainment and joy that the NGO children presumably lacked. Yet as their comportment, dress, and peripheral position in the planning hierarchy indicated, they were not fully accepted members of an elite group who could freely dispense charity and behave appropriately in such venues without explicit instruction. In fact, given that the children's fair was really for promoting "the volunteerism of school children" these middle-class children were the ones for whom the event was structured and whose socialization into such activities was the most important purpose. Although everyone welcomed the NGO children and hoped the event would provide them with a lovely day, the crucial work was to inculcate the government schoolchildren with norms of volunteerism that JCI members and private schools had already mastered. The upper classes instructed the middle class on how to "help" the lowest classes, or those with special needs regardless of class. In that way, the children's fair provided an instructive lesson on who stood where in the class hierarchy and what kinds of expected behavior corresponded with each position.

"For the Children of Gaza"

A similarly illustrative volunteering event occurred a few months later. This time, the events in question occurred more spontaneously. The triggering occurrence was Israel's bombing raid on the Palestinian territory of the Gaza Strip, spanning from early December 2008 to late January 2009. The images of violence and destruction that flooded the Arab world were gruesome and disturbing. Bloodied corpses of children, houses rendered piles of concrete dust, and decrepit hospitals teeming with the living wounded appeared on TVs, the Internet, newspapers, and magazines. The intensity of the bombing did not abate, and as it continued, raw emotion and fury in the Arab world accelerated. In Damascus the tension over the bombings and anger at the perceived injustice boiled. Television sets in stores and homes stayed tuned to the constant footage of the bombings on the Pan-Arab station al-Jazeera. Taxi drivers continually interrogated me about my reaction to the bombings, vainly searching for some explanation of why the international community allowed the violence to continue. Shopkeepers began placing copies of Israeli flags or Stars of David on the pavement in front of shop entrances so that customers might step on them and thus express their disgust. One particularly angered and ambitious shopkeeper compiled a collage of inflammatory images, including Israeli flags imprinted with swastikas and signs stating, "Kindly American citizens are not welcome in this store."

By early January audible and visible expressions of anger over the siege were present on Damascus streets, as the government or other para-governmental organizations arranged protests on an almost daily basis. Given that there was no Israeli presence in Syria, the targets of their rage varied. A crowd of mostly young men marched on the Egyptian embassy, furious at President Hosni Mubarak's decision to refuse Gazans entrance into Egypt. A crowd of schoolchildren and government employees, pushed out of classrooms and offices by official decree, headed for the American embassy. Mostly the protests began and ended at central Damascus squares where the protesters held signs and chanted slogans, primarily for the benefit of the Syrian television stations that filmed them. Posters vilifying Israeli leaders and Arabic chants demanding death to Israel and America were common.

Consistent with their general distancing from nonelite styles of inter-action, commerce and style, and their insistent apolitical stance, JCI members chose not to keep up with the reactions of the majority of Syrian society and the government's official actions. In fact, JCI members seemed remarkably disconnected from the popular forms of protest constantly occurring around them. At a meeting on the same evening as a sched-uled, government-sponsored protest at the American embassy, a member was scheduled to give a short presentation. He was curiously late for over an hour, texting another member to report that he was stuck in traffic. When he finally arrived, breathless and apologetic, he described grid-lock on the streets, for a reason he could not fathom. The other members seemed puzzled too, wondering what would keep someone in a standstill on the road just behind the American embassy, until I finally reminded them that there was an official protest that day. Oh right, they murmured, and returned to their discussion of a business lecture series. Yet despite their disinterest in activities such as protesting in the streets and creating inflammatory signage, they too expressed mounting anger over the bomb-ings of Gaza and began to discuss in their meetings what kind of response would be appropriate for their group.

At a meeting in mid-January, one of the committee chairs announced that they would hold an "action" on behalf of the people of Gaza that com-ing weekend. The event would be a fund-raising drive to collect money on behalf of the Syrian Red Crescent, which had ostensibly been transferring funds and goods to Gaza. It would take place on a Friday afternoon on the side of Damascus's largest and most traversed traffic circle. JCI members would carry boxes and solicit cash donations from passersby who would pull over to donate. A DJ would provide inspiring background music, and the day would conclude with a short performance by a children's choir.

When I arrived at the fund-raiser, I saw that they had positioned their staging area so that we were most likely to catch the cars going to or coming from the most affluent areas of the city, where most JCI members resided. This position would catch the Damascus residents who had the most money to give, but it would also make the JCI action visible to the part of Syrian society who mattered most to them and for whom their branding was relevant and comprehensible. I arrived at 11 a.m. on that Friday, when Damascus is empty, as traffic does not start circulating until after Friday noon prayers. By the time I arrived, JCI members had already established a staging area, marked by two parked vans on the side of the traffic circle. There were two huge banners hung over the vans. One, written with spray paint on a sheet-like banner, proclaimed in Arabic "donate on behalf of the children of Gaza to the Syrian Red Crescent." The sign was charmingly handmade and unsophisticated. It contrasted sharply with the banner hanging over the other parked car. This one, made from an industrial plastic material, featured the crisp, professionally designed JCI logo, in English, printed repeatedly on a bright blue background. The sign was obviously professionally made and well planned to provide JCI's "branding"—as its membership repeatedly called it in English—with maximum visibility. In fact, later when we took a group picture, there were several rounds of reshuffling people to ensure that the JCI logo was visible and legible in the photo. No such interest was taken in the Arabic sign asking people to donate.

As I greeted the JCI members organizing the event, I was given a sashlike scarf that features the iconic black and white check of Palestinian scarves called *kafiyeh* and the word *Gaza* printed in Arabic next to what looked like the outline of a mosque. A JCI member affixed a small button that read in Arabic "on behalf of the children of Gaza." It was tiny and barely legible to anyone standing farther than six inches from the scarf. A member also handed me a large bright blue adhesive sticker that read in English "I'm a volunteer" with JCI and its logo printed below it. Like the larger signage hung over the cars, there was a clear division of labor between English and Arabic in these materials. It was not incidental that JCI's branding, logo, and other materials were written exclusively in English while all information pertaining to donations, the suffering in Gaza, or the Red Crescent were written in Arabic. The limited use of Arabic highlighted the plight of the Gazans but communicated little if any information. JCI's use of its English materials reminded passersby of the prestigious status of the organization, even if the majority of the passersby did not command English sufficiently to comprehend what was written. They could still register the prestige associated with English, and those who did command English—JCI's target audience—would process both the message of prestige and the semantic meaning carried by the English words. Arabic, on the other hand, expressed the more populist and general message of supporting Palestinian children. However, the pervasive presence of English, which many Syrians cannot read, somewhat diluted the universal message of the Arabic signs.

Even the apparel sported by JCI members during the fund-raiser indicated the extent to which JCI was concerned with projecting its elite status at the expense of conveying information about their event and the cause it supported. Members wore crisp gray polo shirts with the JCI logo professionally embroidered on the chest. Some even sported JCI bandanas with the JCI logo in English emblazoned on them. The clear boxes they carried to collect the money featured a large JCI logo on the front, with no mention of Gaza and the beneficiaries of the fund-raiser. The eye-catching bright blue of the JCI logo and buttons dominated the event's visual cues.

As noon prayers ended and Syrians began their weekend, the square was suddenly crammed with cars. The strategy of positioning the fund-raiser to catch the wealthiest cars seemed to succeed, and a flood of BMW, Lexus, and other luxury cars pulled over to deposit money. In many of them were young adults who recognized their JCI friends and stayed for a while to chat. Parents handed money to children to deposit in the containers. As a reward for donating, we distributed the bright blue JCI stickers to people, not the pins using Arabic to express support of the children of

Gaza. After about four hours, the fund-raiser collected several thousand dollars.

In the late afternoon, a children's choir arrived to perform as the concluding event. It was composed of about thirty private school students of varying ages, dressed uniformly in white shirts and black bottoms. They came with an entourage of parents and siblings, all dressed in fashionable clothes and expensive-looking jewelry, clutching the latest digital and video cameras. They stood on the periphery of space designated for the singers but often darted in to fix a wrinkled shirt or brush some messy hair. The choir director, a middle-aged man, immediately began ushering the children into neat rows, speaking mostly Arabic but imploring them with "please" or "thank you" in English. When he hooked up the microphone, he yelled "test" in English to the teenager operating the machinery. This insertion of key English lexical items was in keeping with elite interactional styles. Finally the children were organized and prepared to his satisfaction, and he signaled to start the singing. The parents in the audience recorded the performance intently and many also mouthed the words along with their children.

A few minutes into the performance, a small group of boys ranging in age from about thirteen to six wandered up to the area and looked in curiously. They were dressed in ill-fitting, outdated clothes and had no adult chaperone. Most likely on their way to the mini-bus station nearby, they were clearly from a lower socioeconomic class, and the unlikely sight of identically dressed children singing in neat rows seemed to both intrigue and irritate them. They moved through the crowd until they were standing next to the other children. At this point, the choir was singing a rearranged version of a classic Arabic folk song of solidarity so these boys knew the lyrics if not the tune. They began to sing along loudly and their voices, not in sync with the choir, became louder than the choir. Instantly two female JCI members rushed forward and attempted to usher the newcomers to a spot in the audience. The boys resisted, starting to disagree loudly and argue with them. Eventually several of the larger, more imposing JCI male members came and shepherded them away. They lingered in the audience for a moment or two and then walked on, their voices loud enough to hear them expressing—in Arabic—their anger at their removal.

At the end of the concert, the parents and JCI members rushed to the children in the choir, praising them elaborately, hugging them, and complimenting them on their great talents. The choir director received long applause. The children were rewarded and validated by their participation in the fund-raising effort, which stood in stark contrast to the frosty reception given to the boys who inserted themselves, uninvited, into the performance. For JCI and their community, there was a right way and a wrong way to participate in such volunteer activities. The right way was planned, well organized, visually stylish, composed—and interspersed with English. For the upper-class children who hewed to that mandate, there was verbal praise and acceptance. For the lower-class children who did not understand these norms of volunteering, there was rejection and displacement. This may have been blind charity for the children of Gaza, but it was not a carte blanche for the children of Damascus.

Conclusion

The decade of 2000–2010 in Syria was marked by a new interest in nongovernmental efforts such as civic events, entrepreneurship, and volunteerism. For a country long dominated by an authoritarian regime that stifled civil society, it was easy to conflate such developments with a trend toward a more open, inclusive society. Yet an analysis of even a small number of such events reveals that while they were influential in disseminating new trends and ideas, they brought their own strict hierarchies and insistence on normative social rules. The examples in this chapter point to several facts about civic efforts in Syria like volunteering and fund-raising. First, the possible range of responses and outcomes to something like the events in Gaza was highly differentiated on the basis of socioeconomic class. Second, such moments of response were often venues in which socioeconomic class stratification became visible, audible, and even tangible. The strategic use of English in these settings, like the JCI branding materials or the choir director's English commands, played a critical role in distinguishing upper-class initiatives from lower-class ones and in demarcating class boundaries and preferences. Fund-raisers and other charitable events, like the Children's Fair, by outlining "proper" modes of behavior and by clarifying who may act as a donor or a volunteer and who may not, identified those at the top, middle, and bottom of the class structure. While new elites at the top enthusiastically partook of new opportunities, those with limited social and economic resources found themselves passed from one rigid system to another. These conclusions illuminate why Syrians were divided in their responses to antiregime uprisings, with educated urban elites standing by President Asad and provincial and rural nonelites protesting against the regime. The latter's social standing in Bashar al-Asad's new order might bring them clowns and balloons at a fair, but it did not give them increased access and integration into new social and economic possibilities.

8

God and Nation

The Politics of Islam under Bashar al-Asad

PAULO G. PINTO

The tragic conflict between the forces of the Ba'thist regime and various antigovernment armed groups that gripped Syria, having claimed 100,000 lives by July 2013, put an end to Bashar Asad's image as "reformer," while underlining his determination to preserve the regime. However, little more than a decade earlier, his ascension to the presidency of Syria, after the death of Hafiz al-Asad in 2000, had created great expectations of structural reforms in Syria. The young age of the new president together with his "Western" education were seen as factors that would facilitate change in an otherwise static regime.

In the early years of Bashar's presidency, the economy, the political system, and the struggle for an autonomous civil society were privileged by most analysts as the main arenas wherein to observe the processes of change and continuity unleashed by the new leadership (Droz-Vincent 2001; George 2003; Perthes 2004). However, the apparent stability and durability of both the Ba'thist regime and Bashar's leadership in the face of an increasingly unstable and hostile regional and international arena—and the uneven, slow, and sometimes paradoxical nature of the economic and political reforms—showed the limitations of strictly political and economic analyses (Wieland 2006a) and exposed the extent to which analyses of social dynamics and cultural processes were equally important to understanding the mixture of change and continuity that defined the first decade of Syria under Bashar (Chiffoleau 2006; Dupret, Ghazzal, and al-Dbiyat 2007). Indeed, it was clear since the beginning that Bashar's government would have to deal with Islam as a cultural force in Syrian society and that Islamic practices, beliefs, and identities had an enormous importance in the shaping of Syria during the first decade of Bashar al-Asad's rule.[1]

One can say that the process of affirmation of Islam as a normative framework for both individual trajectories and the public arena had largely been accomplished by the beginning of Bashar al-Asad's rule. This process was achieved not by the Islamization of the state institutions, but rather through the moral reform and discipline of individuals by a variety of religious actors, who ranged from local Sufi shaykhs to high-profile *'ulama*. The result of this process was a high degree of religious pluralism among the Sunni Muslims, who constitute the major religious group in the Syrian population, as various codifications of Islam competed for the religious imaginary of individuals.

The Mobilization of Islamic Rituals

Islamic symbols, norms, and rituals constituted a shared cultural idiom that allowed the participation and positioning of individuals and groups in various social arenas in Syrian society. A good example of this phenomenon was the mobilization of Islamic rituals by some groups in order to renegotiate their relationship to the state during the period of transition in the months that followed the death of Hafiz al-Asad in June 2000 until the confirmation of Bashar as Syria's new president in July of the same year. During the mourning period for Hafiz al-Asad, a Sufi shaykh linked to the *tariqa* (Sufi path), Rifa'iyya, led his disciples through the streets of Qardaha, the deceased president's hometown and site of his mausoleum, in a procession that included the performance of the *darb al-shish* (perforation of the body with skewers) by a Sufi shaykh in a rare public display

---

1. The ethnographic data analyzed here were collected during my fieldwork in the Sufi communities and pilgrimage shrines in Damascus and Aleppo from 1999 to 2001 and during other periods of fieldwork research between 2002 and 2010.

of religious power.[2] The use of this ritual to mourn Hafiz al-Asad strategically established a symbolic connection between the mystical powers of
the Sufi shaykh and the presidential figure. Images of the procession were
broadcast by the Syrian state TV in a clear recognition of the legitimacy of
the religious idiom in which the plea of allegiance was encoded,[3] and were
debated by many Syrians in Aleppo and Damascus.

This implicit recognition by the official media of the use of Islamic
rituals and symbols by religious groups to reaffirm or renegotiate their
particular relation with the state triggered the proliferation of processions
led by Sufi shaykhs and their disciples in Aleppo, who proclaimed their
support of Bashar as Hafiz's successor in the Syrian presidency. In this
sense, the very rituals of compliance to power that inaugurated Bashar's
rule already pointed to a role for Islam more important than before in the
establishment of symbolic and practical links between the Ba'thist regime
and various groups in Syrian society.

The Pious Ruler: Religious Nationalism under Bashar

Since the beginning of Bashar al-Asad's presidency, the regime tried to
use for its own benefit the growing strength of Islam as a shared cultural
idiom in Syrian society. The Ba'thist regime increased its use of Islamic
symbols and vocabulary in an attempt to gain legitimacy and popularity
among pious Sunni Muslims. This strategic recognition of religion started
under Hafiz al-Asad but became more salient in the political discourse of
the Ba'thist regime under Bashar, as it needed to mobilize the support, or
at least the acquiescence, of large sectors of Syrian society in the international context that unfolded after the Anglo-American invasion of Iraq in

2. In the mystical tradition of the *tariqa*, Rifa'iyya's successful performances of the
darb al-shish are seen as miraculous deeds (*karamat*) that are triggered by the shaykh's
baraka (religious power/grace).

3. Manifestations that had cultural idioms considered as "illegitimate" from the
point of view of the regime were strictly forbidden. This was the case of a large manifestation of support for Bashar that was planned by Kurdish organizations in Aleppo in July
2000, but which was prevented by the security services.

2003 and the isolation that Syria faced over the killing of former Lebanese prime minister Rafiq al-Hariri.

After the withdrawal of the Syrian military forces from Lebanon in 2005, which happened under strong international pressure led by the United States and France, billboards displaying a picture of President Bashar al-Asad, a map of Syria with the colors of the national flag, and the sentence "God Protects you, oh Syria" (*Allah yahmiki, ya Suriya*) were erected all over the country. This sentence was uttered in that same year during a presidential speech at the University of Damascus and became part of the official propaganda released by the state in order to foster nationalistic acquiescence among the population.

However, unlike previous Baʿthist slogans, which usually were reproduced by the population as lip service to official discourse (Wedeen 1999), this one was actively appropriated by various groups in Syrian society. Soon it became a formula of patriotic support for Syria in face of the threats to the country posed by the military and political interference of the United States and its allies in the Middle East. Thus the slogan was stamped on billboards paid for by private associations, such as the Chamber of Commerce of Damascus. It was also displayed on more ordinary markers of individual commitment such as posters or bumper stickers, which could be seen in shops, taxis, and buses throughout Syria.

The social circulation and uses of this slogan showed a process of cultural creativity that transformed the official language of the state into vernacular patriotism, with different versions of it appearing, such as "Syria, God protects her" (*Suriya Allah hamiha*), as it was appropriated by groups and individuals. The sentence tended to be reproduced verbatim by groups that had an interest in establishing direct links with the state, such as trade or professional associations, but was significantly altered, sometimes in ungrammatical ways, by those who were expressing a more diffuse relation with Syria as a nation-state.

The fusion of Islamic references and nationalistic discourse allowed this slogan to express meanings, experiences, and expectations linked to a variety of social actors that existed beyond the groups that participated in the Baʿthist system of governance. The capacity of Islamic references to provide a cultural language that was shared by large sectors of Syrian society made them an attractive symbolic and discursive framework to the Ba'thist regime in the period post-2003 when it faced international pressures and internal discontent.[4]

Indeed there was a proliferation of images portraying Bashar al-Asad as a pious Muslim. Together with the iconography of him as a "modern leader" in smart suits and on family holidays, there was the production of images of Bashar praying, holding a *masbah* (string of prayer-beads), and holding or kissing the Qur'an. These kind of images existed already under the presidency of Hafiz al-Asad (1970–2000), but they were used only in moments of heightened religiosity, such as Ramadan, in order to express the president's respect for the Islamic religious festivities. Under Bashar, images portraying the president performing religious activities or in connection with Islamic symbols became permanently displayed on state-owned religious buildings, showing the greater concern over affirming the president's identity as a pious Muslim. One example is the billboard with the picture of Bashar pressing a Qur'an on his forehead, in a sign of respect and devotion to the holy book, which was displayed on the entrance of the Madrasa Khusruwiyya, the main Qur'anic school in Aleppo.

The greater intensity in the use of religious symbols and vocabulary by the Syrian state under Bashar al-Asad led to their incorporation into the public discourse about Syria. However, the regime did not control the range of meanings and values that could be produced and expressed through religiously framed discourses about the nation. A clear example of this lack of control was the use of religious references in the antigovernment protests that spread throughout Syria after February 2011, as well as the overtly sectarian character that the conflict between armed groups and the regime took after 2012.

In the beginning of the uprising, Syrian protesters took secular political slogans from the successful revolutions that had toppled long-standing dictators in Tunisia and Egypt, such as "the people want the downfall of

---

4. Besides the chronic economic crisis faced by Syria, there were episodes of ethnic unrest and violent confrontation between the Syrian government and the Kurds in northern Syria in 2004 and 2005 (see Tejel 2009, 114–32).

the regime" (*al-sha'b yurid isqat al-nizam*), and added their own creations that had explicit religious references. A popular slogan sung in demonstrations all over Syria in the beginning of the anti-Ba'thist uprising was "God, Syria, Freedom and that's enough" (*Allah, Suriya, Huriya wa Bas*), which subverted the Ba'thist ideology by excluding the mandatory reference to the president in the discourse about the nation.

The regime and its supporters tried to answer this challenge with the counter-slogan "God, Syria, Bashar and that's enough," reinstating the president as a central element of the national narrative. Beyond the obvious differences in their political imaginaries, both the Ba'thist regime and the opposition agreed that the moral dimension of the Syrian nation was defined through its link to God. This agreement shows how religiously framed discourses about the nation constitute a cultural idiom shared by both sides of the current political divide.

The Syrian government has highlighted the importance of mosques in the mobilization and organization of the demonstrations and in the use by the protesters of religious chants—such as "God is Great" (*Allahu Akbar*) and "There is no god but God" (*La ilah ila Allah*)—in order to accuse them of being militant Salafis or members of the Muslim Brothers. In addition to the use of unrestrained violence against the protests, the Ba'thist regime tried to portray them through a sectarian prism as an expression of Sunni radicalism in order to divide and isolate the opposition. After some time this strategy succeeded in creating sectarian mistrust and hostility among some sectors of the 'Alawite and Christian communities, as well as among Sunnis Muslims, fueling the radicalization of religious identities that has defined the Syrian conflict after 2012.

From the point of view of the regime, control of the cultural and political power of Islam had been used long before the current uprising as an accessory tool to the national project led by the Ba'thist regime under the Asad family. For example, in May 2010 Bashar stated in an interview that the biggest challenge that he faced was "how can we keep our society as secular as it is today?"[5] Indeed, since 2008, in a reaction to the pervasive

5. http://www.charlierose.com/view/interview/11029, accessed Sept. 9, 2010.

spread of Islamic discourse, the regime had sought to reassert its control over the Islamic religious field.

Official Islam: The Bureaucratization
of the Religious Establishment

The growing use of Islamic rhetoric by the Ba'thist regime before the uprising went in tandem with its efforts to secure the acquiescence of the Sunni religious establishment for its political and social projects. These efforts started much before Bashar's presidency with the interference of the Ba'thist regime in the election of Shaykh Ahmad Kuftaro for the post of Grand Mufti (al-mufti al-'amm) of Syria in 1964. After his election, Shaykh Kuftaro helped the state to consolidate its control over the Sunni Muslim religious establishment. He benefited from this relationship to expand his branch of the Naqshbandiyya, the Kuftariyya, into a transnational Sufi order. At the same time, the government assigned the process of control over the main mosques and the imams that preached in them to the Ministry of Awqaf (Pious Endowments) (Böttcher 1997, 20–22).

Since the presidency of Hafiz al-Asad, the Ba'thist regime has tried to develop indirect ways to influence the religious debate by giving certain key figures easy access to media (radio, television, and Internet) or, simply, by tolerating their public religious activism. The Syrian state did not try to impose a doctrinal or discursive consensus, but, on the contrary, allowed a vast range of competing opinions and positions to be expressed on various religious and social issues. It is in that sense that the "official Islam" inherited by Bashar al-Asad was less a coherent corpus of doctrines and opinions than what Pierre Bourdieu has defined as a "field" or "universe of possible discourses" (Bordieu 1997, 167–71). However, the public discourse on religion was disciplined by the establishment of discursive limits within which different actors could present competing visions.

While Bashar's government continued this policy of indirect interference in the religious field, it also tightened its grip on the official religious establishment. The relative autonomy that the religious establishment had in relation to the state was severely diminished in the process of succession of Shaykh Ahmad Kuftaro, who died in 2004. For more than a year the chief muftis of Syria did not manage to elect a new Grand Mufti. The process ended in July 2005 with Bashar al-Asad's appointment of Shaykh Ahmad Badr al-Din Hassun, who had been the mufti of Aleppo since 2000, as the new Grand Mufti of Syria.

The choice of Shaykh Hassun represented continuity with the legacy of Shaykh Kuftaro, as he also is a Sufi shaykh linked with the *tariqa* Naqshbandiyya. It also represented a new opening to the Sunni universe of Aleppo, which was traditionally viewed with suspicion by the Baʿthist political establishment through its connection with the Islamic opposition to the regime in the 1970s and 1980s. However, the presidential appointment of the new Grand Mufti denied any degree of autonomy to the religious establishment. The effect of making public the direct interference of the Baʿthist regime in the internal functioning of the official religious leadership was to symbolically transform it into a mere extension of the regime-controlled state bureaucracy, at least on its highest official levels.

Notwithstanding its political importance, this display of control over the religious establishment had paradoxical effects. While it assured the acquiescence of the upper echelons of the religious establishment in relation to the Baʿthist national project, it risked making these official religious leaders even less appealing to pious Sunni Muslims outside Damascus. Indeed, most shaykhs tried to construct their religious authority in ways that affirmed their autonomy in relation to other sources of power, such as the state.

In a sense, the idea of complete government control of the religious field was always illusory, as the production of meaning and experiences that give social reality to Islamic norms, symbols, and concepts largely escaped the boundaries set by the official religious elite. It is true that some important religious authorities, such as the mufti Ahmad Badr al-Din Hassun and Shaykh Said Ramadan al-Buti—who was killed in a bomb attack in 2013—became more and more identified with the Baʿthist regime, especially after the uprising began. However, even within the official religious establishment many ʿulama tried to preserve their religious authority by expressing dissent or keeping some distance from unpopular or openly repressive policies. An example of that dissent was the denunciation, in

April 2011, by the mufti of Der'a of the violent repression of the antigovernment protests in the city.

Therefore, it is important to have in mind that during the first decade of Bashar's presidency the production of Islam as cultural idiom, even when it was informed by a particular political project, expressed the cultural dynamics and the power struggles of a variety of actors, institutions, and communities that constituted the religious field. Similarly, the "state" was never a unified and coherent institution, but rather the articulation of several centers of power, prestige, and political imagination that were unequal in importance and in competition for resources and influence. Therefore, instead of talking about a coherent "religious policy" under Bashar, we will be pointing to the processes of translation and appropriation of political realities into the cultural idiom of Islamic discourses, symbols, and practices.

Aleppo, the "Capital of Islamic Culture": Islam and Local Politics

After the ascension of Bashar al-Asad to the presidency, efforts were made to reshape Aleppo's often-conflictive relationship with the Syrian state through the official recognition of its "Islamic tradition." The appointment of Shaykh Ahmad Badr al-Din Hassun, who came from a well-known family of Aleppine shaykhs and had many followers in the Sunni bourgeoisie of Aleppo, Grand Mufti of Syria in 2005 opened the possibility of an alliance between the Ba'thist regime and the religious establishment of Aleppo.

The official celebration of the intimate connection between Aleppo's urban identity and Islam—which happened after the choice of the city as "Capital of Islamic Culture" ('Asima lil-Thaqafa al-Islamiyya) by the Organization of the Islamic Conference in 2006—pointed to a change in the symbolic position of the city within the Ba'thist polity. The shift in the official discourse, which aimed to sanitize the image of Aleppo as a hotbed of Islamic militancy and opposition to the Ba'thist regime and to create a positive image of its religious and urban traditions in the Syrian national narrative, could be seen in a poster hanging on the façade of the neo-Ottoman building of the Ministry of Culture near the Old City, on which it was written "Aleppo the Gray, City of Culture, Tolerance, and National Unity" (Halab al-shahba', madina al-thaqafa wa al-tasamuh wa *al-wahda al-wataniyya*) beside the image of Bashar al-Asad together with Aleppo's Citadel. The state-controlled Syrian press and television gave broad coverage to all the events. Banners, billboards, and plaques were spread throughout Aleppo with slogans that fused references to Islamic symbols, Ba'thist slogans, and Aleppo's urban history. The official valorization of Aleppo's heritage showed an accommodation of the Ba'thist discourse about the nation with the local ideals of identity, meaning, and order that were culturally encoded as the "Aleppine tradition."

The implicit acceptance by the state of traditional forms of sociality, power, and prestige through the preservation of Aleppo's architectural heritage contrasted with the aggressive urbanization implemented by the Syrian state in the 1970s and 1980s, which aimed to reshape the local society according to the Ba'thist ideals expressed in the modernistic reorganization of space. The official inscription of the Aleppine tradition into the Ba'thist national narrative allowed the negotiation of Aleppo's place in the Syrian polity to be also played around nonreligious elements, such as the entrepreneurial character of its elites, for trade and industry are also considered to be part of Aleppo's tradition (Cornand 1994; Droz-Vincent 2004, 92–95; Rabo 2005, 3–12).

However, even this "secular" trend was linked to an intense investment in using Islam as a shared idiom to build trust and negotiate relations that were fundamental for the process of economic liberalization fostered by the government of Bashar al-Asad.[6] The positive image of the entrepreneurial sector in Aleppo as having "social consciousness" was constructed through religious ideals of contribution by businessmen to the common good, such as the practice of charity or the endowment of religious and/or cultural institutions.

Therefore, the construct of Aleppo as an "Islamic city" was mobilized as a cultural idiom by the distinct social actors involved in the negotiation of the city's insertion in the Syrian nation-state. The effects of this

---

6. The private sector in Aleppo had been reluctant to accept the partnership with the Ba'thist regime that is inscribed in the guidelines of the process of economic liberalization since Hafiz al-Asad (Perthes 2004, 27–39; Droz-Vincent 2004, 240–43).

construct could be seen after 2011, as Aleppo's middle classes remained distant from the antigovernment protests. This attitude was seen by many protesters as a betrayal of Aleppo's history of opposition to the Ba'thist regime. A banner in a demonstration in Baniyas in 2011 had written on it "Where are you, Aleppo?" (*Waynak, ya Halab?*),[7] scolding the Aleppines for not staging massive demonstrations against the government. In Homs, in that same year, antigovernment protesters called for a boycott of all goods made in Aleppo. Even after several neighborhoods of Aleppo were taken by the Free Syrian Army and other armed groups, most Aleppines chose not to join the uprising against the Ba'thist regime.

The Specter of Sectarianism:
Shi'is and Sunnis in Syria's Holy Places

Bashar al-Asad also inherited a well-advanced policy of inscription of Shi'i Islam in the Syrian religious landscape. The Syrian and the Iranian states joined efforts in promoting Shi'i holy sites in Syria as the destination for Shi'i pilgrims from Iran, Lebanon, Azerbaijan, Pakistan, India, and the Gulf countries. This promotion was done through the reconfiguration of mosques and shrines that marked these holy places as sanctuaries with a clearly defined Shi'i identity. Usually this meant the replacement of pre-existing structures by lavishly decorated mosques and shrines in Persian neo-Safavid style, as in Sayda Zaynab and Raqqa. When the existing structures had high historical and architectonic value and, therefore, could not be destroyed, they were resignified as Shi'i holy places through the placing of explanatory signs written in Arabic and Persian that connected the building with the Shi'i sacred history of martyrdom of Husayn and his companions in the plains of Karbala (Ababsa 2001; 2005b; Mervin 1996).

The affirmation of Ja'fari Shi'ism in the Syrian religious field had several advantages from the point of view of the Ba'thist regime, which

7. http://www.reuters.com/article/2011/04/22/us-syria-protests-idUSTRE73L1SJ201 10422, accessed Nov. 12, 2011; http://www.reuters.com/article/slideshow/idUSTRE73L1 SJ20110422#a=3, accessed Nov. 12, 2011.

explain the official efforts in promoting it. The establishment of a Shiʻi pilgrimage route linking Iran to Syria gave a religious dimension to the alliance between both countries, which began as a strategic alliance in the geopolitics of the Middle East. The new visibility of Shiʻism in the Syrian religious landscape could help to consolidate the Islamic credentials of the ʻAlawite community,[8] to which the Asad family belonged. Finally, it added another instance of pluralism to the Syrian religious field, which accorded well with the general framework of "official Islam" that was fostered by the regime.

However, the new religious and political realities created by the Anglo-American invasion and occupation of Iraq, such as the sectarian conflict that opposed Sunnis and Shiʻis, fueled religious tensions among Sunni Syrians, whose religious sensibilities were offended and who felt gradually marginalized by the growing Shiʻi presence in the main holy places in Syria. The growing visibility of Shiʻi devotional practices in sacred spaces that were seen as solidly Sunni, such as the Umayyad Mosque in Damascus, led to an increasingly vocal expression of resentment and rejection of the Shiʻi presence by pious Sunni Muslims. The influx of pilgrims was accompanied by the placing of written signs that informed the pilgrims of the identity of the holy figure buried in the place and/or the myth of origin of the holiness of the place that they were visiting. In 2006 a plaque written in Arabic and Persian was put on the shrine of Yahiya's head,[9] incorporating the main hall of the mosque into the circuit of Shiʻi mass pilgrimage.

Indeed, after 2005 the main prayer-hall of the Umayyad Mosque was regularly taken over by Shiʻi pilgrims who performed their rituals, recitating the drama of Karbala and lamenting over the tragic destiny of Husayn and his family members and companions. During a visit to the mosque in

8. In 1973 Musa al-Sadr, the leader of the Shiʻi community in Lebanon, issued a *fatwa* declaring the ʻAlawites as part of Jaʻfari Shiʻism. This fatwa responded to strategic needs of the Hafiz al-Asad government, as the Islamic credentials of the ʻAlawites were being questioned by the Islamic opposition. It also consolidated the process of *taqrib* (doctrinal convergence) that was happening between the ʻAlawite community and Jaʻfari Shiʻism (Mervin 2002).

9. Yahiya is Saint John the Baptist in the Christian tradition.

2006, I spoke with several Syrians who complained about the loud rituals of lamentation disturbing their prayers. Some also pointed to the difficulty of performing rituals around the shrine of Yahiya's head when the Shi'i pilgrims were there, for they "did not know how to show respect, gathering all together around the tomb and not letting any space for other visitors," as one Syrian told me in the mosque.

These tensions heightened to new levels during the worst phase of the sectarian violence in Iraq between 2006 and 2008, when hundreds of thousands of refugees flocked into Syria. The refugees were both Sunnis and Shi'is, but the increasing political power of the Shi'is in Iraq after 2003, together with the alliance of some Shi'i political leaders with the Americans, led to a sense among Sunni Syrians that the Shi'is were some sort of fifth column driven by sectarian hatred against both Sunnism and Arab nationalism. Stories of the horrible violence unleashed by Shi'i militias against Sunnis in Iraq circulated in Syria, where they were seen as the confirmation of the anti-Shi'i stereotypes.[10]

The Shi'i rituals performed in the Umayyad Mosque were sometimes interrupted by angry Sunni Syrians who shouted at the pilgrims that these practices were wrong and sinful (*haram; khati*) and should not be performed in such a holy place. Usually the pilgrims, many of whom did not speak Arabic at all, simply ignored these outbursts of Sunni outrage and continued to perform their rituals. On one occasion one guide of the pilgrims who spoke Arabic had a loud discussion with some Syrians who tried to interrupt his lamentation of Husayn's martyrdom.

In light of the growing discontent of Sunni Syrians in seeing their sacred places, some of which were also national and Damascene "lieux de mémoire," as was the case of the Umayyad Mosque's being transformed into a space of performance of Shi'i religious practices, the Syrian government allowed various local actors, such as the mosque administration, to control and contain Shi'i religiosity. Therefore, new disciplinary measures were taken to regulate behavior in Syria's sacred places. In 2008 signs inviting

---

10. At the same time, stories of Sunni violence against Shi'i civilians in Iraq produced a similar sense of victimization among the Shi'i refugees in Syria.

the male and female visitor/pilgrim (*za'ir, za'ira*) to keep the sacredness (*hurma*) of the Umayyad Mosque were placed in the main entrances of the building. The new "rules of behavior" that were listed on the signs included no loud talking or gatherings within the mosque's prayer-hall, which affected directly the groups of Shi'i pilgrims who have the recitation of the drama of Karbala as one of their main rituals. Within the main hall of the mosque a new fence separating male and female worshipers forced the groups of pilgrims to split by gender in order to perform their rituals.

This rule of gender segregation created smaller groups, which were more easily supervised and controlled in their behavior. However, they disrupted not only the rituals of the Shi'i pilgrims, but also those of the Sunni Syrian visitors to the mosque. The performance of prayers and asking for blessings at the shrine of Yahiya's head, which was the main ritual performed by its visitors, were severely restricted, as the fenced corridor for women only allowed them to approach one side of the tomb.[11] This restriction created several conflicts between the visitors, both Sunni and Shi'i, who wanted to perform their devotional rituals all around the tomb, and the staff of the mosque that tried to prevent them from crossing the boundaries between the newly gendered spaces of the mosque. However, the Shi'i pilgrims were targeted by further restrictive measures: a rigid time schedule was created for them, which reduced their number to a few groups and confined the performance of their devotional rituals to time slots in the mornings. Parallel to these measures, most of the explanatory signs in Arabic and Persian were removed from the mosque, with only those on the shrines of Husayn's head and of Yahiya's head remaining.[12]

11. The enforcement of rigid rules of gender segregation in the main Syrian mosques is a phenomenon that is not only linked to containment of Shi'i devotional practices, but also to the performative affirmation of Syria as a Muslim country in Islamic international arenas. Thus, similar rules of gender segregation were implemented in the Umayyad Mosque of Aleppo in 2006, when the city was chosen "Capital of Islamic Culture" by the Organization of the Islamic Conference. In this case, Shi'i pilgrims were not an issue, as this mosque was not part of their pilgrimage route; the issue was rather the refashioning of religious spaces according to "international" Islamic standards.

12. The plaque left on the shrine of Yahiya's head is written only in Arabic.

These administrative measures tried to restore the character of the Umayyad mosque as a holy place embedded into the cultural logic of local Damascene religiosity, rather than that of transnational Shi'i pilgrimage.[13] There were further measures aiming to reaffirm the Sunni character of the Umayyad mosque. One of them was the granting of permission by the government to certain Sunni shaykhs to teach religious lessons (*dars*) in the main prayer-hall of the mosque. The shaykhs who were allowed to teach in the mosque were usually those linked to the constitution of "official Islam" as a discursive field. For example, in 2008 I saw a large crowd attending a lesson given by a disciple of Shaykh Rajab Dib, who is linked to the Kuftariyya, a Sufi order that was led by the late Grand Mufti, Shaykh Ahmad Kuftaro. To many Syrians, the symbolic and practical effect of these lessons was that of a reclaiming of the sacred space of the mosque by the Syrian Sunnis after it had been "occupied" for a long time by foreign Shi'is.

This trend targeted even the sacred spaces that had a clear Shi'i identity, such as the shrine of Sayyida Zaynab on the outskirts of Damascus. Since 2008, recitations of the drama of Karbala and ritual lamentations could only be performed in the courtyard of the shrine. While the attempts by the staff of the shrine to prevent collective recitations when in the arcade of the shrine were unsuccessful, they managed to reduce collective crying and chest-beating to a minimum.

The containment of the public display of Shi'i religiosity shows the awareness on the part of the regime about the rise of Sunni/Shi'i sectarian tensions in Syria. The growing presence of Shi'i devotional practices in traditional Sunni holy places, such as the Umayyad mosque, resulted in a sense of disfranchisement of the Syrian Sunnis in the face of what they perceived as the loss of control over their sacred spaces. Gradually, Sunni and Shi'i identities were culturally signified as markers of the Syrian/foreigner divide, as well as invested with the dynamics of confrontation that

13. In a visit in November 2009 I could see that some of the signs were back on the walls and new ones were added around the shrine of Husayn's head. However, no new signs were put inside the mosque's main prayer-hall, consolidating it as a Syrian Sunni space.

defined these identities in terms that referred to the sectarian conflict that ravaged Iraq between 2006 and 2009.

Sectarian tensions reappeared in full strength during the uprising, when there was an identification of the Ba'thist regime with Shi'ism and foreign powers such as Iran. The importance of mosques for both the Ba'thist regime and the Syrian society as arenas of dispute and negotiation of religiously framed discourses about the nation can be seen in the role that they acquired during the antigovernment protests that started in March 2011. The Umayyad mosques of Damascus and Aleppo were stages for protests, which were violently repressed by the security forces.[14] The 'Umarī mosque in Der'a, which was also built in the Umayyad period,[15] was the center of the revolt that took control of city during several weeks in March and April 2011. The city was brought under government control through a brutal crackdown on the protesters and the civilian population, which symbolically reinstated state control of the city with the military assault and occupation of the mosque.

The chanting of anti-Iranian and anti-Hezbollah slogans, which targeted the Shi'i political allies of the Ba'thist regime, accompanied the protests in Der'a.[16] Later in the uprising, Shi'i shrines became military and symbolic targets by armed groups fighting the regime. In 2013 the tomb of Amar Ibn Yassin in Raqqa and the shrine of Hujr Ibn Uday in Adra were destroyed by the rebels, and the shrine of Sayyida Zaynab in a suburb of Damascus was attacked with rockets launched by antigovernment

14. For Aleppo, see http://www.youtube.com/watch?v=V3mh-StEuSA; for Damascus, see http://www.youtube.com/watch?v=aOyPDonA30A, accessed Mar. 1, 2012.

15. The fact that the three mosques that acquired a symbolic dimension as arenas of protests had their history linked to the Umayyad dynasty (AD 661–750) was not a coincidence. During the Umayyad period Syria was the center of the Arab-Islamic Empire, which had its capital in Damascus. The Ba'thist historiography refers to this period in order to create a Syrian national narrative fused with a Pan-Arab one, which also includes Islam as a Syrian cultural heritage (Valter 2002, 53–58).

16. See Thomas Pierret's article published in Le Monde, Apr. 7, 2011: http://www.lemonde.fr/idees/article/2011/04/06/le-parcours-du-combattant-des-opposants-syriens_1503828_3232.html, accessed Aug. 6, 2011.

armed groups. It was exactly in order to avoid this kind of political/sectarian amalgam that the regime had moved toward the containment of Shi'i visibility in Syria's holy places.

While the Ba'thist regime was the actual facilitator and even promoter of the inscription of Twelver Shi'ism in the Syrian religious landscape, it could not control the processes that informed the dynamics of its interaction with the other religious identities present in the Syrian society. The limited effectiveness of the state control over the internal dynamics of the religious field becomes visible when one looks at the dynamics of vernacular religion.

Vernacular Religion: The Limits of Bashar's Religious Policies

Charismatic forms of acquiring, displaying, and using power were central to the construction of religious authority in the Syrian religious field.[17] In part this centrality is owing to the widespread influence of Sufism on Sunni religiosity. It also reflects the importance of local cultural processes in the constitution of Sunni Muslim identities, a clear example of which is the religious divide between Aleppo and Damascus in terms of conception, production, and recognition of forms of religious authority, as well as the diversity of understandings, practices, and experiences that give social and cultural reality to Islam. This diversity resulted in an intense fragmentation of the religious universe, with areas under direct control of the state and others that had a high degree of autonomy from the official religious elite (Pierret 2008–9). Therefore the bureaucratization of the religious establishment under Bashar al-Asad had very little effect on the functioning of the religious field in regard to religious practices and identities.

Even the opening toward the religious universe of Aleppo with the appointment of Shaykh Hassun as Grand Mufti did not create solid channels of dialogue with the religious elite in that city. All the shaykhs to whom I talked when I was doing fieldwork in Aleppo in 2006 said that

---

17. I use the concept of charisma to refer to forms of power and authority that are embodied, personalized, and loaded with emotion.

they were happy that Shaykh Hassun became Grand Mufti, but, they added, he was not one of them. This response was all the more surprising because not only had Shaykh Hassun occupied previously the position of mufti of Aleppo, but he also continued to come to Aleppo every Friday to perform his duties as preacher in the Rawda mosque, in the bourgeois neighborhood of Sabil. Furthermore, he was the Sufi shaykh of one of the local branches of the Naqshbandiyya.

One shaykh summarized the arguments, saying, "Yes, he [Shaykh Hassun] is linked to the Naqshbandiyya, but he is not from Aleppo! He is from the countryside [*hwa min al-rif*]. He is a good person and an important shaykh, but he does not share the *silsila* [mystical genealogy] of the Sufis from Aleppo. He lived here, but found his place in Damascus." The refusal to recognize Shaykh Hassun's religious authority, and even Aleppine identity, is an affirmation by the religious leaders of Aleppo of their autonomy. Through their rejection of Shaykh Hassun the Aleppine shaykhs draw a clear boundary between themselves and the Syrian state and its agents, who are defined as external to the city and its traditions.

Also, the distant and nonchalant attitude to the official openings to Islamic traditions of Aleppo, which could be seen during the celebration of the city as Capital of Islamic Culture in 2006, can be understood as a performative strategy that aims to affirm the distinction between the Aleppine religious establishment and the codifications of Islam fostered by the state. On that occasion, while many shaykhs welcomed the official recognition of Aleppo's Islamic tradition and attended some of the events, most of those to whom I talked expressed their dismay at the "pasteurized" official Islam and "folklorization" of Sufism offered by the event for the consumption of Muslim tourists, mostly from the Gulf countries. In June 2006, during a conversation, one shaykh said with irony, after seeing the program of the celebration, "Yes, there is a lot of chanting and talking, but can you see any important shaykh from Aleppo giving a speech?"

However, despite the general contempt for the overtures of the Ba'thist regime toward Aleppo's Islamic tradition, many Muslim leaders and their followers in Aleppo used the greater recognition of the local religious tradition to negotiate new arenas of visibility for their religious practices and discourses. Some Sufi shaykhs started to celebrate the *mawlid* (saint feast) of their communities in the streets in front of their *zawiyas* (ritual lodges), occupying the public space in ways that were not so widespread before.

Other religious arenas created under Bashar al-Asad were the large mosques built in Aleppo and Damascus, usually with funding from Saudi Arabia or the Gulf countries. These mosques clearly had the function of providing a disciplined and controlled space for the performance of collective rituals such as the Friday prayer (*salat al-jum'a*). Notwithstanding the efforts of the state in shaping mosques as controlled sacred spaces, they constitute complex performative arenas that articulate various ritual and discursive spheres of constitution, discipline, and expression of Muslim identities. Furthermore, there are several religious individual and collective activities that happen in the mosques that escape the logic of official Islam, such as the meetings of informal study-circles devoted to the reading and recitation of the Qur'an, or the performance of Sufi rituals.

Owing to the fact that many of the religious authorities in the mosques are Sufi shaykhs, it is not uncommon to have Sufi rituals, such as the *dhikr* (mystical evocation of God), performed there. Sufi forms of Islam are not officially recognized by the Syrian state, which had its religious policies framed by a modernistic conception of religion that saw Sufism as something "popular," "irrational," and "backwards," hence destined to disappear under the rationalizing effect of the state-led modernization of Syrian society. Therefore, despite the alliance between the Ba'thist regime and some Sufi shaykhs in the constitution of the official Islam, Sufi practices and communities are not officially sponsored by the Ministry of Awqaf and, therefore, remain beyond its direct regulation and control.[18]

The relative autonomy of Sufism becomes evident in the Sufi rituals that are performed within the premises of mosques, when one can see clearly the differences between the dynamics of Sufi gatherings in relation to the regular prayer ritual of the mosque. In 2000 I attended a Friday

---

18. This does not mean that Sufi communities or activities are beyond the surveillance or the repressive capacity of the Ba'thist state. The Sufi *hadras*, as all public gatherings in Syria, are regularly monitored by the security services (*mukhabarat*). However, this monitoring is very different from the direct state intervention and control that the Ministry of Awqaf exercises over the religious activities in the mosques.

prayer in a mosque in the Old City of Damascus, when a small audience of thirty men listened to the *khutba* (sermon) as the preacher read a sermon setting a parallel between the fight of the early Muslims against the polytheists in Mekka and the bravery of the Syrian army in its struggle against the Zionist aggression toward the Arab nation. Clearly the text of the sermon followed the official line of Ba'thist propaganda and, as a consequence, audience attention was low, with people talking to each other, falling asleep, or simply looking distracted by other things. After the prayer, a Sufi *hadra* started with the performance of a *Shadhili dhikr* led by the shaykh, with more people arriving to participate in the ritual. Soon there were around 250 men performing the *dhikr* under the guidance of the shaykh,[19] who was transformed from religious bureaucrat into charismatic leader. After the ritual performance was over, the large audience listened attentively while the shaykh delivered a sermon stressing the necessity of proving the inner states (*ahwal*) one achieves through mystical initiation through obedience to the rules of the shari'a in public life.

The appropriation of the space of the mosque by the Sufi ritual withdrew it, at least partially, from state control, for it shifted the framework within which Muslim identities were being produced, expressed, and organized. The state-sanctioned ritual inscribed the Muslim devotee within the moral framework of the Arab nation as incarnated in Ba'thist Syria, while the Sufi *hadra* aimed at producing an autonomous moral agent who could embody the normative principles of Islam and inscribe them in the social order through his/her practices and personal example.

While the religious policies of the Syrian state try to foster the textual spiritualism of "official Islam" as the dominant framework for religious practices and identities, it is widely known and empirically observable that most Sunni mosques in Syria are centers of diffusion of interpretations of Islam that differ from this model, being usually connected to the various mystical traditions of Sufism or, in some cases, conservative trends of the Salafiyya. Therefore, the autonomy of vernacular religious

19. There were also women participating in the ritual from a balcony above the prayer-hall.

practices, discourses, and experiences remained a social and cultural reality in Syria despite the attempts of Bashar al-Asad's government to control their dynamics by enforcing its power over the religious elite or ritual and discursive religious arenas such as mosques.

Conclusion

During the first decade of Bashar al-Asad's rule, the attitude of the Ba'thist regime toward Islam experienced several changes in relation to some areas of the religious field, such as the institutional aspects of Islam and the Shi'i presence in Syria's holy places. Nevertheless, there was a high degree of continuity in other arenas, such as the continued autonomy of vernacular religious practices and discourses in relation to "official Islam." In practice the boundaries between trends of change and continuity were not always clear. For example, there was continuity from Hafiz al-Asad's presidency in the use of Islamic symbols and vocabulary by the state aimed at acquiring some sympathy, or at least acquiescence, to its national project among pious Sunni Muslims. Notwithstanding these similarities with previous times, the use of references to Islam in the official discourse passed through significant changes as well. It became more conspicuous and generalized, going from just the presentation of the president as an observant Muslim to the promotion of religious definitions of the Syrian nation.

The use of Islamic references in the official discourse was also an instrument in Bashar's efforts to co-opt local elites and identities that had had conflictive relations with the Ba'thist regime, such as was the case of Aleppine urban identities and the economic elite. The growing involvement of Bashar al-Asad's government with the use of Islamic symbols and vocabulary manifested a strengthening and more public regime grip on the dynamics of the official Islamic religious elite.

However, the regime certainly did not control the religious dynamics that informed the constitution of Muslim identities in Syria. The religious field in Syria was marked by the existence of multiple realms of discourse and practice that remain beyond the boundaries established by the state or the religious authorities. A clear example of that was the rise of sectarian tensions between Syrian Sunnis and Shi'i pilgrims. While the state managed to impose its direct control over some areas of the religious field, the effects of this policy remained somewhat ambiguous. Indeed, the greater presence of state power in the functioning of the religious field did not create conformity among its participants. Instead, it encouraged the renewal of the strategies of accommodation, subversion, and confrontation that Muslim religious leaders and their communities mobilized in order to maintain various degrees of autonomy during the Ba'thist era. These strategies also allowed these religious actors to create their own political paths and position themselves in relation to the ongoing struggle for Syria. The incomplete control of the regime over the religious field was exposed when Islam became a main discourse for the mobilization of opposition to the regime during the Syrian uprising beginning in 2011.

9

Female Citizenship in Syria

Framing the 2009 Controversy over Personal Status Law

RANIA MAKTABI

On May 21, 2009, the website Syrian Women Observatory (SWO)[1] published the text of a draft law on personal status.[2] The draft was prepared by a committee authorized by the Ministry of Justice to reform the law codified in 1953. Until the publication of the text through the Internet, the existence of the committee that worked on drafting a law for almost two years was unknown to the Syrian public. The committee's work circumvented usual channels of information such as publication in the local press and the Syrian parliament's official website, which Syrians usually rely upon to remain informed of the latest legislation proposed by the

---

1. The SWO's Arabic name is *nisa' suriyya* (Syrian Women); see http://nesasy.org/, accessed May 2013. Established in 2005, the SWO has been—and still is as of March 2014—under the editorship of journalist and human rights activist Bassam al-Kadi. For more on SWO, see Maktabi (2006); and Sands, "Syria Moving Away from Equality: Report," *The National*, 2009, accessed May 15, 2013, http://adurva.blogspot.com/feeds/posts/default?orderby=updated.

2. Personal status law (*qanun al-ahwal ash-shakhsiyya*) regulates a person's judicial and economic rights and duties within the kinship structure such as marriage, divorce, inheritance, custody over children, maintenance, and adoption. "Personal status law" is also referred to as "family law." Both terms are here used interchangeably. The 1953 code applies to all Syrians, but Catholics, Druze, and Jews have autonomy in regulating marriage and divorce.

government. If not for the leak, the public would not have learned of the draft law (*The National*, July 14, 2009).

Finalized in April 2009, the draft law was the first proposal in nearly six decades for major reforms in personal status formulated by the Syrian government.[3] Following its publication, an outcry erupted among Syrians who criticized the "Talibanization" of the code because of the overt use of orthodox religious terminology. The secretive way in which the draft was prepared prompted opponents to accuse the government of backing away from pledges to strengthen the civil rights of women and to initiate reforms that comply with the Convention on the Elimination of all forms of Discrimination Against Women (CEDAW) signed by Syria in 2003.[4]

On July 4, 2009—six weeks after the draft was made known to the public—the Presidency of the Council of Ministers (prime minister's office) announced that the government disagreed with the content and that the draft law had been sent back to the Ministry of Justice for further study. Opponents saw this as a political triumph: their mobilization had impeded the procession of the draft law in parliament. Four months later, on November 8, 2009, the government presented a new and revised draft on personal status that was made public through the SWO the same day. Comments on both drafts continued throughout 2010, albeit at a less intense level.

The 2009 controversy over the draft law on personal status illuminates how the Syrian authoritarian regime balanced its interests with regard to pressures toward social reform amid a self-proclaimed process of political

3. The draft law was finalized on April 5, 2009, and sent to all ministries on April 9, 2009, six weeks before the text was published through the Internet (SWO, July 1, 2009). The draft was bound to be publicly known at a point in time after its release, but probably not at the scale it reached following its publication on the Internet after May 21, 2009.

4. al-Kadi, *"mashru' qanun 'al-ahawal ash-shakhsiyya' al-jadid: 'alkahnut al-dini' yakshufu wajhahu al-haqiqi,"* SWO, May 25, 2009; and *"mithlama qulna 'la' li-mashru' qanun ta'ifi . . . nu'akkid: 'la' li-rudud ta'ifiyya,"* SWO, May 27, 2009; Ghassan al-Miflih, *"mashru' qanun al-ahwal as-shakhsiyya al-jadid min wad' rijal din am rijal 'dawla'?";* Bahiyya Madani, *"al-Kadi: Suriyya satasbahu imaratun talbaniyya ma' mashru' al-ahwal ash-shakhsiyya,"* SWO, June 11, 2009.

liberalization.[5] This chapter addresses the following three questions: (1) What are the textual differences between the current 1953 law and the draft law? (2) Who was mobilized and what were the opinions of different actors? (3) How did Syrian authorities respond to the outcry? I show how the controversy reflects domestic conflicts pertaining to the expansion and contraction of female citizenship that I argue are related to the distribution of public welfare in society; the powers of clerical authorities in regulating family law; and how networking played a central role in politicizing family law and mobilizing Syrians against the draft law.

Regarding methodology, the SWO provided the main overview of activities and articles that comment on the draft law because their website was central in mobilizing the Syrian public.[6] I read all 225 articles published on SWO under the icon "personal status law" between May 21, 2009, and May 21, 2010. Seventy percent of these articles (159) appeared in June and July 2009 when the controversy over the draft law (popularly termed *dajje*) was at its peak.[7]

Gendered Citizenship in Syria
and Pressures for Change Since 2003

In most Arab states, including Syria, family law embodies the clerical imprint of religious law in which male citizens are custodians of female citizens. "Gendered citizenship" denotes the legal incongruence between

5. I focus here on public reaction toward the first draft code made public in May 2009 and not on the second draft presented in November 2009.

6. SWO articles are for the most part written by academics specialized in the subjects they write about, by intellectuals, and by freelance journalists. Many articles are also excerpts from daily newspapers and magazines.

7. By September 2010, articles published under the icon "personal status law" stretched over a period of four years (March 23, 2006–May 21, 2010) and totaled 279 articles, of which 80 percent (225 articles) appeared in the period under study, that is, between May 21, 2009, and May 21, 2010. See Maktabi 2010 for an analysis of female citizenship based on fieldwork in Damascus (November 2006 and April 2007), where I interviewed representatives of women's advocacy groups, lawyers, religious scholars, and judges in religious courts.

constitutional laws—where Article 45 guarantees equal rights for males and females—and gendered state laws that are permeated by female legal subordination in three main spheres: citizenship law, criminal law, and family law. In citizenship law, a Syrian woman cannot pass Syrian citizenship to her children if married to a non-Syrian, while a Syrian man has this right if married to a non-Syrian. In criminal law, Article 548 establishes an understanding that femicide, that is, the killing of a woman by a male relative, differs from homicide. Accordingly, prison sentences are no more than two years for femicide and up to fifteen years for homicide. For Muslims, the 1953 family law grants the husband the right to have four wives and unilateral divorce. A wife is required to raise a case in court if she demands divorce. While the legal marriage age is set at eighteen for a boy and seventeen for a girl, youngsters are allowed to marry at the age of fifteen for a boy and thirteen for a girl provided that a male guardian agrees. The patrilineal family is empowered to take charge of the financial rights of children if the father is dead, although the mother may have custody right. Article 12 stipulates that the testimony of a woman counts half that of a man's. In matters of inheritance, daughters inherit half the share of sons (Itri 2006).

After Syria signed CEDAW in 2003, albeit with reservations,[8] the convention started playing an important role in reframing demands regarding gender equality. The Syrian Commission for Family Affairs (SCFA) was immediately established with direct organizational links to the Council of Ministers headed by the prime minister.[9] The commission coordinated the work of international organizations such as UNIFEM (United Nations Fund for Women), UNICEF (United Nations Children's Fund), and the UNDP (United Nations Human Development Program), and was mandated to raise national consciousness pertaining to women's and children's rights. In collaboration with the largest women's union, the Syrian

8. Reservations pertain to abolishing laws and practices that discriminate against women (art. 2), gender equality in nationality laws (art. 9), regulation of marriage and divorce (art. 16), freedom of movement, and of residence and domicile (Art. 15), and Art. 29 concerning arbitration between states in the event of dispute.

9. The more routine and expected organizational link would have been the Ministry of Social Affairs, which traditionally addresses women's issues.

General Union of Women,[10] the SCFA proposed a draft law on personal status that would safeguard the civil rights of women and children with reference to CEDAW and the UN Children's Convention. The SCFA draft included three projects, which the commission had prepared in collaboration with lawyers, the Women's Union, and religious scholars. The projects included an alimony fund envisioned to channel custody and maintenance fees to divorced mothers and children through the state, a housing scheme for divorced mothers, and the establishment of family courts specialized in family law.[11] Other pressures for change also proliferated. For instance, the Association for Social Initiative (ASI) was central in the passage of Law 18 in October 2003 that prolonged the period of children under their divorced mother's custody by two years (sons up to thirteen and daughters up to fifteen). This was the first amendment to a family law since 1975.

Three years later parliament accepted a new Catholic family law (Law 31, *Official Gazette*, July 5, 2006). Internal reform started in 1990 when the Law of Oriental Churches addressed international conventions on the rights of women and children. Changes suggested by those mandated to draft the law were congruent with the liberalization agenda of the new president at the turn of the millennium wherein the regime was eager to accommodate religious pluralism (Nome 2006). Changes stipulated the principle of equality between daughters and sons (in matters of inheritance) and mothers and fathers (in relation to their children). The financial rights of Catholic women were considerably strengthened.

10. The SWGU (hereafter called "the Women's Union") was established in 1967 and represents 114 women's unions and associations in all social and economic fields, making it the biggest women's organization in Syria.

11. These projects were discussed during a seminar held at the premises of the Women's Union on August 10–11, 2006. For more on the projects, see at-the-time lecturer at the Faculty of Law at Damascus University, and minister of social affairs as of February 2013, Dr. Kinda al-Shamat: *"mashru' qanun al-nafaqa,"* SWO, Nov. 30, 2006; *"tajarub 'arabiyya fi mawdu' mahakim al-usra,"* SWO, Dec. 18, 2006; and *"al-tajarub al-'arabaiyya fi majal sunduq al-nafaqa,"* SWO, Jan. 3, 2007; Rahada 'Abdoush, *"sunduq al-nafaqa wal-takaful al-ijtima'i ila ish'ar akhar,"* SWO, Apr. 13, 2009; *Al-Thara E Magazine,* Jan. 30, 2009.

In between these two legal reforms, family law issues were widely discussed in Syrian society. A nationwide public campaign on violence against women was a tangible result of the government's commitment to gender-specific issues, yielding the publication of a study in 2005 and the establishment of public shelter homes for abused women in each governorate in 2009.[12] Networking also facilitated the first nationally publicized civil campaign against femicide, launched in 2005 by the SWO as a direct response to the killing of a young Druze woman who had married a Sunni Muslim and thus had broken the Druze family law, which prohibits extracommunal marriage.

Five years of vibrant focus on female issues changed when state authorities adopted repressive measures against political activists after 2006 (Pierret 2013, 207–9. In February 2007, Syrian authorities withdrew the ASI's license to operate as a civil society following allegations by a neoconservative shaykh who accused the ASI of instigating war against the family by conducting a survey on personal status issues. The government's subtle support for conservative religious forces was exposed in June 2009 when the SWO disclosed the draft code that a ministerial committee had been working on secretly for nearly two years.

Facing Pressures: The Syrian Government's Janus-Faced Response

The "secret" committee mandated to work on a draft for a new family law can usefully be seen in the light of pressures by social groups (such as women's and human rights groups and the Catholic Church) for reform in family law. Through Prime Ministerial Order 2437, the Ministry of Justice appointed five members (still publicly unknown)[13] on June 7, 2007, that were to work on a project entitled "Syrian personal status law proj-

---

12. See *Dirasat midaniyya hawlal-unf al-waqi' 'alal-mar'a* (Fieldwork study on violence against women), a joint report by the Syrian Central Bureau of Statistics (CBS), UNIFEM, the SCFA, and the Women's Union.

13. Five persons were allegedly chosen by former Minister of Justice Mohammad al-Ghufri. Only one of those five, Hassan Awad, a professor at the shari'a law school in Damascus, came forward on public radio (*The National*, July 14, 2009).

ect" (*mashruʻ qanun al-ahwal ash-shakhsiyya*). The date is particularly informative. It reveals that the committee was established less than a week before Law 31 extended the autonomous powers of the Catholic Church in reformulating its family law and three months after the ban on the ASI in February 2007. Apparently, criticism by representatives of the Sunni orthodox clergy of pressures to reform the 1953 code sent a message of disapproval to Syrian authorities. Coupled with skepticism toward changes in the Catholic family law that widened the differences between rights granted to Muslim and to Christian citizens, the Sunni orthodox clergy sought to counter further reforms.

By 2007 these conservative pressures for changes in family law had reached a stage that alarmed opponents, who saw reforms as infringements on the 1953 personal status code. The Syrian regime had in a remarkably short period of five years addressed sensitive and gender-specific issues. At the same time, state authorities were attentive to critical voices by the Sunni orthodox clergy. The establishment of a ministerial commission mandated to draft a law on personal status indicated a Janus-faced approach toward enhanced female citizenship. Syrian political authorities showed a will to address women's issues but not at a price that compromised the interests of the Sunni clergy.

The Draft Law of April 2009 Compared to the Current 1953 Code

The one-hundred-page-long text of the draft law published in May 2009 contains 665 articles envisaged to replace the 308 articles of the existing 1953 code.[14] Among the most noticeable features of the draft compared to the 1953 code is the overt display of Sunni Islamic doctrinal terminology based on orthodox interpretations of shariʻa principles and jurisprudence (*fiqh*). Terms such as *thimmi* (non-Muslim), *kitabiyya* and *kitabi* (female and male member of the "People of the Book," that is, Christian or Jew),

---

14. The first version of the draft code was published by SWO on May 21, 2009, and is found on http://nesasy.org/content/view/7366/336/. The 1953 Code is found on http://nesasy.org/index.php/-79/41--------591953, both codes last accessed May 15, 2013.

and *murtadd* and *murtadda* (female and male apostate) are for example found in Articles 63 and 92. Islamic doctrinal tenets are also reflected through the explicit legitimizing of polygyny in Articles 71 to 75. Whereas the 1953 code sets restrictive conditions for a Muslim man to marry more than one wife, the draft law only restricts a Muslim man from marrying "a fifth woman until he divorces one of his four wives" (art. 66). The draft is lenient toward extrajudicial marriage (art. 84), contravening thereby conditions that limited polygyny in 1975. The dissolution of marriage is explained as being constituted in mainly four forms (art. 164–239), one of which allows universal divorce by the husband but not the wife.[15] The draft law maintains male guardianship and custody (*wilaya* and *wisaya*) over females and children, perpetuating thereby the curtailment of full legal capacity for female citizens as adults and as mothers. Marriage between minors (thirteen years for girls and fifteen years for boys)—a point heavily criticized by human rights activists as institutionalizing child marriage— is sustained in Articles 44 and 45.[16]

With regard to religious minorities, the draft introduces major changes. While the 1953 code grants general exemptions to Christian denominations (art. 308), the draft law strengthens the state's control over marriage and divorce by specifying no fewer than thirty-five legal regulations for Christian denominations (art. 620–55), restricting thereby the authority of the Christian clergy. No major change is proposed to rules regulating the Druze community.

Two new institutions are introduced. The Family Insurance Fund (*sunduq al-takaful al-usari*) in Article 23 is meant to alleviate the financial burdens of divorcees, orphans, and widowers with no male guardians (*la 'a'il lahum*). The other—more politically intriguing—institution suggested is *an-niyaba al-'amma ash-shar'iyya* (art. 21). Roughly translated as the "General Legal Agency," it is envisaged to monitor illicit marriage

---

15. Article 164 states that separation (*firqa*) between a married couple occurs, first, by the will of the husband (*talaq*); second, by the will of the married couple (*mukhala'a*); third, through a court decision (*tatliq* or *faskh*); and fourth, through death.

16. See lawyer Muna As'ad's article "*dirasat muqarana bayna mashru' qanun al-ahwal ash-shakhsiyya al-jadid wa akam ad-dutur as-suri*," SWO, June 2, 2009.

on behalf of the state (*az-zawaj bil-muharramat*).[17] In this regard, prohibition against mixed marriages deemed illicit (*zawaj batil*) by state law is specified in several articles (Art. 21, 63, 92). Regulations also include state-imposed and enforced separation of a married couple owing to difference in faith (*tafriq li-ikhtilaf ad-din*)[18] and allegations of apostasy (*radda*), that is, conversion from Islam to Christianity (art. 230–34).

In short, the draft introduces overt orthodox religious references into the law. It provides for stricter enforcement of family law under the auspices of state power. The picture portrayed is of a state that encourages religious pluralism at communal group level, but not its practice through individual choice by adult citizens who wish to engage in cross-religious marital relationships without converting.

Public Reactions to the Draft Law

The dajje that evolved after the disclosure of the draft was mainly voiced by intellectuals and scholars in the cities of Damascus, Homs, and Aleppo. Broadly painted, three groups with different ideological viewpoints regarding gender roles, religious pluralism, and political participation can be identified.

First, orthodox views were articulated by Sunni clerics (*shaykhs*) and scholars (*'ulama*) who claimed to represent the interests of the Sunni

17. Article 48 of the 1953 code prohibits marriage between a Muslim woman and a non-Muslim, and article 318 prohibits a Druze woman from marrying a non-Druze.

18. There exist cases where officials have appealed through court against what Syrian authorities deem as illicit interfaith marriages. Lawyer Rukniya Schadeh has, for instance, handled a case where the Political Security Division required a previously Muslim Syrian woman who had, according to the Syrian family law, illicitly converted to Christianity in Lebanon (where religious conversion from Islam to Christianity is permitted) to divorce her husband, a Syrian Christian, after twenty-two years. (Letter no. 25963 sent by the Political Security Division (*shi'bat al-amn as-siyasi*) to the Personal Civil Registry in Damascus (*amanat as-sijl al-madani bi-dimashq*), dated Dec. 18, 2005). On June 14, 2006, Schadeh raised a counter case against the minister of justice (Case 5245/2006). State authorities penalize such marital engagements by denying children born of these unions registration in official personal registries, a denial that renders children de facto stateless.

majority population. Some had fundamentalist revivalist agendas, some enjoyed governmental positions such as mosque sheikhs (most notably Mohammed Sa'id Ramadan al-Buti, who headed the Umayyad mosque between 2008 until his death by a suicide attack in March 2013[19]), while others held nongovernmental but socially influential positions as religious teachers. What characterizes the religious orientation of these groups was a text-oriented version of Sufi Islam (Pierret 2009, 71) wherein traditional gender roles prevailed.

Second, a conglomerate of commentators can be seen as "traditionalists," "conservatives," and "pragmatic" reformers who do not oppose the clerical imprint nor the judicial basis of religious pluralism in the Syrian code. What they demand are reforms that address contemporary social problems such as financial negligence by males related to divorce and abandonment, legal reforms that attend to the needs of working mothers, and increased awareness regarding violence against women and femicide. The Women's Union and the SCFA were two institutions that represented such demands. Others were pragmatic religious figures with a reformist agenda such as State Mufti Ahmad Hassoun; MP and leader of the Islamic Study Centre, Dr. Muhammad al-Habash; leader of the Association of Syrian Women, Asma' Kuftaro;[20] and Catholic bishop and judge Antun Mosleh, who spearheaded the enactment of the 2006 Catholic family law.

Third were "secularists" who sought to remove the clerical imprint embedded in the code. They wanted to establish civic and secular standards of equality between women and men that harmonize with the constitution and international conventions. Civil society groups with a secular agenda include the ASI, the Syrian Women's League (*rabitat an-nisa' as-suriyyat*), and some intellectuals within human rights groups.

While the first and third groups were polarized into two ideologically opposing camps, the second group was fairly large and represented

19. Top pro-regime cleric killed in Syria blast, accessed May 15, 2013, http://www.aljazeera.com/news/middleeast/2013/03/2013321174113479353.html.

20. Asma' Kuftaro is married to MP Muhammad al-Habash and is grandchild of the late Grand Mufti of Syria Ahmad Kuftaro (1964–2004).

a mix of viewpoints that, interestingly, reflected the Ba'thist religio-secularist agenda. Many of their arguments, for instance, ran along secularist lines advocating individually based citizenship not mediated by a person's membership in a religious group. At the same time, the same critics emphasized the importance of group-based rights such as minority religious rights and wanted matters related to marriage and divorce maintained, which they wanted to remain under communal religious autonomy. For instance, lawyer 'Abir 'Allum, in a lecture at the Democratic Youth Union on March 5, 2010, argued for the need to separate the state from religion and to protect the personal status law against the interpretations of clerics. At the same time she maintained that civil society organizations demand "a modern code based on citizenship that conforms with the basics of religions."[21] 'Allum's views probably reflect a certain degree of self-censorship. Her moderation illustrates, however, the restraint that characterizes statements by representatives of the second group: they seek to advance women's and children's rights, but they do not want to discredit what they perceive as the sanctity of religious tenets in family laws.

The following section presents the opinions of the different groups.

The Dajje Articulated

Upon the disclosure of the draft through SWO, the Internet portal's editor, Bassam al-Kadi—a secularist—published a series of commentaries in which he accused the drafters of creating "sectarian religious emirates" in which a citizen is categorized according to religious belief. Readers were called upon to "raise their voice in revealing the disgraceful project."[22]

---

21. The original sentence reads, "*qanun 'asri yaqum 'ala asas al-muwatana wa yansajim ma' maqasid al-adyan wal-'aqa'id al-samiyya, kama yatawafaq ma' karamat al-dawla as-suriyya wa iltizamiha bil-ittifaqiyyat al-dawliyya]*" (*al- Nur*, Mar. 24, 2010, rendered in SWO, Apr. 3, 2010).

22. "*Mashru' al-qanun al-ahwal ash- shakhsiyya al-jadid: al-kahnut al-dini yakshufu wajhuhu al-haqiqi,*" SWO, May 24, 2009; "*risalat maftuha ila ri'asat majlis alwuzara' hal tamma tajawuz mashru' qanun al-ahwal al-shakhsiyya?*" (SWO, May 26, 2009); and

A week after the disclosure of the draft, four open letters signed by ten prominent civil society groups were addressed to President Bashar al-Asad, First Lady Asma al-Asad, the SCFA, and the Women's Union.[23] The signatories demand that broader segments of the population—such as specialists in law, development studies and labor unions—be included in forming a code consistent with international conventions and Syria's Tenth Five-Year Plan (SWO, May 30, 2009).

Not surprisingly, lawyers were the most active critics. Among the first to react was Abdallah S. Ali, who criticized the sustaining of the principle of male guardianship and the strengthening of men's prerogatives (*imtiayazat*). Ali pointed out two features he considered dangerous. First, *hisba* trials—that is, apostasy trials—were allowed in Articles 21 and 22 wherein citizens raise cases against persons believed to be apostates (*murtadd*) following illicit cross-religious marriages. Second was the sectarian segregation (*tatyif*) of Syrian society in ways that makes Christians feel like second-class citizens. He concluded that the draft opened up the danger of "islamization by law" (*al-ta'aslum qanuniyyan*).[24]

Other commentators wondered why the SCFA, the Women's Union, researchers, and concerned religious leaders were not included as participants in the law's drafting and accused the drafting committee of being

---

"*mithlama qulna 'la' limashru' qanun ta'ifi . . . nu'akkid. 'la' li-rudud ta'ifiyya*," SWO, May 27, 2009.

23. The ten signatories included seven civil society groups (*al-jam'iyya al-wataniyya litatwir dawr al-mar'a, rahibat al-ra'i as-salih, rabitat an-nisa' as-suriyyat, al-mubadara an-nisa'iyya, al-muntada al-fikri, lajnat da'm qadaya al-mar'a, muntada suriyyat al-islami*), and three electronic sites (*Thara, Ishtar,* and SWO).

24. See "*al-tatyif wa saif al-hisba ahamm mashru' qannun al-awhal al-shakhsiyya*," SWO, May 30, 2009; "*qira'a fi mashru' qanun al-ahwal al-shakhsiyya al-muqtarah (1/2): ikhtilaf al-din wa al-radda*," SWO, June 2, 2009; and "*qira'at fi mashru' qanun al-ahwal al-shakhsiyya al-muqtarah (2/2): al-ta'aslum qaninuniyyan*," SWO, June 8, 2009. Ali points at the Egyptian case of Dr. Nasr Hamed Abu Zeid, in which an individual raised a case of *hisba* in 1994 against Zeid requesting the court to separate him from his wife on the basis of Zeid's being an apostate (*murtadd*). On more critique of *hisba*-cases in Syria, see Wadad Sallum, "*al-usuliyya hiya nahj fit-tafkir: al-hisba namuthajan*," SWO, July 17, 2009.

"stone age men" (*rijal al-kuhuf*) and a "tripartite lobby" consisting of the Ministry of Justice, the Ministry of Religious Endowments, and the Council of Ministers.[25]

A protagonist of the draft, Khalid Rashwan, a lawyer who specialized in criminal and shari'a law, maintained that "personal status laws should follow shari'a law and in shari'a law the rights of women are specified, so we should accept this. Why is it being likened to the Taliban?" (quoted in *Syria Today*, August 2009). Another representative, Zuheir Salem, who leads the Orient Arab Institute for Development Studies (*markaz ash-sharq al-'arabi lil-dirasat al-hadariyya*), argued that

> those who follow the public interest with regards to the impact of the imperial project on our region know that the destruction of the family, . . . is the target which international organizations are working on continuously . . . under different titles such as . . . defense of women's rights and what is referred to as individual rights (*hurriyat fardiyya*) . . . We do not deny that this law perhaps needs some . . . adjustments here and there . . . , provided that this is done by taking care of primal shari'a sources and not through the whim and will of those [who support] international clubs and its militants in the land of Islam.[26]

The first newspaper to reject the draft code was the Communist Party's *an-Nur*, which urged "concerned authorities to consider the draft law to be a step backwards in the social sphere [which] does not serve the interests of economic development and modernization" (SWO, June 2, 2009). The announcement was welcomed by the SWO, whose editorial wondered why

25. '*Awdat ila mashru' qanun al-taqaddum . . . ilal-khalf*, SWO June 2, 2009; Dib, Bashir and Qurzan, "*la takad takhlu maddat minal 665 mawad min intiqad mashru' qanun al-ahwal al-shakhsiyya 'an ta'ami hawiyyat al-mujtama' as-suri*," in *al-Azmina*, reprinted in SWO, July 9, 2009; Bassam al-Kadi: "*ri'asat majlis al-wuzara' tastakhdim "al-amana as-suriyya liltanmiya" li-tard khamsat khubara' kibar min al-hay'a al-suriyya*," personal page, Aug. 1, 2009; Nabuwwa, "*min ajl qanun 'asri lil-ahwal al-shakhsiyya*," *an-Nour*, Aug. 19, 2009, rendered in SWO, Aug. 23, 2009.

26. Quoted in al-Kadi, "*as-syyid "salem", min "rubu' al-inhilal wal-imla'at": fa-l-taqtu' al-'ayyid wa-l-arjul min khilaf*," SWO, June 22, 2009.

other political parties and human rights associations remained silent on the issue.[27] Two weeks later the central newspaper mouthpiece of the ruling authorities, *al-Ba'th*, published an article on the draft law in which the leader of the Women's Union, Majeda Quteit, asserted that the draft law did not correspond with the development of women's position in Syria. She remarked that the Women's Union had formulated revisions to the code that were consistent with the contemporary needs of women and children (*al-Ba'th*, June 15, 2009; reproduced in SWO, June 17, 2009).

Two days later, the mufti of Aleppo, Dr. Mahmoud Akkam, a legal scholar in personal status law and member of the working group on family law issues at the SCFA, was among the first religious clerics to criticize the draft law in public. In a radio interview he said that he was surprised for two reasons: the draft law consultations should have included the Syrian people because it affects all aspects of their life, and also it neglected the efforts by the SCFA during the past five years in formulating a draft law. Akkam insisted that the code be based on Article 45 of the Syrian constitution, which grants Syrian women and men equal rights (*Sham FM* on June 17, 2009; reproduced in SWO, June 22, 2009).

Looking at the debate in retrospect, the *al-Ba'th* article printed on June 15 and the mufti of Aleppo's arguments two days later appear to have lowered the threshold of permissible comments by prominent public figures. Nearly half of all articles of the one-year period under study (approximately sixty articles) were published between June 16 and July 1, namely, after comments by the leader of the Women's Union and the mufti of Aleppo.

The Draft Law Halted in Parliament

On July 1, 2009, a SWO editorial launched a sweeping critique against Prime Minister al-Otri following his appeal that the debate be carried out within the confines of a democratic dialogue:

27. "*An-nur tantaqid mashru' qanun al-ahwal, wal-ahzab wal-qiwa wa munaththamat huquq al-insan . . . samita*," SWO, June 3, 2009.

[D]o you believe that the legalization of appeals that enforce separation from my wife . . . to be a democratic dialogue? . . . [Does] the debasement of Muslims and their portrayal as racists [resemble] a democratic dialogue? . . . [Does] the curtailment of women's rights, . . . the rape of children . . . , represent an exchange of ideas? . . . Why has your office threatened to take severe measures against journalists in all official media if they dared to bring up this issue? . . . Why have private media corporations received tacit intimidations if anyone opens his mouth against this dark project?[28]

This verbal attack came at the same time as the draft law was halted in a parliamentary session. Within five days three somewhat conflicting official statements appeared: On June 29, 2009, the president of the Assembly, Dr. Mahmud al-Abrash, declared that the draft law was canceled; another parliamentary statement announced that parliament had sent the draft back to the Ministry of Justice for a fresh look; in a third, Prime Minister al-Otri commented that the draft law was still a working paper.[29] On July 4, 2009, the Syrian Arab News Agency (SANA) publicized the following statement by al-Otri, who sought to downplay the role of the former minister of justice who had mandated the work of the secret committee:

In order to provide the public with accurate information and correct the misconception about this issue . . . we feel the urge to clarify the following: The government started in 2000 to make a comprehensive evaluation of the regulations in place now in order to modernize them so they match . . . the process of social and economic development. . . . To achieve this aim the ministers called for the Justice Ministry to amend some laws including the Personal Status Law. . . . The Ministry submitted a number of drafts, including the Personal Status Draft Law. Upon studying this draft, the Presidency of the Council of Ministers returned the draft to the Ministry of Justice for it to study again this issue in

28. "'An ayy hiwar dimuqrati wa ra'y akhar tatahaddathu ya siyadat ra'is al-hukuma?" SWO, July 1, 2009.

29. The National, July 14, 2009; al-Thara, Dec. 26, 2009; and SWO newsletters dated July 4, 2009, and Aug. 3, 2009.

coordination with all the authorized and concerned factions. [The draft] will be studied according to the usual procedures, i.e. it will be submitted to the specialized ministerial committees and then to the Council of Ministers . . . and then it will be submitted to the People's Assembly . . . and discussed in the same way like any other legislation. (Reproduced in SWO, July 4, 2009)[30]

By the end of July, five senior workers at the SCFA—pivotal in preparing an alternative personal status law—were fired, apparently penalized for sending a two-page note to the Council of Ministers in which they criticized the disclosed draft law (SWO, Aug. 3, 2009).

Framing the Controversy: The Politicization of the Public Discourse on Reforms in Family Law

Debates over family law are multifaceted. On the one hand, they should be understood as fundamental individual and group struggles for welfare, since in the absence of expansive welfare states, the family remains the essential guarantor of individual welfare in Arab societies. Seen from this perspective, equal female citizenship is intimately linked to conditions that enable a female citizen to obtain minimal legal and economic powers within the family on an autonomous and individual basis.

Second, personal status laws have a profound impact on the authority of religious leaders. Reforms in family law alter the extent to which religious authorities, that is, the Sunni clergy as well as communal leaders of minority religious groups, are enabled by state authorities to exert influence on their members, namely Syrian citizens, in regulating legal and financial dispositions laid in family law regarding their living conditions.

Finally, the way in which Syrian authorities responded to criticism following the outcry illustrates how an authoritarian regime undergoing political liberalization attempts to cope with conflicting demands. As such, the controversy over the draft code reveals the maneuvering room

30. English translation as rendered in SWO newsletter. See also SWO, June 30, 2009, which cites the prime minister.

within which authoritarian rule nurtures and structures its survival. I elaborate on these three points in order to shed light on why family law created a political crisis in a relatively short period of time.

Civil Society and Welfare Issues: Feminized Political Opposition?

The primacy of kinship-based systems in Syria (as well as in all states where public welfare schemes are rudimentary) accentuates the importance of family laws because of the profound social and economic impact of these laws on the quality of life of all family members, including females who are predominantly outside the waged labor market. Discussions regarding the establishment of an alimony fund—primarily a welfare issue—can therefore also be understood as a political issue through which the civil and economic rights of female citizens and children are advanced on the domestic political agenda.

As a response to pressure groups that address social problems, the Ministry of Awqaf presented a set of notes entitled "Observations on Social Solidarity" in 2009.[31] The notes demonstrated the ministry's lack of support for the SCFA's work with personal status issues. The *awqaf* criticized further the establishment of the state-run alimony fund as suggested by the SCFA and argued that it was a conspiracy against poor women and children that would cause the collapse of the family. In the notes, the ministry opposed the lifting of CEDAW reservations, which the SCFA supports, and described the activity of the SCFA and other NGOs as promoting irresponsible and unacceptable social change. The awqaf presented its vision of social welfare reflected in both draft laws in the form of a family insurance fund (*sunduq al-takaful al-usari*) wherein male relatives retain judicial and financial custody of children.

---

31. See Rahada 'Abdoush, *"sunduq al-nafaqa wa-l-takaful al-ijtima'i ila ish'ar akhar,"* SWO, Apr. 13, 2009; and Yahya Alous, "The Ministry of Endowments—Where Is It Going?" *Al-Thara E-Magazine*, no. 218, Jan. 30, 2010. The exact date of the notes on social welfare rendered by the awqaf is unclear from the article.

In other words, two alternative welfare models were suggested by different parts of the state apparatus. While mutually congruent in target (both sought to alleviate social destitution), they were incongruent in method and ideological rationale. The SCFA and civil society groups pressed for institutionalized rights-based social welfare in which the state guaranteed financial transfers (such as alimony and custody fees) to women and children. The awqaf sought to buttress a traditional understanding of poverty alleviation based on charity and privately extracted funds to the "needy," that is, poor women and children who have no male relatives (*la 'a'il lahum*) (art. 167). Theirs was a model that lent less support to women in obtaining individually based financial rights and made women primarily dependent on male relatives.

The upsurge in Islamic charitable activities, as Thomas Pierret indicates (2009), sheds light on the awqaf's flexing of muscles with regard to alleviating poverty in ways it defines appropriate. He points out that the increase in charitable associations, partly sponsored by businessmen who subsidize expenses related to food, surgeries, and marriage, had evolved in the wake of worsened economic and social conditions since the 1990s. The regime was caught between its ban on charitable Islamic organizations since the 1980s, with the underlying legitimacy problem embedded in such a ban, and its practical need to rely on work done by Islamic charity groups (2009, 77).

Buttressing the Power of Communal Religious Leaders

The controversy over the draft laws indicates that—although a majority of commentators argued for equal and individually based rights—clear-cut secular justifications were rare. Syrians were markedly unwilling to support orthodox interpretations of religious law, but the public at large concurred on retaining a family law with a clerical imprint.

My reading of the controversy over the draft laws is one in which concerned citizens sought to safeguard religious moderation. Critical and concerned voices addressed problems connected with social transformation by interpreting religious laws and tenets in ways that strengthened the civil rights of females and children within the confines of religious tenets.

Moderation came, however, at a price. The power of communal leaders and their authority over the interpretation of religious law were buttressed. The dajje thus signaled opposition toward orthodoxy, but within a fairly conservative framework of argumentation. Islamic scholar and MP al-Habash serves as an example of conservative moderation in his reservation against Syria's lifting of Article 16 of the CEDAW regarding marriage, divorce, and polygyny. He made his stance clear that female citizens cannot have the same legal authority as male citizens in matters regarding marriage and divorce:

> Absolute equity in rights and responsibilities in marriage and divorce is not conceivable because the wife's responsibilities in pregnancy, breast-feeding and custody differ from the husband's duties in economic maintenance. Islamic law states a man's right to polygyny, but a woman can never be granted the same right. The [CEDAW] article grants a woman unilateral divorce on an equal footing with men. This is out of the question in terms of Islamic jurisprudence. The shari'a grants a woman the right to abolish a marriage through court and not by individual will. I believe reservation on this article is necessary and absolute. (2005, 22)

Profiled as a liberal Islamic scholar (Heck n.d.), al-Habash's clarification illustrates that although the style of argument may be new, he maintains a patriarchal understanding of gender roles.[32]

The Syrian Religio-Political Conundrum: State Feminism under Authoritarian Rule

Pressures for or against reforms in the Syrian family law became a "keystone of the state's commitment to Islam" (Moors 1999, 159). This pressure

---

32. After the uprising, MP al-Habash defected gradually from the regime. In February 2012 he moved to Dubai and urged President al-Asad to resign (Pierret 2013, 225–26).

put the authority of the secular-oriented Baʿthist regime, headed by the ʿAlawite minority, constantly to the test with regard to changes that extend female citizenship. Can we detect an "Islamized" transformation in the foundation of Syrian authoritarianism as Salwa Ismael indicates (2009, 26–27)?

The language used in the draft provides a textual foundation for such a conclusion. There are, however, reasons to emphasize the power play at stake rather than the Islamic mantle with which political considerations are draped. Inherent in the organization of the Syrian legal and institutional structure were spaces where political discord was easily "religionized." State-mandated registration of religious identity, family law, and the inherent religious authority that was embedded in communal religious leaders were such spaces. Pressures for reforms in family law were, more specifically, arenas where disparate ideological opinions—political in nature—are easily and recurrently politicized. I argue that diverging and conflicting interests are easily defined as "religious" by both proponents and opponents of change. However, these interests nevertheless represented divergent ideological standpoints with regard to the distribution of legal and economic assets in society. These assets are political in nature and intimately related to the enactment of citizenship as a relationship between citizens and state (Mayer 2003; Mouffe 2005, 152–53). In Syria, the secular ideology of the state and the clerical imprint of family law lived side by side in paradoxical but remarkably adaptive ways.

The aftermath of the discourse on family law in 2009 indicates that religious authority per se was not challenged, though its orthodox expressions certainly were. The government responded to the dajje by presenting a revised second draft in November 2009, six months after the first draft code leaked out in May 2009. Sunni orthodox elements of the first draft were removed and the judicial authority of religious leaders of minority religious denominations over marriage and divorce was rebolstered in the second draft. Political authorities had sufficient backing from the public uproar to withstand pressures from the alliance between the Sunni clergy at the awqaf who had allied with the Ministry of Justice in reformulating the Syrian family law along more orthodox lines.

Conclusion

Three main observations can be discerned following the public outcry: First, the controversy exposes the strength as well as the weakness of social forces in pre-2011-uprising Syrian society that sought to expand female citizenship. In terms of weakness, the appointment of the secret committee revealed a political will to conciliate the interests of Sunni orthodoxy that evidently constrain and limit the civil rights of Syrian women. The manner in which the Internet emerged as a medium of mobilization demonstrated, however, the potential strength of civil society as a means of supporting political demands, even in fairly autocratic polities such as Syria. Authoritarian rule, however, caught up with this development. In April 2010, less than a year after the dajje broke out, the government signaled that it was working on a draft Law on Electronic Broadcasting (*qanun al-i'lam al-iliktroni*) that sought to regulate electronic media. This step helped tighten—or restore—the regime's grip on freedom of expression and communication.[33] Since 2005 the SWO had been able to operate as a significant critical actor in articulating social demands and representing comments on the position of women in Syrian society. By the end of 2010 the SWO had not been censored nor closed down, as was the fate of some 160 websites in 2008 (Pace and Landis 2009, 138). The disclosure of the draft law on the Internet in 2009, however, precipitated limitations on Internet-based mobilization activities on the scale witnessed during the controversy over the draft family law.[34]

33. *"Limataha la tanshuru al-musaddaqa itha kuntum sadiqin?"* SWO, May 1, 2010; *"marsad nisa' suriyya yarfudu qanun al-i'lam al-iliktroni al-yawm wa ghadan,"* SWO, May 3, 2010.

34. At a conference held April 13–16, 2010, under the auspices of Communication Minister Mohammad Sabuni and Deputy to the Minister of Information Nabil al-Dibs, media actors were urged to show "responsible freedom" (*al-hurriya al-mas'ula*). In exchange, licensed Internet portals would receive financial support, the ministers argued. Commenting on this offer, Bassam al-Kadi points to the imminent danger of putting electronic sites under the control of the state by regulating their activities through a law that disregards the very essence of networking (SWO, May 3, 2010).

Second, the controversy over the code showed the tacit tug-of-war between political and religious authorities in Syria. Discrepancies in policy orientation between the dominant Sunni majority and the secularly oriented 'Alawite-dominated regime were particularly discernible in debates in which family law constituted an ideological battleground. Seen by opponents of the draft laws as gatekeepers of "issues Islamic," the Ministry of Justice and the awqaf were the two main state-bureaucratic institutions that expressed the ideological viewpoints of the Sunni clergy and citizens with orthodox ideological views on social issues, including gender equality. The hasty way in which the prime minister responded to the disclosure of the draft law and the presentation of a new version within four months revealed an overt disagreement between the Ministry of Justice and the presidency of the Council of Ministers, if not in policy orientation then at least over content and form.

With regard to a potential legislative process for family law reforms in Syria, the public display of different arguments during the dajje provided a background that portrayed the ideological opinions of different segments within Syrian society. Zoheir Ghazzal and colleagues (2009) pointed out that despite President Asad's legislative powers, which overshadowed those of parliament, there was a deliberative process within the Syrian parliament that involved collaboration of representatives who "draw practical maps that delineate borders between what is permitted and what is forbidden within the institutional framework. Such maps leave open a broad margin of uncertainty" (2009, 67–68). I suggest that in the aftermath of the 2009 controversy, the scope of uncertainty regarding substantial changes within family law in parliament was narrowed. Ideological frontiers had been publicly displayed during the dajje. A mobilized broad alliance of individuals and groups confronted overtly orthodox views and demanded religious moderation, but did not oppose the clerical imprint of family law. As such, political mobilization revealed fairly conservative leanings that bolstered the authority of religious scholars, including the authority of heads of religious minorities, in defining family law.

Third, political authorities in Syria approached opposing groups in a variety of ways: aligning with some groups and distancing themselves from others, spearheading changes in the law, and, at times, switching their support among different factions. The controversy in 2009 shows the Syrian ruling authority's will and success in dealing different kinds of cards (political agendas and mandates) to various players (social pressure groups), and orchestrating finely tuned co-optation strategies in different governmental institutions: Two institutions, the SCFA and the Women's Union, were until the controversy erupted in 2009 mandated to play the progressive and secular game for strengthened female civil rights, while two other institutions, the Ministry of Justice and the Ministry of Religious Endowments, were provided the part of playing out the role of gate-keepers of faith politics.

Support to expanded female citizenship was prevalent under secular Ba'thist rule after 2003. The controversy over the draft law in 2009 reveals, however, that this support was contained and contingent on political calculations regarding regime survival. Pressures for reforms that strengthened female citizenship were less probable by the end of 2010 because political rule nurtured, and was nurtured by, the support of clerical authorities and conservative forces within the state apparatus. The president was strong enough to hold power, but not strong enough to support reforms that widened the civil rights of Syrian women. Reforms were constrained by an ostensibly secular regime still inclined to maintain and buttress the clerical powers of those seen as primal definers and interpreters of family law as state law.

The Syrian uprising, in polarizing Syria and undermining the middle ground between secularists and minorities on the one hand, and increasingly radicalized Sunni Islamists on the other hand, is likely, as well, to leave its imprint on debates over female citizenship and family law. Already in so-called "liberated" areas, new authorities seek to impose orthodox versions of the shari'a law, sparking resistance by moderates and secularists. The regime, in turn, depicts itself as the protector of minorities and moderates against fundamentalist Islam. As such, the uprising reflects how women's and children's civil rights are part and parcel of, and hostage to, the power distribution within an emerging order shaped under the auspices of accentuated Islamic clerical orthodoxy. The outcome of the civil war is bound to have profound implications for female citizenship.

10

The End of a World

Drought and Agrarian Transformation
in Northeast Syria (2007–2010)

MYRIAM ABABSA

The years 2007 to 2009 were three terribly dry years in the Middle East. Syria had to receive international aid and food supplies for one million peasants living in the northeastern provinces of Raqqa, Hassaka, and Deir ez-Zor (the Jezira), the poorest region in Syria. The country's emergency cereals reserves had been used but were not sufficient to cope with all the population's needs. Tens of thousands of farmers fled to main cities' suburbs in search of informal jobs. In the Jezira, the source of two-thirds of Syria's cereals and cotton production, the consequences were dramatic. According to a report by the International Institute for Sustainable Development, between 160 to 220 villages were abandoned because of drying up of wells and harsh windblown sand that invaded the houses (Brown and Crawford 2009; DIS and ACCORD 2010). About 300,000 families were driven to Damascus, Aleppo, and other cities in one of the "largest internal displacements in the Middle East in recent years" (OCHA 2010). The government launched an emergency program to reduce the consequences of the drought, but only a third of the requested 43 million dollars necessary were donated by the international community. As a consequence, the World Food Program had to reduce food distribution to 200,000 persons in 2009, compared to 300,000 in 2008.[1]

---

1. IRIN, "Syria Drought Pushing Millions into Poverty," Sept. 9, 2010, accessed Oct. 2010, http://www.irinnews.org/report.aspx?reportid=90442.

The drought accentuated the decline of the agrarian sector, already weakened by the dismantlement of its former socialist structures. Even before the drought, between 2002 and 2008 Syria had lost 40 percent of its agricultural workforce, dropping from 1.4 million to 800,000 workers (Aita 2010b). Although workforce statistics have in the past shown wide fluctuations, in this case it appears to have partly been owing to mismanagement of water and land resources and partly because of a new agrarian relation law. Promulgated on December 29, 2004, Law 56 allowed landowners to terminate, after three years, all tenancy contracts and to replace them with temporary contracts. Applied in December 2007, this law resulted in the expulsion of hundreds of tenants and workers, especially on the coast in Tartous and Lattakia (Sarkis Fernández 2011).

The aim of this chapter is to provide an overview of the agrarian transformations in Bashar al-Asad's Syria as a general context within which the 2007–9 drought occurred. It examines the drought and the government strategy to cope with its consequences, as well as the pace of restructuring in the agriculture sector. Its main argument is that political reasons are at least as important as climatic ones in explaining developments in the Jezira. The most important of these is the policy of high subsidization of cotton production that consumed up to one-third of the country's water resources, salinized the soils because of the inefficient drainage system, and used considerable amounts of fertilizers. The second reason is the dismantlement of all state farms starting from 2001 and their distribution to former landowners, farmers, and civil servants. The third political reason is the promulgation of Decree 49 in 2008, which forbade all land sales at the border with Turkey to "foreigners" as well as to several categories of Kurds in Hassaka governorate, where the "Arab belt" of forty-one villages was created in 1974. The purpose of this decree was to further pursue the arabization policy and to reduce the number of Kurdish landowners. The fourth reason is the new agrarian relations law noted above.

The Jezira: A Century of Village Creation, Latifundia Development, and Land Distribution (1864–2007)

Formerly a pastoral area for nomadic and seminomadic tribes located between the Tigris and the Euphrates at the borders of historical Bilad ash-Sham, the Jezira was, since the 1950s, Syria's pioneering agricultural and energy site. It is in this region that the great Euphrates and Khabour Project was implemented in the seventies, and where the main national hydrocarbon reserves have been exploited since 1985 (Ababsa 2009). The Jezira is a highly strategic region for Syria. It covers 40 percent of its territory, producing two-thirds of the country's cereals (70 percent of wheat or 3 millions metric tons) and three-quarters of its hydrocarbons. Its population makes up 17 percent of Syria's overall population (three million out of twenty-one million in 2008). However, it is also the region with the highest proportion of poor and the highest illiteracy rate. The Jezira hosted 58 percent of Syria's poor population before the advent of the 2004 drought, and the percentage thereafter increased: The de Schutter report stated that poverty reached up to 80 percent of the Jezira inhabitants in 2010 (UNGA 2011).[2] The level of unemployment was high (25 percent compared to 11 percent at a national level in 2004) since the land could no longer provide jobs for all the youth, and the region only hosted 7 percent of Syria's industrial installations. The industrial underdevelopment of the Jezira was striking: whereas, pre-uprising, the region produced 69 percent of Syrian cotton, only 10 percent of cotton threads were spun there.[3]

This region is inhabited by Arabs and Kurds, especially in Hassaka governorate where Kurds form nearly half of the population (1,395,000 inhabitants in 2007).[4] This strategic zone has been heavily controlled by successive Ba'thist regimes that have relied on medium-scale landowners from the

2. http://www.alertnet.org/thenews/newsdesk/IRIN/c9ae22f3b93f3b621bdc7f83ea82 94da.htm, accessed Oct. 2010.

3. The center was Aleppo, with seven of the sixteen state-owned spinning plants. Deir ez-Zor and Hassaka each had only one spinning plant, and therefore farmers had to transport their seed cotton more than 200 kilometers (Westlake 2001).

4. The Kurds form more than 10 percent of Syria's population, or two millions persons (low estimation), more than half of them living in the Jezira and Afrin regions, and the rest in suburbs of Aleppo and Damascus. The national statistics do not specify the ethnic origin of the population. Several French scholars studied Kurdish villages during the French Mandate (Poidebard 1927; Rondot 1938) and in the 1980s (Velud 1985 and 1991).

seminomadic tribes of the valleys of the Euphrates, the Balikh, and the Khabour in order to carry out their development objectives.

The Jezira underwent a boom at the end of the nineteenth century, owing to the Ottoman policy of land endowment of Bedouin chiefs and the settling of the Euphrates seminomadic tribes. This policy was continued by the French Mandate with relative success, in a zone that in 1920 was divided between Syria, Turkey, and Iraq. Vast landed estates were formed in the Syrian Jezira, controlled by Bedouin shaykhs, by the chiefs of the Euphrates tribes who had registered collective lands in their names, and lastly by the inhabitants of Raqqa (*Raqqawi*) and Deir ez-Zor (*Deiri*) who offered usurious loans to small landowners and confiscated their lands when repayments were not made (Hannoyer 1982; Ababsa-Al-Husseini 2002). In 1951, 90 percent of the Jezira's agricultural land was owned by forty Bedouin chiefs and town notables. Ten of them, including the Najjar and Asfar families and the shaykh of the Shammar (the main Bedouin confederation), Dahham al-Hadi, owned 70 percent of the irrigated land of the Euphrates (Khader 1984, 66).

The Jezira's first economic boom came about at the initiative of Aleppo merchants (*khanji*) at the time of the cotton boom in the fifties. Thirteen thousand motor-driven pumps were installed along the Euphrates by entrepreneurs from Aleppo, Raqqa, and Deir ez-Zor to irrigate the upper terraces of the Euphrates. Irrigation without draining the land and monoculture led to the impoverishment of this new agricultural land within a

Table 10.1

Land Ownership Structure in the Jezira and on the Euphrates in 1945

	Euphrates		Jezira	
Properties <10 ha	15%	178,000 ha	5%	56,000 ha
Properties 10–100 ha	32%	286,000 ha	52%	528,000 ha
Properties >100 ha	28%	246,000 ha	34%	343,000 ha
State Properties	25%	224,000 ha	9%	96,000 ha

Source: *Service technique du cadastre et d'amélioration foncière*, 1945, in Khader 1984, 189.

decade. Yet, at the same time, middle-scale owners grew extremely rich. They began to question the domination of the old shaykhs (Khalaf 1981). New figures emerged within tribes, especially wealthy middle-scale land-owners who subscribed to the Ba'ath Party from 1963 onward.

The 1958 land reform was only partially implemented in the North-east of Syria. Its limited application in the main zone of Syria's latifundia was owing to technical obstacles—the absence of a land register, lack of staff, and the division of land between heirs—as well as to political rea-sons. From 1963, the Ba'th regimes adopted a pragmatic policy toward the Jezira that consisted in promoting the emergence of a class of middle-scale tribal landowners who were loyal supporters of the party, while allowing the great "feudal landowners" to keep the basis of their wealth.[5] At the end of the land reforms process, less than a fifth of the arable lands of the Raqqa governorate (18.5 percent) and of the Deir ez-Zor governorate (14.5 percent) had been expropriated. Only one-third of the fertile lands located in the Euphrates valley were affected by the land reform. As for the remaining two-thirds, either their ownership was relatively egalitarian (with farms below the 55-hectare ownership limit of 1963), or, most often, their shaykhs were sufficiently influential to deter the distribution com-mittee from expropriating them (Bauer et al. 1990, 10). As for the bigger landowners of Raqqa (with more than 20 irrigated hectares or more than 80 unirrigated hectares), although they counted for only 5 percent of land-owners, they still owned 37 percent of the land of the governorate, while the 83 percent of small-scale landowners (with fewer than 8 irrigated hect-ares or 30 unirrigated hectares) shared 40 percent of the land (Hinnebusch 1989, 234). A quarter of Raqqa's farming families received no land. In the

5. Thus an amendment to the land reform law was enforced in 1966, protect-ing recently irrigated lands from expropriation. This amendment was inspired by neo-Ba'thist militants from Deir ez-Zor, who were small- and middle-scale landowners, anxious to oppose the cities' middle classes, counting not on the peasantry, but on their kind, other middle-scale landowners, at least according to Petran (1972, 183). Their aim was to control a region that was 92 percent rural and 96 percent of whose inhabitants were illiterate, and to create favorable conditions for the implementation of the great Euphrates and Khabour Project.

middle valley of the Euphrates, large-scale landowners managed to retain up to 55 hectares of the most fertile land, located all along the valley, while leaving the semiarid plateau lands to be expropriated and distributed.

The Effect of the 2007–2010 Drought on the Jezira

The Drop in Production

Raqqa, Deir ez-Zor, and Hassaka governorates accounted for 80 percent of the country's total irrigated wheat acreage, or 680,000 hectares, and produced in a good year (such as 2003–4) roughly 2.7 millions tons of irrigated wheat and 0.8 million tons of rain-fed wheat[6] (PECAD 2008). But in 2008 the production fell to 1.3 million tons, with no production in the *badia* (steppe). According to the Food and Agricultural Organization of the United Nations drought appeal of 2008, up to 75 percent of the Jezira farmers suffered total crop failure during the 2007–8 planting season (FAO 2008). Wheat and barley yields dropped by 47 and 67 percent, respectively, compared to the previous year. In the nonirrigated areas, production dropped by 82 percent, and the barley harvest failed entirely.

The main reason for this drop is that 80 percent of irrigation depends on underground wells and rivers in the Jezira (94 percent in Hassaka governorate, 75 percent in Deir ez-Zor governorate, and 50 percent in Raqqa governorate where the Euphrates Project was implemented with all its dams and canals [table 10.3]). Syria had become self-sufficient in wheat in 1991, thanks not only to its state irrigation projects, but also to the multiplication of private wells. The number of wells was estimated to have increased from around 135,089 in 1999 to more than 213,335 in 2007.[7] In 2001 the cost of a 270-meter-deep well was 16,000 euros in Raqqa governorate, an investment that only tribe shaykhs and big landowners could

6. 1.7 millions hectares of wheat were cultivated every year, of which 45 percent, or 850,000, was irrigated, mainly in the Jezira (PECAD 2008).

7. According to figures from the National Agricultural Policy Centre (NAPC), accessed Oct. 2010, http://www.syria-today.com/index.php/focus/5266-mining-the-deep.

Table 10.2

The Evolution of Cereals and Vegetables Production, 2004–2008 (in tons)

Cereals	2004	2006	2008
Wheat	4,537,000	4,931,500	2,139,000
Barley	527,200	1,202,400	261,000
Maize	210,200	159,000	281,300
Vegetables			
Lentils	125,300	180,700	34,100
Chick Peas	45,300	51,900	27,100
Dry Broad Beans	35,800	30,600	38,100

Source: *Agriculture Yearbook 2009*, table 14/4, accessed Oct. 2010, www.cbssyr.org/year book/2009/chapter4-EN.htm.

afford. In 2005, because of groundwater depletion, a new law was issued forbidding new well drilling, but it was not enforced. In 2007 Syria consumed 19.2 billion cubic meters of water, which was 3.5 billion more than the amount of water replenished naturally, with the deficit coming from groundwater and reservoirs, according to the Ministry of Irrigation.[8]

The overuse of underground water resources led to a depletion of the water table and the death of historic rivers such as the Balikh, which dried up in the middle of the 1990s, and the Khabour River, which dried up in 2001. From 60 cubic meters per second, its flow decreased to zero, and agriculture was carried on with 6 cubic meters per second of underground water.

In the 2008 and 2009 drought crisis, precipitation was reduced to a third of the normal amount. Many herders had to sell their livestock at 60 percent below cost. As the fodder prices rose in January 2008 by 75 percent, the flocks were reduced by a 50 percent increase in animal mortality and a 70 percent reduction in fertility rates (FAO 2008).

As a consequence of water table depletion and the extraordinary rise in fodder prices, in 2008 some farmers preferred to rent out fully vegetated

8. http://www.alertnet.org/thenews/newsdesk/IRIN/75f137c33f473e665eb4e969186 84e1a.htm, accessed Oct. 2010.

Table 10.3

Irrigation Methods in Northeast Syria in 2008 (in thousands)

	Water				Modern Irrigation Methods		
Governorate	Rivers, Springs	Wells Underground	Dams	Total	Sprinkler	Drip	Total
Aleppo	28	92	86	206	25	10	35
Raqqa	43	51	94	188	5	1	6
Deir ez-Zor	76	39	37	152	—	1	1
Hassaka	29	341	21	391	41	4	45
Syria	208	760	387	1 355	162	91	253

Source: *Agriculture Yearbook 2009*, table 10/4, accessed Oct. 2010, www.cbssyr.org/year book/2009/chapter4-EN.htm.

irrigated wheat fields for grazing of sheep at the high cost of US$15 per *donum*[9] (PECAD 2008).

The Rise of Fuel and Fodder Prices

The drought's consequences were aggravated by the rise of fodder prices worldwide and by the government decision to stop subsidizing fuel, as Syrian smugglers were selling fuel at seven times its price in Lebanon and Jordan. In January 2008 bread and fodder prices increased by 75 percent, and in May 2008 the government stopped subsidizing fuel. Its price rose by 350 percent (from 7 to 25 Syrian pounds (SYP) per liter). This rise in price had a strong impact on middle-scale farmers using motor pumps to extract water and run tractors. The situation got even worse for "middle" shepherds who used to drive water tanks to their flocks in order to graze anywhere in the badia (the "degradation kit" according to International Center for Agricultural Research in the Dry Areas [ICARDA] experts). The government created an Agriculture Support Fund to compensate for

9. In Syria, farmers have used the unit *donum* for centuries. It corresponds to 0.1 hectare. The PECAD report mentions $600 per acre (0.4 hectare).

this price rise and allowed international agencies to distribute food to the poorest of the victims. Small herders and farmers had no choice but to sell all their meager material and move to the cities to look for ill-paid jobs in the informal sectors and in plastic greenhouses in the Der'a region and on the coast.

The Yellow Rust Epidemic of 2010

In addition, in 2010 production was hit by the plague of yellow rust that affected two-thirds of the soft wheat fields.[10] Paradoxically, the good weather conditions that prevailed during the 2009–10 winter (with above normal rainfall and mild temperatures) coincided throughout the entire Middle East with the outbreak of a virulent new strain of yellow rust that affected the soft wheat crop previously resistant to this fungus.[11] As no preventive fungicides had been distributed to the farmers, "the 2010/11 wheat production may have fallen as low as 3.3 million tons, an 18 percent reduction from the previous year and 35 percent below record levels thought possible a month ago. . . . Government estimates in late April indicate[d] that rust-infected wheat acreage totaled 442,000 hectares, of which 300,000 hectares were un-harvestable (total loss)" (PECAD 2010).

Massive Internal Migration

The drought put an end to decades of development in the fields of health and education in the Jezira, and the sanitary situation became dramatic. In 2009, 42 percent of Raqqa governorate suffered from anemia owing to a shortages of dairy products, vegetables, and fruit. Malnutrition among pregnant women and children under five doubled between 2007 and 2009

10. Soft wheat is cultivated to produce bread. Hard durum wheat is cultivated for pasta production. Forty percent of Syrian wheat production is of soft wheat, more vulnerable to the yellow rust.

11. ICARDA research on wheat led to the creation of the highly productive al Cham variety resistant to fungus, thanks to the incorporation of a gene called Yr27 (PECAD 2010).

(OCHA 2009). To complicate matters, vegetable and fruit growers in dry northern Syria used polluted river water to irrigate their crops, causing outbreaks of food poisoning among consumers, according to environmental and medical experts. Experts pointed out that the problem stemmed from sewage and chemicals allowed to reach rivers in rural areas near Aleppo, Lattakia, and Raqqa.[12]

Small-scale farmers (less than 10 donums) and herders (less than 50 head) were already vulnerable because their livelihoods depended on agriculture, a sector characterized by low productivity and an irregular demand for labor. According to a 2004 United Nations Development Program poverty survey, 77 percent of the poor rural people were landless but had some cattle, sheep, and goats. Around 59,000 families, each owning one hundred head of cattle or less, lost half their herds. Herders and farmers sold off productive assets, eroding their source of livelihoods and earnings.

As they were suffering from malnutrition and lack of income, small-scale farmers and herders and landless peasants stopped sending their children to school. According to a UN needs assessment, enrollment in some schools in eastern Syria decreased by 70 percent after April 2008.[13] This decrease reversed decades of literacy efforts and school creation in the Jezira, where the illiteracy rates were the highest in the country: 38.3 percent in Raqqa governorate, 35.1 percent in Hassaka governorate, and 34.8 percent in Deir ez-Zor governorate. More than a third of the active population was illiterate, including more than half of the female active population.

Between 160 and 220 villages were abandoned in Hassaka governorate. The wells dried up and the population could not afford to bring water from private tankers at a cost of 2,000 SYP per month (about 30 euros).

12. http://www.ens-newswire.com/ens/mar2010/2010-03-08-02.html, accessed Oct. 2010.

13. A government report on drought impact in Hassaka governorate, prepared in June 2009, states that nineteen schools closed in the districts of Tel Tamer, Al Shadadi, Tal Hamis, Amuda, Qamishli, and Ras Al Eim. In Hassaka governorate, 7,380 children dropped out of school. In Deir ez-Zor governorate, at least 13,250 students dropped out of school in the 2007–8 and 2008–9 academic years (OCHA 2009, 18).

Table 10.4

Illiteracy Rates for Active Syrian Population in 2004 (population more than fifteen years old)

Governorate	Male (%)	Female (%)	Total (%)
Damascus	4.2	10.2	7.2
Aleppo	16.8	30.9	23.7
Raqqa	26.2	51.4	38.3
Deir ez-Zor	23.1	46.8	34.8
Hassaka	23.3	47.1	35.1
Syria	12.1	26.1	19

Source: UNESCO 2009, 11, accessed Oct. 2010, http://www.unesco.org/fileadmin/MULTI MEDIA/INSTITUTES/UIL/confintea/pdf/National_Reports/Arab%20States/Syrian_Arab _Republic__English_.pdf.

Dust-bowl conditions and sandstorms were reported. According to the United Nations Office for the Coordination of Humanitarian Affairs, one of the "largest internal displacements in the Middle East in recent years" occurred during the drought, with 65,000 families being driven to the cities of Damascus, Aleppo, Hama, Raqqa, and Deir ez-Zor (OCHA 2010; UNGA 2011). Another UN source estimated that between 30,000 and 50,000 families left the rural areas every year after 2008. With farmers abandoning their villages and selling their assets, 80 percent of Syria became susceptible to desertification according to Abdulla Tahir Bin Yehia,[14] FAO head in Syria.

In 2009, UNICEF conducted a survey of twenty-five tent settlements in rural Damascus governorate, established by persons internally displaced because of drought, such as Sa'sa camp near Damascus. It seems that many of these internally displaced persons found work in greenhouses on the

14. Desertification is defined by FAO as "the sum of the geological, climatic, biological and human factors which lead to the degradation of the physical, chemical and biological potential of lands in arid and semi-arid zones, and endanger biodiversity and the survival of human communities," accessed Oct. 2010, http://www.greenprophet.com /2010/06/syria-drought-2/.

coast in Tartous and Lattakia, and in the Der'a region. They were paid by a share—mostly a third—of the production (*al-hissa*), and lived with their families in small houses in the field. They did not take part in the revolts in Der'a and on the coast, being too poor to get politicized according to many observers. Nevertheless, the presence of so many displaced peasants, proof of the failure of the Jezira development, was an important context element in which the revolts occurred.

Change in Land Tenure in the Jezira

Another force impacting the Jezira was regime-initiated changes in the structure of land tenure during Bashar al-Asad's age of liberalization.

The New Agrarian Relations Law 56 of 2004

Between 2006 and 2010, the total workers employed in agriculture dropped in the Jezira by 20 percent, from 274,475 to 221,440, while in Hassaka governorate this drop was by 30 percent (from 110,335 to 77,547). This reduction is even more striking as the demographic growth rate was high during this period.

As we have seen, the drought had a strong impact, especially in the Jezira, but another likely reason for rural poverty and unrest was the introduction of a new law on agrarian relations, Law 56 of December 29, 2004,

Table 10.5
The Drop in the Agriculture Labor Force in the Jezira

	2006	2007	2009	2010
Hassaka	110,335	103,152	74,132	77,547
Raqqa	80,577	73,718	64,951	68,280
Deir ez-Zor	83,563	91,889	74,662	75,613

Source: Central Bureau of Statistics, *Labor Force Survey* 2010, 2009, 2007, 2006, accessed Oct. 2010, http://www.cbssyr.org/work/2010/ALL-2010/TAB13.htm.

which applied nationwide. In order to foster investment in the agricultural sector, landowners received the right to terminate tenants' contracts and expel the peasants from the land they had been working on for two generations. The aim of the law was to "reach a more efficient agriculture for the wealth of the nation and better economic and social relations" (*bi-hadaf al istithmar al-ardh bi-sura saliha li-tanmia al-tharwa al-qawmia wa iqama 'alaqat iqtisadiyya wa ijtima'iyya 'adila*) (paragraph 2, Law 56, December 29, 2004). This complex law, containing 167 paragraphs, allowed landowners to terminate any contract, applicable from December 2007 onward, in exchange for meager indemnities, calculated on the number of years tenants had spent working the land. According to paragraph 106, indemnities were calculated at 2 percent of land value per year worked, and they could not be less than 20 percent of the land value and not more than 40 percent. Paragraphs 96 and 163 were especially controversial. Paragraph 96 stipulates that the contract must be on paper and signed by a signature or a fingerprint while paragraph 163 allows the cancellation of the contract without indemnities if it was an oral contract. Most of the work in the greenhouses (where refugees from the Jezira drought had sought work) was based on informal oral contracts (al-hissa), which gave workers 20 percent of the production's sales price (Sarkis Fernández 2011, 155).

One of the consequences of the law was increasing speculation on agricultural land located at the edges of villages and cities. On the coast, near Banyas, peasants were expelled from the land on which they had built their houses, planted trees, and drilled wells, and the land was sold at 20,000 to 30,000 SYP per square meter (*Tishreen*, Sept. 28, 2009), that is, a thousand times the cost of agricultural land at 30,000 SYP per donum). The fear was that this law would have the same consequences as Law 96 of 1992 in Egypt, which led to the expulsion of elderly and women farmers and accelerated the rural exodus to the cities (Bush 2002).

The ensuing protests were so high, as the Communist Party's online petitions relate, that President Bashar al-Asad had to promulgate an amendment to Law 56 allowing farmers to give oral proofs of their former work, such as neighbors' testimonies. But this did not change the intention of the law to allow landowners to expel farmers as they wished.

The Euphrates Project, State Farms, and Their Privatization

The decade of economic liberalization launched by President Bashar al-Asad also took on a radical form in the domain of public agriculture: that of a distribution of state farmland and the renting out of undistributed land confiscated during the land reforms.

The State General Administration for Land was created in 1986 within the Ministry of Agriculture to administer nine big projects (*munkhat*) and five agricultural units throughout nine governorates.[15] It administrated 114,040 hectares (ha), of which 62,188 ha were exploited. In 2004, 6,307 permanent workers and around 10,000 temporary workers were employed in what had been state farms (*Tishreen*, Sept. 1, 2004). In the northeastern provinces of Aleppo, Raqqa, Deir ez-Zor, and Hassaka, state farms had covered 68,146 ha of which 21,011 ha (fifteen farms) were irrigated land in the Pilot Euphrates Project. A further 45,862 ha were uncultivable land that was also included in the state farms (*Tishreen*, June 23, 2003).

With the beginning of the economic opening under Hafiz al-Asad in 1991 (*infitah*), the Syrian state launched a renewal of private economic initiative. It also insisted, however, that some sectors be protected from liberalization for strategic reasons, especially the agriculture sector. One innovation was that in 1992, a new production system was introduced in the state farms. This system allowed for sharecropping contracts, which gave 20 percent of the production to the cultivator. A new category of owners thus appeared alongside the formerly dominant farm laborers and the various engineers and technicians: that of the holders of an exploitation contract (*musharikin*).

Under Bashar al-Asad the deepening of economic liberalization spread to the agricultural sector. Combined with a severe decline in agricultural production and extensive corruption in the state farms, the new policy

15. These big projects are: 8th March Project in the Damascus countryside; Hurriya Project in Lattakia; Asad and Abu Firas Hamdani Projects in Aleppo governorate; Rachid Project in Raqqa governorate; Si'lo Project in Deir ez-Zor; and Ras al-Ain Project, Manajir and Tiger in Hassaka governorate. The five agricultural units are located in Quneitra, Der'a, Suweida, and Hassaka governorates.

Table 10.6
State Farm Surfaces Evolution (1970–2000)

Year	State Farms Total Surface	Cultivated Surface
1970	138,000 ha	64,132 ha
1983	67,666 ha	10,378 ha
2000	68,146 ha	21,011 ha

Sources: Hinnebusch 1989, 203; Ministry of Irrigation 2001; *al- Thawra*, Feb. 5, 2002.

led to the privatization of all Syrian state lands by virtue of Decision 83 on December 16, 2000. According to this decision, the state farmland was parceled out in shares of 3 ha for irrigated land and 8 ha for nonirrigated land. The decision formally allocated "right of use," and not property. It also called for land to be distributed to, in order of priority, the former owners, the farm workers, and employees of the General Administration of the Euphrates Basin (GADEB).

In the Jezira, the decision triggered considerable tension and competition among these three categories, as each feared being excluded from the land redistribution process. As implementation proceeded, more than 250 letters of complaint were addressed to the Syrian president's office. Critically, this decision was made by the Ba'th Party and then transmitted to the Agriculture Ministry and to the Irrigation Ministry (and the GADEB). However, Decision 83 was not accompanied by the cancellation of the preceding decrees (1971 and 1983),[16] which relate to the distribution of ownership. This led to confusion regarding the rights of the former owners, the agrarian reform recipients, the workers, and the technicians (Ababsa 2010).

The bulk of the distributions took place within the Pilot Project of the Raqqa governorate and the large Bassal al-Asad farm of Meskene,

16. In 1983, Decree 1033 limited the private property in the State irrigation projects to 160 donums. Also, 3,100 ha were expropriated and transformed into state land that was rented for 75 SYP a donum per year (Bauer et al. 1990: 38).

Table 10.7

Syrian State Farm Distribution in September 2009

Project Name	State Farm Distributed Surfaces	Number of Beneficiaries (average surface)
Pilot Project	15,802 ha	6,046 (2.6 ha)
Asad Farm	15,511 ha (12,628 *baal*)	3,486 (4.4 ha nonirrigated)
Meskene	12,809 ha	6,533 (1.9 ha)
Meskene Est	980 ha	700 (1.4 ha)
Suweidi	934 ha	526 (1.7 ha)
Tell Saman	164 ha	302 (0.5 ha)
Total	46,200 ha (only 33,000 ha irrigated)	17,593 (2.6 ha)

Source: www.sana.sy, Sept. 16, 2009, accessed Oct. 2010.

located in the Aleppo governorate. In total in 2009, 38,650 irrigated ha were redistributed to 12,500 beneficiaries in the Jezira (12,809 irrigated ha were distributed to 6,533 beneficiaries in Asad Farm–Meskene).[17] According to Hassan Suleiman, director of agriculture in Raqqa governorate, more than 20,000 families, or 100,000 persons, profited from the distribution of state farms (SANA, Sept. 2009). The total land surface redistributed reached 33,662 ha (20,836 ha irrigated and 12,826 ha nonirrigated—*baal*). In the Pilot Project, 15,802 ha were distributed to 6,046 families, 652 ha were kept for a training center, and 2,168 ha were planted with trees.

The decree at least allowed recovery of a satisfactory level of productivity at the farms. According to the head of the Department of Agriculture of the Raqqa governorate, one of the direct positive consequences of dismantling the farms was the fivefold increase in revenue from total agricultural production of the Raqqa governorate between 2000 and 2003 (Ababsa 2010).

17. http://www.albaathmedia.sy/, Aug. 8, 2009, accessed Oct. 2010.

Land Resale and Latifundia Reformation
by Members of the Euphrates Tribes Contractors

In fact, the state farms reform created many conflicts between family members, that is, between heirs who regained land and those who did not.[18] There were also conflicts between those who received "bad" and those who received more productive plots of land. Moreover, the reform led to an extreme scattering of land parcels (most of the recipients obtained plots far from their former and current properties). As a consequence, an informal "rationalization" process took place through plot sale or exchange. Following the parceling out of the land and its distribution, many recipients either rented or sold their plots. Since both selling and hiring of state farm plots were illegal, the contracts were confidential and engaged only private individuals. The exposure risk weighed on the original land recipient and not on the man who rented or bought it.

A double process resulted from the practice of selling or hiring the Pilot Project fields. On the one hand, there was a reinforcement of large contractor capacities, mainly members of the Euphrates tribes but also Raqqawi, who had the means to rent and exploit large surfaces, and who were able to keep their property during the agrarian reform by giving it to their heirs. These contractors had access to low-cost Euphrates water through the Euphrates Project canals. On the other hand, there was a resumption of large latifundia estates exceeding all property ceilings set by the successive land reform laws. Thus the change in the property structures and the nature of exploitation was radical. Land passed from state farms to large private domains, which the Ba'th Party ideology had wished to limit. It was indeed a form of counterrevolution (Bush 2002).

18. While some landowners registered their land in the name of their heirs before the distribution process, many did not. Consequently, a father who registered his sons received 3 donums for each of them, whereas a father who did not only received 3 donums in total.

The Arab Belt Policy Continued: Decree 49 of 2008

In Hassaka governorate, the effects of the drought as a push factor for migration were worsened by Presidential Decree 49 of 2008, which restricted the ability of people living in certain border areas of Syria to sell or purchase property without prior approval of the authorities. In Hassaka governorate, this decree was extended in practice to the entire governorate. The border region was a sensitive one, as its population consisted mainly of Kurds until the 1970s, when the government decided to create an Arab belt of forty-one villages, where four thousand Arab families from the Walda tribe, whose land was submerged by the Euphrates dam, were settled (Meyer 1990). Most of the Kurdish tribes were seminomadic, moving freely along and across the Turkish-Syrian border at this time. The Syrian authorities argued that, during the implementation of the agrarian reform, many Kurds came from Turkey hoping to obtain distributed land. For this reason, in 1962, the chief of Hassaka Political Police, Mohammed Talib Hilâl, conceived the Arab Belt Plan to expropriate Kurds and deprive them of their citizenship rights in a 350-kilometer-long and 15-kilometer-wide band along the Turkish border. He organized an exceptional census on October 5, 1962, after which 120,000 Kurds lost their Syrian citizenship under the pretext that they were not able to prove their presence in Syria before 1945 (Seurat 1980, 104). They were given a red identity card, classifying them as *ajanib* (foreigner), whereas their Syrian-born children became *maktumin* (hidden). Statistics indicate that their numbers rose particularly during the agrarian reform period; but a lot of Syrian Kurds were deprived of their legitimate citizenship. Ajanib and maktumin had no choice but to settle in the poor suburbs of Qamishli and Hassaka. Thirty thousand Kurdish peasants were moved to Aleppo and Damascus cities by the government.

After the March 2004 riots in Qamishli, President Bashar al-Asad announced that 90,000 Syrian Kurds would obtain their citizenship. Interviews were conducted in February 2005 by the government, but the risk of a Kurdish irredentism in the context of the growing autonomy of Iraqi Kurdistan slowed down the process. In 2010 opposition Kurdish parties still claimed that the rights of 75,000 maktumin and around 150,000 ajanib had not been restored.

In this context, the issuing of Decree 49 was interpreted as a new policy to arabize the Jezira. According to a report by the Danish Immigration Service,

> [The decree] has frozen the economic activity, construction work and land sales within an area of 25 km from the border, and it has as well had a negative impact on agricultural activities. Furthermore, the area affected by the decree has been expanded to the entire Hassaka province. Therefore, it is de facto impossible to sell or buy property in the area, unless one is informant for the security services or a prominent member of the Ba'ath party. [A] source however assumed that the decree does not apply to Arabs in order to promote an influx of Arabs to the region. (DIS and ACCORD 2010, 10).

In April 2011 President Asad announced that citizenship would be restored for some of the stateless Kurds, but implementing this measure was not a priority in the context of the revolt that hit Syria in March 2011.

Relief and Development Policies

International Undermobilization for Syria

Several international agencies such as the World Food Program proposed to provide assistance to Syria to help cope with the drought. In August 2010 Special Rapporteur for Food Security Olivier de Schutter made a ten-day field trip to the Jezira. His main concern was that the 2008 Syrian drought appeal launched by FAO had only received a third of the required funds because of Syria's bad relations with donor countries. "As a result of recent droughts, between two and three million" Syrians were "living in extreme poverty in the country" compared to 2.02 million in 2003–4 (UNGA 2011). In October 2009, 11,500 families in the Hassaka governorate, 10,500 in the Raqqa governorate, and 9,000 in the Deir ez-Zor governorate received food baskets distributed by the World Food Program.[19] The European Commis-

---

19. Each basket contained 150 kilograms (kg) flour, 25 kg sugar, 25 kg bourgoul, and 10 kg lentils. www.esyria.sy/eraqqa, accessed June 2011.

sion paid two millions euros to fund the food distribution in 2010. The World Food Program received only half of the 22 million dollars required for distribution to 300,000 persons. As a consequence, only 200,000 received food baskets in 2010, leaving 110,000 without help.[20]

In order to mitigate the impact on agriculture of the drought and of higher diesel prices, in 2008 the government raised all public wages by 25 percent and established the Agricultural Support Fund. The ASF was allocated 10 billion SYP in the 2009 budget. In 2008, the ASF distributed diesel coupons allowing each household to buy 1,000 liters of diesel at a reduced price. But in 2009 these coupons were replaced by 10,000 SYP cash transfers to vulnerable households. The eligibility criteria for transfers were based on income, asset ownership, and utility bills. Approximately half of the Syrian households were thought likely to benefit from these transfers (IMF 2009).[21] People protested that this cash transfer was not enough to compensate for the augmentation of their diesel bills. Diesel consumption was sharply reduced, whether because people could not afford it or because of the end of the "cross-border leakage of subsidies" through smuggling. The authorities were determined to continue to modernize the subsidies system to further limit the cost to the treasury (IMF 2009).

In the context of the Arab Spring, Syria accelerated the creation of a National Social Aid Fund that had been under consideration for several years. It was created by Decree 9 of January 14, 2011, and started its first cash distribution in mid-February 2011 to 420,000 households living below the poverty line. Those deemed eligible to receive support were classified into four categories based on their income levels. The poorest group was to receive three payments totaling SYP 42,000 (US$913) annually. The subsequent three groups would receive annual subsidies of 30,000 SYP (US$652), 12,000 SYP (US$217), and 6,000 SYP (US$130), respectively.[22] The beneficiaries had to prove that their children were still enrolled at school and vaccinated, which is difficult in the Jezira, where some people had become so

20. http://www.eubusiness.com/news-eu/syria-drought-food.58w/, accessed June 2011.

21. http://www.imf.org/external/pubs/cat/longres.cfm?sk=22702.0, accessed June 2011.

22. http://www.syria-today.com/index.php/news/14478-social-aid-fund-begins-distri bution, accessed June 2011.

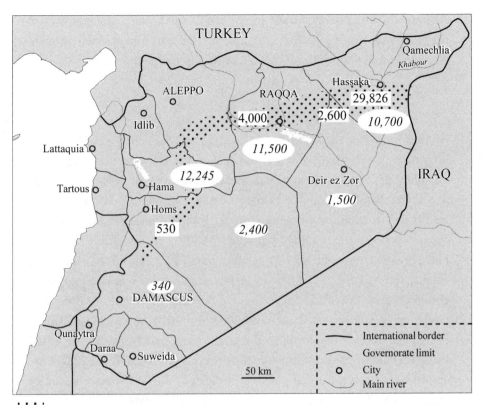

Drought Severely Affected Herders with Ownership of Less than 50 head, in Agroecological Zone 5

1,500 Drought Severely Affected Herders

530 Drought Severely Affected Farmers

10.1. Population severely affected by drought in Syria, 2009. Map conception and design by M. Ababsa, 2014, based on OCHA 2009 and data from the UN World Food Programme and the Ministry of Agriculture and Agrarian Reform (FAO 2008).

poor that they could not afford clothes to dress their children. Furthermore, all illiterates had to attend literacy classes as a condition for receiving aid, which was again a huge constraint in the Jezira.[23] With this policy, the government hoped to stop migration to the main cities of Damascus and

23. http://www.nsaf.gov.sy/forms/faqs/viewAllFaqs.php?pageLang=en, accessed June 2011.

Aleppo, and even to encourage the return of migrants to the Jezira since migrants were not eligible for social aid. But the government had to provide employment opportunities if this return was to happen.

The New Irrigation Programs

By the middle of the 2000–2010 decade, Syria launched new irrigation programs in the Northeast aimed at extending the irrigated perimeters and demonstrating to the international community that Syria was entitled to a higher total share of the Euphrates water, whose flow was controlled by Turkey. In 2008, by virtue of Decree 51, the General Organization for Land Development (GOLD) replaced GADEB, created in 1981, which had previously created 117 km of main canal and 350 km of secondary canals, and had organized fifty-three peasant cooperatives in a pilot project. According to GOLD's new director, Abdallah Darwish, 43,805 ha of land were newly irrigated between 2006 and 2010, at a very rapid pace during the worst of the drought. The total irrigated surfaces administrated by GOLD along the Euphrates with its several dams stood at 222,079 ha; 40,005 ha were in the process of being irrigated, and 94,000 ha were under study (with 40,000 ha feasible).

In the context of the drought, the state accelerated land reclamation and irrigation in Ressafa and Balikh number 2, projects planned in 1975, in order to provide the new beneficiaries of the state farm distribution

Table 10.8

Irrigated Surfaces Administrated by the General Organization of Land Development (GOLD) in August 2010 (by governorate)

	Land Irrigated by GOLD	Under Project in 2010
Aleppo Governorate	72,394 ha	14,041 ha
Raqqa Governorate	107,111 ha	21,329 ha
Deir ez-Zor Governorate	42,574 ha	12,923 ha
Total	222,079 ha	48,293 ha

Source: www.an-nour.com, Aug. 17, 2010, no. 448, accessed Oct. 2010.

with water to convert their dry land into irrigated land. Yet much tension emerged as people contested the distribution and criticized the slow pace of the irrigation work. In addition, in March 2011 President al-Asad laid the foundation stone of the Tigris Water Diversion Project, a 2.1-billion-dollar irrigation project, aiming at drawing 1.25 billion cubic meters of water from the Tigris River to Hassaka governorate and to the Khabour River. The project was planned to include several pumping stations and 181 km of canals. It was an eighteen-year project aiming at irrigating 150,000 ha of land in Hassaka governorate, plus providing water to the 63,000 ha on the banks of the dried-up Khabour. However, these fairly long-term projects would be able to offer relief to only a small proportion of the victims of the drought and were among the development casualties of the uprising.

Conclusion

The terrible drought of 2007–9 is comparable in severity to that of 1958–61 that led to the death of half of Syria's cattle and the forced settlement of nomads (Lewis 1987). Sixty years later, Syrian cattle numbers were again reduced from 21 to 14 millions head. As the groundwater reserves meanwhile dried up, farmers had no choice but to migrate to Aleppo, Damascus, Der'a, and the coast. The government started to distribute cash aid in spring 2011, hoping to bring the internally displaced persons back.

However, the problem was more structural, as during the 2000–2010 decade employment dropped significantly in agriculture. This drop was partly owing to the implementation of the new agrarian relation Law 56 of 2004, which allowed landowners to terminate farming contracts. This law was highly contested as it is a highly capitalist, antisocialist one in favor of landowners, and thus constituted a real element of agrarian counter-reform. Furthermore, the drought crisis was used to encourage migration out of the Jezira, especially poor Kurdish tenants and workers, as a law forbade them to buy and sell land at the Turkish border.

Syrian agriculture was going through a harsh crisis. In September 2010 Dr. Adel Safar, then minister of agriculture and agrarian reform, who became prime minister in April 2011, discussed openly with Olivier de

Schutter, UN Special Rapporteur for Food Security, the means of easing the damaging effects of the drought. The minister attributed some of the adverse effects to a "structural problem of the conversion of State planned agriculture to a more indicative planning," that is, the economic liberalization of the sector (SANA, Sept. 7, 2010). Although more research on the issue is needed, it seems likely that in neglecting, during this transition period, the system of agricultural planning and support developed in the seventies, the regime was left unprepared to cope with the worst effects not only of the drought but also of its neoliberal policies. This lack of preparedness, in turn, enervated its rural support base and made it more vulnerable to the mobilization of opposition among the rural population during the Syrian uprising.

PART THREE

Coping with Regional and International Challenges

11

The Ancien Regime's Policy Paradox

International Emergence versus Domestic Suppression

CARSTEN WIELAND

Not long before the wave of Arab protests reached Syria, the regime in Damascus had started to regain the initiative in foreign policy. European governments and even the US administration seemed to have come to the conclusion that Syria was at least a stable, politically approachable, and important geostrategic player in the Middle East whose president was on the path of piecemeal reforms. It was hard work for Bashar al-Asad to get to this point after years of isolation and stigmatization following the Iraq war. What many Western governments did not see—or did not want to grant importance—was that in the shadow of a more proactive approach and considerable successes in amplifying spaces of maneuver abroad, the regime in Damascus had launched a new wave of suppression at home against human rights activists and mostly secular opposition forces long before the unprecedented street protests started in March 2011. The hope did not materialize that a less threatening international environment would allow a more relaxed stance toward domestic dissent.

Against this background, the cautious but strategically reasonable engagement of Syria by Western governments at that time became a matter of debate: was Syria, as some argued, escaping from its pariah role too easily or, as others emphasized, had Syria been stigmatized for years without due reason and relations were merely being normalized. From 2011 onward, however, benevolent voices gradually fell silent. The dimensions of Syria's domestic struggle dwarfed any other political problem in the region, and Asad's foreign policy successes lay in shatters.

This chapter focuses on Syria's foreign policy, in particular its emergence from isolation in 2008, by looking at Syria's relationship with several key countries; it also explores the relationship between Syria's external situation and internal repression or relaxation.

International Factors and Three Waves of Domestic Suppression

Syria's post-2008 development is best understood in the context of the wider pattern of relationship between external threat and internal repression in the 2000–2010 decade. Classifying Bashar al-Asad's first ten years in office in domestic and foreign policy phases (see table 11.1) suggests the possible links between outside and inside. The earlier periods up to 2008 will first be briefly discussed before turning to the post-2008 period.

In the first years of Bashar al-Asad's presidency, the new leadership was still determining its foreign policy orientation. No major changes were taking place either in discourse or in major foreign policy initiatives. Nevertheless, there were lively debates within the leadership on the course of Syria's foreign policy, basically between European or westward-looking protagonists and eastward-oriented figures that favored contacts with Russia, Iran, and China.

The *first wave of repression* took place in 2001 as a clampdown on the mushrooming debating clubs of the Civil Society Movement. The leading figure imprisoned at that time was entrepreneur and ex-Member of Parliament Riyad Seif, who dared to announce the foundation of a new social democratic party. This was a redline, and the regime feared another perestroika that would destabilize it, a fear especially shared by hard-liners such as Vice President Abdul Halim Khaddam (who defected to Paris after the Hariri killing in 2005). Not long after the Damascus Spring was suppressed in 2001, it became clear that economic reform remained the lowest common denominator within the regime after political and administrative reforms were gradually discarded.

But domestic developments might have turned out better if international events had not posed considerable threat to Syria. Among these

Table 11.1

Phases of Bashar al-Asad's Rule

	Foreign Policy		Domestic Policy
2000–2002	Orientation • No significant steps, continuation of known problems and discourses.	2000–mid-2001	Cautious Opening • Damascus Spring, debating clubs, Civil Society Movement
2003–2005	Ideologization • Stiff ideological positioning against the Iraq war, isolation, strengthening ties with Iran but mending relations with Turkey from 2004 onward.	mid-2001-2002	First clampdown • Suppression of the Damascus Spring, first losses of the Civil Society Movement, arrest of Riyad Seif.
		2003–2004	Stagnation • Civil Society Movement simmers.
2005–2007	Contraction • Hariri assassination and consequences, withdrawal from Lebanon, further isolation also by Europeans (France) and Arabs (Saudi Arabia).	2005–2006	Confrontation • Opposition gains courage, Damascus Declaration (Oct. 2005), confrontational course between regime and Civil Society Movement; rising influence of Islamists.
		2006	Second clampdown • End of open confrontation, silencing of the Civil Society Movement, arrest of Michel Kilo, Anwar al-Bounni.

(continued)

Table 11.1 (*Cont.*)
Phases of Bashar al-Asad's Rule

	Foreign Policy		Domestic Policy
2008–2010	Re-emergence • Start of liberation from foreign policy dead-ends and pariah status, back on the international stage, well-thought alliances and decisions (Turkey, Lebanon, Saudi Arabia), consolidation of the regime.	2007–2009	Silence • The comeback of fear to the streets, rest-opposition is in the underground; continued rise of Islamist influence.
		2009–2010	Third Clampdown • Arrest of further senior opposition members and HR activists like Haytham al-Maleh, rising suppression of secularists and secular ideas; increased influence of Islamists up to the legislative level.
Since 2011	Fallback into isolation	Since 2011	Existential regime crisis and military crackdown on mass protests, internal war and possible state collapse.

events were the 9/11 attacks that changed the whole board game in the Middle East and beyond, the military approach of the US administration under George W. Bush, the US economic sanctions on Syria that began with the preparations for the Iraq war, the subsequent war in Iraq in 2003 and its violent repercussions, the wave of Iraqi refugees that hit Syria in particular, the French-US-Saudi-Sunni connection to expel Syria from Lebanon in 2004–5, and the war between Hezbollah and Israel in 2006. In a context of US-American threats of regime change, no democratic experiments could be expected.

Nevertheless, hope for change persisted even through the years of 2003 and 2004 when the Syrian Ba'th regime was entrenched in harsh ideological opposition to the Iraq war. With increasing pressure on Syria especially by Saudi Arabia, France, and the United States to leave Lebanon (underlined by UN Resolution 1559) and the Hariri assassination in February 2005, and in view of the obvious weakness of Asad's regime, the secular opposition caught momentum and was encouraged by Western diplomats and politicians. At that time a historical step toward a more unified opposition was achieved through the Damascus Declaration of October 16, 2005. For the first time, all major opposition groups, reaching from the secular Civil Society Movement to Kurdish activists, moderate Muslims, and even the outlawed Muslim Brotherhood in London, issued a broad call for democratic change in Syria. The lengthy document called for an end to the emergency laws and other forms of political repression, for a national conference on democratic change, and for a constituent assembly.[1]

The *second wave of suppression* followed in the first half of 2006 when those who had been spared in 2001, like Michel Kilo, who drew up the Damascus Declaration, and human rights lawyer Anwar al-Bounni, were arrested. The hunt for signatories of the Damascus Declaration was linked to the accusation of pursuing the agenda of Western interests at a time when the Syrian regime suffered from the "Lebanon trauma" of increased isolation and stigmatization.

If the first two waves of repression followed some logic—that no internal dissent could be tolerated at a time of external siege—the same could not be said for the *third wave* of suppression against secular opposition and human rights activists that started at the end of 2009 when Syria had already celebrated its reemergence onto the international stage.

---

1. More on the developments in and around Syria from 2000 to 2006 can be found in Wieland 2006a, 2006b, and 2012.

Foreign Policy After 2008: Agility on Many Fronts

By the end of the 2000–2010 period, Syria had taken its head out of the noose of isolation that had been tightened by the United States first and consequently also by European countries after the Iraq war. The cause of the regime's success lay in a series of decisions that, on the one hand, reflected a break with past dogmas and implied changes of paradigm, and, on the other hand, displayed a growing maturity of President Bashar al-Asad in foreign policy matters. There was a new Syrian pragmatism after a phase of ideological encrustation during the Iraq war. The latter falling back into old Pan-Arab and intransigently anti-US positions with a dosage of clash-of-civilization rhetoric (especially by Asad's adviser Bouthaina Shaaban) had not left any doors open for backstage diplomacy as Bashar's father Hafiz would have done. On the other hand, the defensive stance of the regime during and after the Iraq war in general can be explained by both raison d'état and emotional desperation in an environment that had put the existence of the Syrian regime in danger.

Interestingly, the new agility in Damascus was not linked with Barack Obama's ascent to the presidency of the United States. The most important decisions for this new course were taken in 2008, long before it was clear who would become the new occupant of the White House. From a Syrian perspective, any change in Washington was to represent a glimpse of hope after the simplistic good-bad rhetoric and exclusively military approach of former President George W. Bush, who placed Syria within the extended "Axis of Evil," despite Syria's intelligence cooperation against militant Islamists after the 9/11 attacks that lasted until long into 2003. Many chances had been missed in the West to keep constructive relations with Syria and to lend support to West-centric elements within Syria's power circles.[2]

Until the beginning of 2011, Syria had rebounded from its worst shocks. The most significant developments in Syria's foreign policy in the years since 2008 can be summed up as follows:

---

2. A critical summary on the interaction of US foreign policy and Syria's development in the past decade can be found in Hinnebusch 2010.

◆ Syria's historical separation from Lebanon both on the level of ideology and in constitutional terms through bilateral recognition, exchange of embassies, and clarification of borders. There was also a startup of talks and personal encounters with representatives of anti-Syrian camps in Lebanon. This, of course, did not exclude the continued exertion of Syrian strategic-political influence in Lebanon.

◆ Indirect negotiations with Israel about the Golan Heights via Turkey, although they were interrupted shortly before they could turn into direct talks owing to the war in Gaza in 2008–9.

◆ The rapid deepening of relations with Turkey.

◆ The start of diplomatic relations with Iraq and bilateral cooperation in the fields of economy and security, although not without frictions.

◆ Détente with Saudi Arabia and thus with the Hariri camp in Lebanon.

◆ Silent resumption of intelligence cooperation with the United States and the United Kingdom that had been interrupted in 2003.

◆ Syria's becoming presentable again in most European capitals, especially in Paris, and being invited to the Mediterranean Conference there in July 2008.

Lebanon

Few were willing to bet on Bashar al-Asad's political future after the assassination of Lebanon's president Rafiq al-Hariri in February 2005, a man who had voiced growing criticism against Syria in his last months. International pressure on Syria grew and caused a hasty military withdrawal from Lebanon, where Syrian troops had been present since 1976.

The 2006 Israel-Lebanon war was one turning point that rescued Asad's fortunes. His ally, Hezbollah, acquired more political influence over Lebanon's state institutions after the summer war, which was a disaster for Israel from a public diplomacy perspective. Afterward, United Nations Interim Force In Lebanon (UNIFIL) troops took up their observation positions in southern Lebanon, but no one dared to mention Hezbollah's disarmament. Even many non-Shi'ites and Hezbollah critics saw the militia of the Party of God as a guarantee of Lebanese sovereignty against Israel, as the country's state organs remained fragile, including a military unable to defend the country. Other Lebanese, however, resented Hezbollah and the war, and its aftermath deepened political and thus sectarian polarization in Lebanon. Polarization took a sharp upturn in May 2008 when Hezbollah's fighters for the first time turned their weapons inward and occupied several Beirut neighborhoods, stopping just short of a coup d'état.

However, the deeply divided Lebanese parties managed to negotiate a breakthrough in the Doha Agreement in May 2008. Thus they cleared the way for the presidential election, and in November 2009, after another tough tug-of-war, the government of National Unity under Saad al-Hariri of the anti-Syrian camp, but also including Syria's allies, could take up its work.

This Hariri-led government was very different from his former anti-Syrian administration. Even "pro-Western" Hariri in April 2010 had contradicted Washington and Israel in declaring that Syria had *not* channeled Scud missiles into Lebanon. On March 24, 2010, the Lebanese newspaper *Al-Akhbar* quoted Hariri as warning representatives of his media outlets: "I have made the decision of building a special relationship with Syria. And in the same way that it is forbidden to [negatively] allude to Saudi Arabia in our media institutions, you must know that from now on, [negative] allusions to Syria will be unacceptable under any form." Anyone who violates this rule should be leaving.[3]

Hariri also uttered increasingly cautious statements concerning the International Tribunal, an indication of the extent to which he was already moving within the Syrian orbit.[4] For the sake of domestic peace, both Hariri and Walid Jumblatt apologized for having blamed Syria for Rafiq al-Hariri's assassination. Hariri feared civil strife and the consequences of this strife for his position. He might have learned from Jumblatt's biography that in this delicate region one can seek the truth but not justice. It seemed unlikely that justice would be done after this assassination even

3. "Hariri to his media staff: 'Those who want to criticize Syria must resign,'" *Al-Akhbar*, Mar. 24, 2010 (quoted according to Mideast Wire).

4. Hariri in a press conference on his visit to Italy; see "Hariri: Scuds Story Similar to US Claims of Iraq WMDs," *Daily Star*, Apr. 21, 2010.

if the Tribunal named the real culprits. So hedging against further negative repercussions became the order of the day. The International Tribunal
therefore turned into a thorn in the eye of each camp for different reasons, given the delicate situation in Lebanon and the region, and given
the blunders made by the Tribunal itself with heavy costs to its credibility, especially in its early years. What started out as a hopeful example of
international law and justice turned into a potential disaster for political
stability in the region.

In 2009 and 2010 Asad had gained confidence and even felt secure
enough to openly concede Syrian mistakes in Lebanon and to receive
then–prime minister Saad al-Hariri, son of the late Rafiq, in Damascus
with a state reception that included a visit to the well-secured presidential
palace. Even Druze leader Walid Jumblatt, who in the preceding years had
been one of the harshest and most eloquent critics of Syria in Lebanon,
traveled to Syria and met Asad for an icebreaking encounter.

For the first time in postcolonial history, Syria and Lebanon became
two sovereign countries that exchanged ambassadors and agreed on bilateral border drawing. This had been one of the main demands of Western
actors toward Damascus. Step by step, the countries established a relationship that would have been unthinkable only a few years ago. After a long
period of political bickering, Syria finally played a constructive role in the
difficult formation of a Lebanese government.

From their perspective, Syrians complained about a lack of recognition from Western states, given the significant change of direction in their
policies toward Lebanon. The government in Damascus had given up
Greater Syria as an ideological premise of Syrian nationalism. Still today,
many Syrians see Lebanon as a French colonial construct rather than a
full-fledged state because of tight family bonds, cultural relations, and the
lively economic exchange between both countries.

At the same time, Syria did not stop exerting political influence in
Lebanon. The game was simply played with different means, notably
via an alliance with Hezbollah. As long as the conflict with Israel is not
solved, the tiny neighboring state will continue to represent an indispensable strategic space. Syria always knew that it would not have any chance
in a direct military confrontation with Israel because of the Syrian army's

corrupt leadership, technically obsolete weapons, and underpaid regular draft troops. The country had always been in need of Hezbollah's asymmetric guerrilla capabilities and, up until today, there is for the regime no alternative to this alliance. Therefore, the continued influence of the Shi'ite organization in Lebanon's domestic politics remained a vital Syrian interest.

Meanwhile, Iran's direct influence in Lebanon so rose that it even alarmed Syria that it could be reduced to a logistical interface between Iran and Hezbollah. Iran's direct influence in Lebanon was rising while Hezbollah was becoming more astute in lessening its dependence on Syria through deepening of direct links to Iran. The overwhelming welcome of Iran's President Ahmadinejad in Lebanon in mid-October 2010 was the more visible aspect of this development. During Ahmadinejad's visit, the British daily *Telegraph* headlined "A Landlord Visiting His Domain."[5]

After the ousting of Prime Minister Saad al-Hariri and the change of government, with moderate pro-Hezbollah businessman Najib Mikati in charge from January 2011 to March 2013, Hezbollah—and Syria—managed to tighten their grip on Lebanon even more. From a Syrian perspective, this power constellation came about just at the right time: it proved crucial to keep the Lebanese flank quiet during the escalating popular revolts in Syria, and kept Lebanon supportive of Syria in the Arab League as well as in the critical debates in the United Nations.

Israel

In contrast to the changes in its neighborhood, Israel was caught in political stagnation. Since the war in the Gaza Strip, Israel had not made any discernible gestures toward its neighboring Arab countries or toward the Palestinians. Turkey's confidence in Israel was deeply shattered by the Gaza war, and the problems in the Gaza Strip and the West Bank were far from resolved.

---

5. Damien McElroy, "Mahmoud Ahmadinejad in Lebanon: 'A landlord Visiting His Domain,'" *Telegraph*, Oct. 14, 2010.

There was no visible Israeli strategy except a continued push to extend Jewish settlements in the West Bank and the Jewish presence in East Jerusalem. As Israel continued to feel very little pressure, time was running in favor of political hard-liners. The security situation was relatively stable in comparison to previous years when Palestinian suicide bombers took their toll on Israeli civilians almost monthly. This stability was true despite the occasional launching of rockets from Hamas positions in the Gaza Strip. A relative satisfaction with the status quo on the Palestinian issue was coupled with a lack of serious initiatives from Washington owing to domestic policy priorities and deep divisions within the Israeli government itself.

Both the Asad regime in Syria and various governments in Israel (at least in words by senior figures) declared at various times that they would be interested in negotiations. The Netanyahu government pushed for a change of procedure to hand over annexed land, which made it more difficult that either the Golan Heights or East Jerusalem would ever be handed back to Syria and the Palestinians, respectively. According to this new law approved by the Knesset at the end of November 2010, the Israeli parliament needs a two-thirds majority for such a decision or a national referendum has to be held for approval. Moreover, as long as no reform of the election law stabilizes the party spectrum in Israel, strong unpopular decisions would remain difficult, and an external enemy would be beneficial to advance domestic agendas. Finally, divisions within Israel over peace with Syria were sharp. Prime Minister Benjamin Netanyahu tried to keep the door open to negotiations with the Syrian regime, including over the Golan Heights, believing a settlement with Syria would give him a free hand to be tough with the Palestinians; by contrast, his former hard-line foreign minister Avigdor Liebermann warned Syria at the beginning of the popular upheaval in 2011 that if a war broke out, Israel's goal would be nothing short of the collapse of the Asad dynasty. Moreover, he admonished, Syria should stop dreaming of recovering the Golan Heights.[6]

---

6. Associated Press, "Israel Warns Syria It Would Lose Future War," Feb. 4, 2010; *Al-Akhbar*, "Why Did Al-Muallem Warn Israel against Attacking Syria or South Lebanon?"

During the first decade of Bashar al-Asad's rule, the Syrian regime tried to send positive signals toward Washington to demonstrate its readiness to negotiate with Israel in the hope of ending the sanctions imposed by George W. Bush. Given Israel's positions, however, Syria soon claimed that there was no serious negotiating partner on the Israeli side. As for Syria's terms for a settlement with Israel, Asad hinted in a conversation with US journalist Seymour M. Hersh at the end of December 2009 that even a return of the Golan Heights would not lead to friendly relations if the Palestine problem remained unresolved. "If they [the Israelis] say you can have the entire Golan back, we will have a peace treaty. But they cannot expect me to give them the peace they expect" as long as other problems remained unsolved.[7]

Two theses existed among pundits with regard to Syria that seemed to contradict each other at first glance: (1) Bashar al-Asad needed the tug-of-war over the Golan Heights for his ideological legitimacy as the Arab voice against Israel and to divert domestic problems; and/or (2) the "liberation" of the Golan Heights would boost his legitimacy more than the existing limbo. In fact, Asad had to swallow several foreign policy defeats that raised doubts about his capability to represent adequately the interests of his country. A perceived just settlement over the Golan Heights could have improved his domestic and international standing if things had not changed so unexpectedly in 2011.

Turkey

Relations between Turkey and Syria changed radically after Asad's groundbreaking visit to Turkey in January 2004 and Turkish president Ahmet Necdet Sezer's visit in 2005. From being at the edge of war because of the Kurdish problem and water issues, both started to hold regular high-level

Feb. 5, 2010 (Mideast Wire); *NZZ-Online*, "Israels Aussenminister droht Asad mit Sturz," NZZ-Online, Feb. 4, 2010.

7. Conversation of Bashar al-Asad with Seymour M. Hersh, *New Yorker Online*, accessed Feb. 3, 2010, www.newyorker.com/online.

consultations. There was a free exchange of trade, and citizens of both countries were allowed to cross the common border without a visa. In particular for Syria, which has been a closed country for decades, this exchange meant a lot. In Syria, only Iranian travelers enjoyed the same privileges.

Almost unnoticeably, Syria recognized the normative power of realities by giving up its demands on the Antakya region that, from a Syrian perspective, forms part of Syria that the colonial French ceded to Turkey in 1939. Maps with a Turkish Antakya even appeared in Syrian government papers. Syria's advantages from a friendship with Turkey were greater than the potential rewards from national revisionism. Neither country signed anything official on their borders, but they agreed on keeping quiet on the Antakya issue.

Animosities from Ottoman times seemed forgotten as well. While both once faced each other with a high degree of suspicion, since the middle of the 2000–2010 decade each acknowledged a feeling and duty of "family bonds"—if one believes the words of leading politicians from both sides up to the beginning of 2011.

This family affair made certain details appear politically inopportune. One of them is the oddity, as a Syrian analyst mentioned, that some of Turkish Prime Minister Tayyip Erdogan's writings that allude to Turkish "imperialism" were forbidden in Syria. Another issue was that Turkish goods flooded the Syrian market and damaged weak Syrian industry and craftsmanship even more, aggravating the economic impact of other free trade agreements such as GAFTA, not to mention Chinese imports. But political gains for Syria outweighed any of those difficulties and contradictions.

Syria had changed, but so had Turkey. The moderate Islamist AKP (Justice and Development Party) government under Erdogan started the difficult task of de-ethnicizing the Turkish understanding of nation. Thus religion became more meaningful again as a connecting link within the Turkish population and between them and their Arab neighbors, without the intention of renouncing Turkey's close Western ties. The Turkish-Syrian cooperation suddenly appeared in the light of a fertile common past.

The Turkish foreign policy of "zero problems" with all its neighbors made Turkey a growing influential factor in the interface between Europe and the Middle East. Although the Turkish discourse—both in the street and in politics—approached the Arab one, including on the emotional level when it came to the occupation of the Palestinian territories, and although the relations with Israel cooled down considerably, Turkey for a long time still enjoyed enough confidence on both sides to play the broker between Syria and Israel.

The shuttle diplomacy that started in May 2008 was just about to enter direct Israeli-Syrian talks in Turkey when the Israeli delegation packed its suitcases with little explanation in December 2008. Shortly afterward, Israel started to bomb the Gaza Strip with the aim of stopping the launching of rockets against Israel from Hamas positions. Turkey interpreted this Israeli behavior as a profound breach of confidence. What followed were verbal attacks by Erdogan against Israel's President Shimon Peres at the World Economic Summit in Davos in January 2009. Swiftly, the Turkish head of government turned into the hero of Arab public opinion since he condemned the Israeli line of action in the Gaza Strip as no Arab head of state (except Syria's) had dared to do.

The shortsighted war in Iraq in 2003 led to results that, in many ways, were in the interest of neither the United States nor Israel, but rather endangered their security interests. One of many points in question was the Kurdish issue. A very practical community of interest emerged in the latter part of the 2000–2010 period between the Syrian regime, Turkey, and Iran because of the fragmentation of Iraq and Kurdish ambitions for autonomy in northern Iraq. All these states felt threatened by Kurdish nationalism.

Syria's good relationship with Turkey certainly represented the greatest success for Syria in the pre-uprising years. Damascus had aptly managed to diversify its foreign policy. In this respect, Syria's escape from isolation had a regional component too.

Iran

The relationship between Syria and Iran was shaped more by short-term political opportunism than by a far-reaching congruence of interests or by shared ideology. However, it was illusionary to try, as the West did, to push Syria to give up its cooperation with Iran. The country was Syria's staunch ally in time of urgent need after 2003 as the world (including most Arab governments) turned away from Damascus and the voices of regime change became stronger in Washington. The more Syrian politicians felt dictated to from Western capitals, the more defensive of their independence they became and the more they relied on Iran, especially when incentives to break with Iran were missing.

Having said this, Syria had diversified its foreign policy and eased its dependence on Iran through its friendship with Turkey. It always remained open how far Syria would have gone to defend Iran. Syria had shied away from a defense pact requiring aiding Iran in case Iran was attacked. But above all, it was in Iraq where dangers lurked for the bilateral relationship between Syria and Iran. Analysts in Damascus privately conceded that there was a potential breaking point in the Iranian-Syrian relationship that could become more visible in the coming years. Syria—as well as Turkey—was interested in keeping the Iraqi state intact whereas Tehran was gradually widening its influence in Iraq's Shi'ite south. If one day the Shi'ites were to demand autonomy or at least strive for an ideological union with Iran, the Kurds would certainly use the opportunity to leave the state structure. Such a scenario would have put a heavy strain on Syrian-Iranian relations. In addition, Iran's rising ambitions in Lebanon made Syria feel uncomfortable after decades of clear Syrian predominance there. Iran's influence could even jeopardize Syria's national interests if it provoked tensions in the region; indicative of this danger is that it took all Asad's art of persuasion to keep Ahmadinejad from visiting the border fence with Israel during his visit to southern Lebanon, where he wanted to throw stones at the Zionist enemy. Representatives of the old school of Syrian diplomacy rejected the term "alliance" with regard to Iran, which believed an overly close alignment with Iran would damage Syria in the long run. Iran was not even able to serve as an ideal partner when it came to keeping Syria's military halfway up to date. However, Hezbollah—apart from an anti-American stance—remained the strongest common interest between Syria and Iran. After 2011, Iran and Hezbollah ended up being a life insurance policy for the Asad regime.

Iraq

Syria's view of Iraq changed late in the 2000–2010 period. Initially the regime in Damascus was interested in encouraging unrest in the neighboring country to keep the Americans tied down and diverted from Damascus. It was opportune for Damascus to let militant Islamists travel to Iraq and be killed by the Americans. Asad made it clear that Syria could do more to secure the border with Iraq but would not do it for free. In the secret cables unveiled by Wikileaks, he said that he demanded an end to sanctions that banned the sale of commercial airplanes and their parts to Syria.[8]

Cooperation attempts with the United States under George W. Bush bore no fruit. But in late 2008, Syria's interest in preventing the fragmentation of Iraq started to prevail in its policy as a matter of self-protection. After twenty-four years of interruption, both countries took up diplomatic relations in 2006. They started to cooperate in the fields of trade and security, although not without periodic friction. Depending on the situation, Syria was able to exert constructive or destabilizing influence on Iraq's security. Therefore, the changed interest in favor of a stable Iraq as part of Syria's raison d'état was a positive sign for their relationship. Certainly, relations between the countries were much improved over what they had been under presidents Saddam Hussein and Hafiz al-Asad, who had competed for the ideological leadership of Pan-Arab Ba'thism in the Arab world.

Saudi Arabia

The geopolitical strengthening of Iran after the Iraq war brought the issue of Arab solidarity back on the table again. The Saudi-Syrian animosity (with Egypt under then-president Mubarak in the anti-Syrian camp) had long been a determining factor after the assassination of Lebanese prime minister Rafiq al-Hariri, who had strong economic links to Saudi Arabia

---

8. Meris Lutz, "Syria's Assad Seems to Suggest Backing for Hamas Negotiable, Leaked Cables Say," *Chicago Tribune*, Dec. 2, 2010.

and carried a Saudi passport. At times this animosity led to a paralysis of the already fragile Pan-Arab cooperation, as demonstrated during the wide boycott of the Arab League summit in Damascus in March 2008.

Beginning in 2008, relations improved. President Bashar al-Asad and King Abdullah bin Abd al-Aziz exchanged a series of letters, political delegations, and even personal visits. The détente in Lebanon between the pro-Syrian and pro-Saudi-Western camps was a consequence of more pragmatic relations between both countries. Riyadh and Damascus were still ideological and sociopolitical antipodes. But to Riyadh, in case of a war against Iran, being on better terms with Damascus was of strategic significance. Although developments in Lebanon, namely, the Hariri Tribunal, still endangered Syrian-Saudi reconciliation, the wave of pro-democracy protests in the Arab world initially created common ground between the Syrian and Saudi autocrats. Not surprisingly, in 2011, Syria declared the Saudi military intervention in Bahrain to suppress the protests there to be justified (separating itself in this regard from Iran).

The United States

Although Syria and Israel had entered negotiations with the mediation of Turkey during the more peaceful years of Asad's rule, all participants knew that an agreement between the archenemies could not be reached and or upheld without guarantees from the United States. Syria, in particular, was interested in walking the last mile with the United States because no one else could press Israel for compromises. The possibility of a tilt away from Bush's hard-line, pro-Israeli policy was raised by the new president, Barak Obama's, apparent early interest in an Arab-Israeli settlement. In his conversation with Seymour M. Hersh in 2010, Asad underlined that, with regard to the global balance of power, a strong United States is better for the world than a weak one.

Yet the United States under Obama was far from playing a dynamic role in the Middle East. Despite its changed tone toward the Muslim world, many Arabs were disappointed by the US administration. The expectations were high, and it appears that Obama gave his Cairo speech too early, long before he could start to put into practice his new intentions.

This situation owed less to a lack of consciousness with regard to the problems, as Obama knew that his two predecessors had been caught up in failed Middle East diplomacy in their last months in office. Apart from a general lack of appetite to engage in long-lasting international struggles, it was domestic hurdles within the United States that made impossible a new Middle East policy. The crisis of the economy and other domestic issues were Obama's priorities. As soon as he tried to raise stakes in the Middle East conflict, the political constellations at home would change even more to his disadvantage. Obama needed to resolve the most important domestic projects first before trying to find allies in political Washington to put pressure on Israel's leadership, to stop the building of settlements, or to enter into concrete negotiations with the Palestinians and Syria. Otherwise, he would endanger his entire political legacy. He would have to build alliances in Congress, too, which became even more difficult after the sweeping victory of conservative Republicans in the November 2010 midterm elections.

Nevertheless, before the uprising, important progress was visible in US-Syria relations: Syria declared itself ready again to take up an exchange of information with the CIA and the British MI6. At the same time, Asad made clear that cooperation could not be a one-way street as it used to be under George W. Bush. Otherwise, Syria would once again stop its cooperation.[9]

After a vacuum of six years, a US ambassador returned to Syria in January 2011. The US president was so convinced that Ambassador Robert Ford had to go to Damascus that he sidelined a Syria-skeptical Congress by making this decision. This was the last major foreign policy victory for the Syrian regime before the popular protests broke out barely two months later. Without any doubt, a US ambassador in place was an important investment in bilateral relations because the reestablishment of eye-level

9. Conversation between Bashar al-Asad and Seymour M. Hersh at the end of December 2009, quotes published online; see Hersh in *New Yorker Online*, accessed Feb. 3, 2010, www.newyorker.com/online, 2010.

politics represented a factor for Syrians that could not be underestimated. Obama's decision came just in time.

Domestic Repression in spite of International Success

In spite of the radical reduction in threat from Syria's external environment, the regime, far from responding with a corresponding internal political relaxation, took advantage of the situation to eliminate remaining domestic opposition. Thus a third wave of repression started with the arrest of senior human rights advocate Haytham al-Maleh, head of the Human Rights Association of Syria (HRAS), in October 2009 and continued with various travel bans and intimidations of intellectuals. This repression included many less renowned figures who were arrested in 2009 and 2010. In particular, secular-minded intellectuals had been threatened with travel bans as a first warning, often preceding arrests.

During that period—that is, well before the beginning of the uprising—Western embassies as well as development and cultural organizations reported increasing difficulties in getting access to government. Diplomats said that communication with Syrian authorities had become more difficult; travel restrictions increased; questions to the administration were ignored or answers dragged on for simple administrative matters as much as for highly sensitive issues such as human rights. According to various reports, it had become increasingly difficult to get access to prisoners of double nationality, and foreign observers in military tribunals (where political defendants are mostly judged) were banned in 2009. Their cooperation with analytical voices that had previously been approved by the government had become more difficult too. The Orient Centre for International Studies (OCIS), a think tank initiated by the foreign ministry and headed by Samir Altaqi, was closed in 2010. Apparently their analysts became too frank regarding critical issues, and their contacts with foreigners could be misinterpreted as track-two diplomacy. A disappointed observer suggested that the government was not interested in professional analysis any longer but restricted itself to discussions within its small closed circle.

The case of Anwar al-Bounni exemplified these domestic developments. Bounni was supposed to run an EU-supported academy of human
rights in Damascus. Although he was arrested partly because of this
endeavor, the mere fact of this project shows that the European Commission in Damascus held plausible the establishment of such a human rights
center in Damascus at that time. Such an endeavor would hardly be think-
able under conditions soon after. At the same time, several opposition figures expressed sadness that, in their impression, imprisoned activists had
been "abandoned" by the Europeans. "It will be hard to find anyone who
is ready to engage with the Europeans to build up a human rights center
again be it in Syria or in any other Arab country," as one of the al-Bounni
family lamented.[10] Given these facts, there was uneasiness that after years
of all too popular "Syria bashing," the pendulum in Western dealings with
the regime was swinging too much toward the side of routine political
business while turning a blind eye to persisting human rights violations.

Attempts at explanation of the regime's behavior proved difficult. A
leading secular intellectual of the Civil Society Movement pointed to the
"trauma of Lebanon," when more or less the whole world—Western and
Arab countries—were standing against Syria after the assassination of
Lebanon's Prime Minister Hariri in February 2005. This situation underlined the perception of persisting nervousness in the regime as the reason
for the overall tightening of redlines. It was also an indication of an ongoing pluralization of power centers in favor of the secret services. Redlines
became difficult to anticipate because they periodically shifted. Sometimes different ministries or different branches of the secret services drew
different limits. Contradictions even occurred within one and the same
institution or on different levels of hierarchy. "Bashar is not the regime," a
leading opposition figure said, and others agreed. The increased strength
that Asad had gained in foreign policy matters but also in domestic popularity and standing was not necessarily reflected in his overall influence in
domestic affairs and routine matters at that time. The regime was a complex web of direct or subtle influences, priorities, jealousies, and power

10. Interview with the author, Oct. 27, 2010, in Damascus.

struggles. There were indications that at times the president was incapable of enforcing his decisions or even fulfilling promises, because others were calling the shots. The opposition figure claimed that Asad was left to act freely in foreign policy only, whereas domestically the secret services, the Ba'th Party, his clan, and big business representatives were controlling events.[11] Incoherence affected all kinds of policy realms including the issue of political prisoners. Some imprisoned opposition figures were given indications of being released but other influences prevented it; or, on the positive side, judges sentenced political captives to fewer years than a branch of the secret service wanted.

Thus the hope that Syria would adopt domestic reforms if it did not continue to feel threatened from abroad did not materialize. In years prior to the foreign policy détente of 2008–10, the thesis was plausible that with Syria's isolation and existential threat against the regime, the political leadership was less ready for experiments and cracked down all the more on opposition movements. The reversal of this thesis did not come true. Despite a relaxation in international affairs and Syria's reemergence on the Arab and international stage, the suppression of political dissenters and human rights defenders actually increased after 2008. Correlations between domestic and foreign policies that were visible in the past were replaced by contradictions between the realms. Against this background, the regime's reflexes against the upheaval starting in 2011 were a logical reaction completely in line with its uncompromising philosophy and practice throughout the previous decade(s) to maintain power and suppress dissenters.

The Uprising: Back to International Threat and Domestic Repression

With the uprising, Syria's foreign relations underwent another revolution, corresponding with domestic repression and civil war. Improving relations with the United States were a first casualty of the conflict, as relations

11. Interview with the author on Oct. 23, 2010, in Damascus.

soured because of the brutal suppression of popular protests. Nevertheless, the United States turned against Asad only hesitantly while hoping for a political solution in Syria. Stability on Israel's northern flank was one part of the explanation for the US stance. In a TV interview on March 26, 2011, then–secretary of state Hillary Clinton still declined to condemn the repression in the harsh terms used in the Libyan case, much less to entertain talk of intervention. Clinton said, "There's a different leader in Syria now. Many of the members of Congress from both parties who have gone to Syria in recent months have said they believe he's a reformer." This tone was dramatically different from the rhetoric employed by ex-president Bush. Asad and the people surrounding him squandered this window of opportunity. With the death toll rising in Syrian streets, international condemnations and sanctions escalated.

In an unusual move, US Ambassador Ford supported the Hama demonstrations with his physical presence in mid-July 2011. This was a sign that the US administration no longer put much value on long-term working relations with the Syrian regime. The oppositional Local Coordination Committee in Hama helped to guarantee Ford's security. Who would have thought that one day a US representative would be more welcome and more secure in a Syrian city than a representative of the Syrian regime?

Shortly afterward, Clinton made clear that the United States had changed sides when she claimed that Asad had lost his legitimacy to rule. "President Assad is not indispensable, and we have absolutely nothing invested in him remaining in power," Clinton said in July 2011.[12] Within only three months Asad had lost yet another important opportunity to become part of the solution instead of remaining part of the problem in Syria and the troubled region.

Syrian-Saudi relations were yet another example of lost chances for Bashar al-Asad. What he had painstakingly constructed in the years

12. Nicole Gaouette and Massoud Derhally, "Assad Has 'Lost Legitimacy,' Clinton Says," *Bloomberg*, July 12, 2011, accessed July 22, 2014, www.bloomberg.com/news/2011-07-11/clinton-says-assad-lost-legitimacy-after-mob-attacks-embassy.html.

before 2011 collapsed within a few months. Asad's uncompromising stand against the uprising and against real reforms in 2011 weakened his position to the extent that old enemies seized the opportunity to engage in favor of the opposition. Saudi Arabia and Qatar emerged among the staunchest supporters of the Sunni Islamist branches of the armed opposition in the Syrian war. The regional interests of the Sunni autocracies added a flavor of Sunni-Shi'a divide to a conflict that originally started out as a confrontation between the Asad regime and great parts of its population, no matter what religion they were affiliated to.

The popular uprising in Syria put Turkey's pro-democracy stance to a test. Criticism of Asad from Ankara rose with the escalation of violence in Syria. It seemed that the rhetoric of "family bonds" between Turkey and Syria was rather meant to address the people of both countries and not necessarily their governments when one of them paid for stability with the blood of its own people.

Meanwhile, as the Syrian regime became isolated from both Western and Arab states, it became heavily dependent on Iran's financial and military support for survival, and Tehran did everything it could to prevent the fall of its only ally among the Arab states. Hezbollah also became an active player in support of the regime against the opposition. The fact that Syria was in the process of disintegrating strengthened the Hezbollah-Iran axis, representing almost an "alliance of losers" as a result of the Arab Spring in general and the Syrian war in particular. Their alliance would become even more significant in case of a Hezbollah-hostile and more Sunni-oriented new political regime in Syria. Therefore, after keeping a rather low profile, Hezbollah stepped up its risky engagement in the Syrian war on Syrian territory in favor of the Asad forces. Syria-Lebanon relations had turned upside down: now Syria became a battlefield of proxy wars for Lebanese actors and not vice versa.

Also, the good relations with Iraq's government that had started late in the 2000–2010 period, especially with Iraq's Prime Minister Nouri al-Maliki, paid off for Asad in difficult times. Arms, personnel, and logistical support flowed almost freely from Iran via Iraq's territory and air space into Syria to assist Asad's struggle against the rebels. Iraq did not take part in the condemnation of the Asad regime, neither in the Arab League nor internationally. On the other hand, the Islamist fighters that Asad had allowed to go to fight in Iraq after 2003 started to return, more radicalized and armed, to continue their jihad against the Asad regime itself.

Most problematic were the consequences of the Syrian uprising for Israel and Syria-Israel relations. Several times earlier in his political career, Netanyahu had hinted that he was open to a deal with Syria. But after the destabilization of Syria and the bankruptcy of the Asad dynasty, Israel's strategists faced tough questions: would there be anyone left with whom to sign bilateral agreements? And if so, would a peace with Syria—under whichever government—still be the key to the pacification of the region as it was considered to be in the past? After the demise of the Asad regime, who would replace the moderating and pragmatic force that Asad's Syria has played on Hezbollah, and even on Iran?

All this meant dim prospects for Israel's security scenarios at the hitherto calm northeastern front. The rhetoric of the regime in Damascus vis-à-vis Israel hardened. Damascus claimed from the beginning that the Syrian civil war had been "imposed on us" by Israel; if Israel had initiated a conspiracy against Syria, it would harvest a regional war with a scope it would not be able to control. The fear was that the more Asad was pushed to the wall, the more likely the regime would lash out to make its dire predictions come true. At the same time, the empowerment of jihadis in the Syrian civil war could pose a threat to Israel.

With the weakening or even collapse of the Syrian state, any political arrangement that included Israel's handing-over of the Golan Heights to Syria became more unlikely. No matter what kind of government would represent Syria in the future (if Syria still existed), the Golan Heights would likely remain an issue and a tool of domestic and foreign policies for both sides. Even in the unlikely event of a peace treaty, Israel and Syria would find enough arguments to keep the image of the external enemy alive in order to divert attention from domestic problems. From the Syrian point of view, Israel would remain an occupying power because of the unresolved conflict with the Palestinians. For Israel, on the other hand, Syria would likely remain an anti-Zionist mouthpiece.

Conclusion

The history of relationships between domestic and foreign policy in Syria suggests that the driving factor has always been domestic regime survival, and that foreign policy has been used to serve this end. On the other hand, foreign policy does affect domestic politics: when the regime felt threatened from without, it was intolerant of domestic dissent; yet when external pressures were relieved, it took this as an opportunity to eradicate the remnants of opposition, hence missing an opportunity for the kind of political reform that might have avoided the uprising against it.

12

Iraqi Migrants' Impact on a City

The Case of Damascus (2006–2011)

MOHAMED KAMEL DORAÏ
AND MARTINE ZEUTHEN

Blocks of flats under construction, pressure on the infrastructure, and crowded public spaces could be found all over Damascus in the first decade of the twenty-first century. However, during the last years of the decade specific areas underwent particularly intense developments. These were mainly linked to internal and international migration movements. Since the fall of Saddam Hussein's regime in 2003, the conflict in Iraq was ongoing, and hundreds of thousands of Iraqis were forced to leave their country and moved in great numbers to Syria. The vast majority of the Iraqis came from the main cities in Iraq, and especially from Baghdad, and they settled in the suburbs of the Syrian capital.

This chapter, based on an in-depth examination of change in areas with a high concentration of Iraqi refugees as well as the personal itineraries of Iraqi refugees, sets out to explore how everyday life in Damascus was changing in the 2000–2010 period. By looking into the public spaces and into how areas previously seen as small villages expanded and became an integrated part of the city, the chapter points to the important linkages between migration and urban development in contemporary Damascus.

When the Iraqi refugees started to arrive in Syria after the 2003 US invasion, neither Syria nor the United Nations High Commissioner for Refugees (UNHCR) had opened camps to accommodate the Iraqi refugees. Therefore they sought living quarters in the suburbs of Damascus and became one of the largest groups of urban refugees throughout the world. Damascus had a long experience of hosting refugees and forcibly displaced population such as the Palestinians, Syrians from the Golan Heights, and Lebanese. After 2006 Damascus became a safe haven for Iraqis who fled from violence and extremely difficult living conditions in Iraq. Most of them lived in Damascus but hoped for asylum elsewhere. In addition to these refugees, Damascus became a major destination for Shiʿi pilgrims mainly coming from Iraq and Iran. Tens of thousands of Iraqis lived in or transited through Syria in the decade after the Iraq war.

These different migrations, be they temporary or long-lasting, significantly transformed neighborhoods of the city. The Iraqis, here labeled as *urban refugees*, settled all over the city. However, some areas were more intensely inhabited by the arriving Iraqis, some areas becoming known as mainly Iraqi, such as Sayda Zaynab and Jaramana. These are the urban refugee areas that are the focus of this chapter. It strives to analyze the role of migrants in recent urban development of Damascus's underprivileged suburbs.

The data analyzed here were collected by the two researchers during fieldwork over a period of time from 2006 to 2009, and therefore information about the situation after that time is limited and gathered from phone calls with organizations still in Syria assisting the refugees and from other reports available. Both researchers carried out ethnographic data collection through participant observation of everyday life in various households, as well as through undertaking of structured and semi-structured interviews with a number of interlocutors of different genders, ages, religious backgrounds, and geographic origins. In this chapter these data are combined with accessible statistical data from organizations such as the UNHCR.

Iraqi Refugees and the Urbanization Process in Damascus

Developing countries, whether signatories of the Geneva Convention or not, tend to promote temporary reception policies toward refugees, keeping them in temporary statuses. Thus they are often considered as temporary guests who have to return to their country of origin once the causes of their departure have disappeared, whether it is insecurity, civil war, or persecutions (Fábos and Kibreab 2007; Kagan 2007). Syria developed such a policy regarding Iraqis by offering them a temporary status of guest based on touristic visa regulations. However, contrary to the policies implemented in numerous developing countries to accommodate refugees in specific areas such as camps, Syria opted—as did Jordan, Egypt, and Lebanon—to allow the free settlement of the Iraqis in the main cities of the country.

As a nonsignatory of the UN refugee conventions, Syria dealt with the refugees in its own way. The regime permitted UNHCR to work in the country as long as it followed a special cooperation agreement. Similar restrictions concerned the fourteen NGOs that were given permission to work in Syria to assist the Iraqi refugees. This unique situation led to a haphazard, even contradictory categorization of the refugees: they were accepted by the regime but not recognized as refugees; however, they registered with UNHCR as refugees and they could be enrolled in the refugee resettlement system. Their situation and the unique categorization system influenced the conditions and context for refugees' lives in Damascus, which was characterized by a feeling of temporality. Though the official way of dealing with the refugees implied temporality, the refugee presence, as we will argue in this chapter, seemed over time to become more permanent.

Refugees as Drivers of Urban Development

Migration is a key issue in most of the Middle Eastern countries affected by both a high rate of emigration and increasing immigration. Because of political instability, the region has experienced one of the highest refugee and internally displaced populations in the world, mainly constituted by Palestinians and Iraqis. These migrant populations are mostly living in diverse urban settings in Cairo, Amman, Beirut, or Damascus. The urban population in these cities increased from one quarter of the total population in the 1950s to more than 60 percent in 2005. Migrants—domestic and international, forced or not—are one of the main factors in this urban development (Al-Ali 2004; Fargues 2009; Tabutin and Schoumaker 2005).

Refugee movements are generally long-lasting, and the end of conflicts is not always followed by a wave of return of the entire refugee population. The more or less permanent settlement of refugee populations in neighboring countries generates deep changes of entire neighborhoods. Therefore it is here argued that refugees should not be considered only as recipients of humanitarian assistance, waiting for an eventual return or resettlement in a third country, but also as actors who contribute, through their initiatives and coping strategies, to the development of the cities that host them. As mentioned by Catherine Brun, "The here and now should also be present when analysing situations of forced migration. Though many refugees and migrants feel that they live, or want to live, their lives elsewhere, they have a present life, where they need to survive, to make their livelihood, and thus through their actions construct the place where they are physically present" (Brun 2001, 19).

Most of the southern suburbs of Beirut are examples of how areas change following migration: they were constituted by Palestinian refugees in 1948 and later by internally displaced Lebanese originating from south Lebanon (Clerc 2006). Two Palestinian refugee camps were surrounded by large neighborhoods where internally displaced Lebanese Shi'i from South Lebanon settled after the Israeli invasions in 1978 and 1982. Shi'i Lebanese, who had mostly been living in rural regions of Lebanon, became city dwellers. Cities like Amman also experienced deep urban changes with the arrival of 300,000 Palestinians expelled from Kuwait after the Iraqi invasion in 1990. The western part of Amman witnessed a massive and rapid change after the arrival of this new population who brought with them money to build houses but also the way of life they had in the Gulf countries. New restaurants, cafés, and shopping malls opened (Van Hear 2005).

The same tendency was to be found in Damascus, where some neighborhoods were profoundly transformed by the settlement of refugees. These contained both internal Syrian migrants and the influx of migrants from abroad, who settled in the suburbs of the city. Since 1948—putting aside waves prior to the country's independence—Damascus has been a place of settlement for different groups of refugees, mainly from the Arab world. The proportion of refugees and displaced persons compared to the total population of the Syrian capital was very high. It was mainly composed of Palestinians (more than 350,000 individuals in the Damascus area). However, the refugee population also contained several hundred Somalis, Afghans, Sudanese, and Yemenis (UNHCR 2009), and the large displaced population from the occupied Syrian Golan estimated at 300,000 individuals (IDMC 2007). Then hundreds of thousands of Iraqi refugees settled, escaping war, violence, and economic difficulties since the 1990s and on a larger scale since 2003 (Doraï 2009).[1] In the absence of refugee camps to accommodate them, more than two-thirds of the Iraqis registered at the UNHCR lived in the suburbs of Damascus. The proportion of refugee and displaced population was very high for a city of just over four million inhabitants.

The settlement of Iraqis in Damascus contributed to major change in the character of the city itself. As Barbara Drieskens and Franck Mermier describe the wider processes, "urban expansion . . . [not only has] an impact on the urban morphology and on relation between centre and periphery, but also redefine[s] social frontiers within the city. These are translated into spatial practices, introducing a multiplicity of implicit and permeable frontiers" (2007, 16).

Damascus and the Development of Iraqi Neighborhoods

In the southern suburb of Sayda Zaynab, the role of migrants and displaced persons is a key element in understanding urban development. According to the Syrian census of 2004, Sayda Zaynab had 136,000 inhabitants. In the 1950s, it was a small village built around the shrine of Sayda Zaynab. After the 1967 war, a Palestinian refugee camp was built and accommodated

1. The actual number of Iraqi refugees in Syria is a sensitive issue. There is the tendency of some international organizations and the Syrian authorities to overestimate the number of Iraqis. In the absence of a census, there is a debate on the actual number. Syrian authorities claim that around 1.2 to 1.5 million Iraqis are in Syria, whereas the UNHCR has registered around 200,000 since 2003. According to many observers, the actual number should be closer to those registered with the UNHCR (for more details on this debate, see International Crisis Group 2008; Leenders 2008).

20,000 Palestinian refugees. Close to the camp a large neighborhood developed where those internally displaced from the Golan Heights settled. A large covered market, where Syrian peasants from villages came to sell their products, separated both spaces. Later, the shrine was renovated, and thousands of Shi'i pilgrims, originating mainly from Iran but also from Pakistan, Lebanon, or Bahrain, came to visit the shrine and buy goods in the *suq* that developed around the mosque. A large part of the suburb came to be dedicated to the pilgrims, with hotels, guesthouses, *hawzat* (Shi'i schools), and a large bus station with connections abroad.

Since the 1970s Syria has hosted opponents of Saddam Hussein's regime, and Iraqi Shi'a also settled and developed the first Iraqi neighborhood. In 1992, after the first Gulf war, the situation changed and the majority of the Iraqis who arrived in Syria, mostly young men, had left Iraq because of the political and economic instability. Most of them worked as hired laborers or street sellers, but some developed small businesses. The poorest stayed in Syria until and after 2003, while the richest or those who connected to migratory networks managed to emigrate to Europe, North America, or Australia (Doraï 2009). Others, such as the political opponents of Saddam Hussein's regime, returned to Iraq after his fall. An Iraqi diaspora developed for several decades, constituted by various waves of migrants, of refugees, or of both (Al-Ali 2007; Chatelard 2005; Sassoon 2009).

The vast majority of Iraqis in Syria were of urban origin, Baghdad being the main origin of the exodus. The majority of Iraqis settled in Damascus because it was easier to find employment and because of the proximity of the international agencies and NGOs. The Iraqi presence in Damascus concentrated in neighborhoods such as Sayda Zaynab, Jaramana, Sahnaya, Massaken Barzeh, Yarmouk, and Qodsiyyeh, and in more remote localities where house rents were lower such as Sednaya or Tell, and to a lesser extent in other cities such as Aleppo, Lattakia, or Deir ez-Zor.

Many families were divided and lived in several countries of exile in the Middle East and beyond. The period spent in Damascus did not constitute a simple waiting time but played an important role in the elaboration of the migratory project. Most of the interviewed refugees planned to directly migrate to Western countries when they left Iraq, but few of them had the possibility of doing so. In Syria, they gathered information on different destination countries, tried to connect with other Iraqis abroad or with people smugglers, and collected money to pay for the trip. Not all the members of the same family would leave Iraq at the same time. The family reunification process often occurred in Damascus, activating the solidarity networks and facilitating settlement in the host country. Forms of solidarity developed in a transnational migratory field, which supported and accelerated the emigration process. Thomas Faist (2000) notes that the installation of earlier migrants is a central element that permits the development of migratory networks because they condense their social capital. Migration develops when social capital does not function only on a local scale but also as a *transnational transmission belt* (Faist 2000). Previous Iraqi migration contributed to determining the subsequent concentration of migration flows toward specific locations (for example, Sweden, Australia, United States). The latest newcomers to Syria benefited from accommodation with the rest of their family and faced fewer difficulties finding employment. They lived looking forward to another departure toward a third country; however, the actual number of resettlements undertaken by the UNHCR remains low.

For illustration, we will describe the situation of an Assyrian family living in Damascus. The family struggled with a very difficult economic and social situation. The husband was a photographer and shopkeeper but had to stop his activity because of the Iraq war. In 2005 he fled alone to Damascus where his wife's parents lived. His wife fled Iraq in 2006 with their two children. In Damascus the family shared their apartment with the husband's parents. Three of the wife's brothers were in Australia, where they claimed asylum after they left Iraq for Turkey and then Greece. Recently arrived in Australia, they were not yet able to send money to their family in Damascus. They were trying to cope with their own resettlement and furthermore they had to pay off the significant expenses generated by their emigration journey.

The family in Damascus had to pay a 10,000-Syrian-pound (US$200) rent each month. They managed to pay it thanks to the pension that the father-in-law of the husband—who resided in Syria—still received and which was regularly sent to them from Iraq. The part of the family that remained in Iraq also sent them basic food products, like rice, via the taxis that connected Iraq to Damascus. The geographical dispersion of the different family members as well as the precariousness of their legal and economic situations led to a dislocation of the family system of solidarity, but new survival strategies and solidarity networks developed around provision of daily needs.

From Exile to Temporary Settlement: Being Iraqi in Damascus

In the following part of the chapter we examine some Iraqi personal cases with the aim of describing their everyday struggle in the urban Damascene environment. This examination will illustrate how varied the lives of the Iraqis were but still describe what it meant to be Iraqi in Damascus. Through these cases we look into subjective experiences in order to avoid seeing "refugees" as a universalizing terminology (Malkki 1995, 497). We are enabled to understand what it means to be "a refugee" in an urban context, trying to make a living alongside other urban poor and displaced groupings. The examples expose specific problems in the lives of Iraqi refugees owing to the difficult living conditions, such as the lack of work permits, marginalization from the rest of the society, and lack of opportunities to influence their future; but the cases also illustrate the general struggle marginalized people living in an urban context are facing.

The Iraqis who settled in Damascus came from different backgrounds and their experience varied according to their financial situation and personal network. Some came to Syria with savings while others had sold everything they owned in Iraq to be able to leave their country. Causes of Iraqi migration were also diverse, ranging from refugees fleeing persecution, to individuals or families leaving Iraq because of the general insecurity, to shopkeepers or entrepreneurs fleeing economic difficulties. This diversity gave the Iraqi community an opportunity to recompose in exile and to adapt to their host society. Nonetheless, forced exile generated a general degradation of the standard of living of Iraqi refugees as well as tensions with Syrians because of the large Iraqi presence in certain districts. The largest wave of Iraqis arrived in Syria in 2006 and 2007, and the cases we investigate both belong to this group. Many of those who arrived during that period were middle-class, well-educated Iraqis, who left Iraq for a mix of reasons but mainly owing to insecurity from the increased violence in the country. The following stories will show the extent to which the refugees over time got better at coping in their new environment and found ways of starting a new life in their new surroundings.

Lack of Opportunities and Social Prejudices Reinforce Temporality

The first story we want to unfold is about a young girl, called Sara.[2] Initially, when we were introduced, she explained that she felt a strong apathy because of the prolonged waiting time for a reply from the UNHCR about resettlement as well as waiting for other opportunities to move on toward a final destination. The feeling of not being able to change her situation made Sara feel apathetic; she slept a lot, did not make any friends, and was very unhappy. Sara often explained that she felt that her life was put on "pause." The way Sara as well as many other Iraqis engaged with the host community and Damascus in general was influenced by their feeling of not wanting to settle, because they were hoping to move on quickly. They therefore made few friends and did not make any effort, almost the contrary, to become a part of the local community and engage with the society around them.

During one of many interviews Sara explained how her family had settled in Damascus and the challenges they had faced. It was very important for her to explain why they had fled Iraq and to share with me the kind of life they had lived there. They had lived with her cousin's family and one day her cousin was killed by a Shi'i militia; because the family is Sunni they came to fear for their lives. Not long after, her father started receiving threatening letters because he worked for an international company. Because of the letters and the killing of the cousin, the family felt increasingly insecure and finally decided to leave.

2. All names of people described in this article are changed to avoid putting them in danger.

Sara arrived in Syria in 2006 and lived with her mother, father, and brother. She was twenty-six years old when we first met about a year and a half after she had arrived in Damascus. Because of Syrian laws she was not allowed to work or to finish her university degree; in Iraq she had been studying for a bachelor's degree in English literature at Baghdad University. Sara loved languages and was therefore trying to learn French. She explained that her plan to learn French was really "just to do something," but generally when we first met she was spending most of her time at home. In Iraq she used to go out a lot and had many friends, but in Syria she did not feel like it, could not afford it, and did not have any friends to meet. Because Sara did not plan to stay in Syria and because she officially was not allowed to study or work and therefore could not do the things she used to do, she felt depressed and upset. She often explained that she was struggling to find hope for the future.

During this period Sara lived with her family in a Sunni-dominated suburb of Damascus: Sahnaya. They lived in a small basement flat because it was the cheapest. They were trying to make the money last as long as possible as they felt insecure about their future. Sahnaya had recently been inhabited by many Iraqi refugees. Most of them had lived awhile in Sayda Zaynab, but since Sayda Zaynab was mainly inhabited by Shi'i Muslims and pilgrims, other religious groupings tended to move out when they found other affordable places to stay.

Sahnaya used to be inhabited by Christian Syrians. It was built around a main street with a small shopping area, a couple of restaurants, medical clinics, and some churches. The surroundings of the center around the main street changed fast and new buildings rose everywhere. Most of the new blocks were half empty and half inhabited—being built and inhabited simultaneously—the system was to complete a full floor and as soon as it was finished one family could move in. From the rent and other income the owner of the building finished the flats one by one so that as soon a flat was finished, a new family could move in and start paying for the next. The area is not particularly attractive since it is located on the outskirts of Damascus on the road to Jordan. The area had a problem with water supply, and the poor quality of the buildings, inadequate heating, and high costs of petroleum made the living costs high especially during winter.

All members of Sara's family were registered with the UNHCR and hoped and waited for resettlement, and by the time I met them they had already waited for years.[3] The time spent waiting was hard for everyone in the family. The health of Sara's mother worsened, her father was increasingly frustrated, and her brother got more and more introverted, sitting in front of his computer constantly chatting with friends back in Iraq. As I got to know Sara better, she told me a lot about how she felt about her life in Damascus. She explained how hard she felt it was for her to be accepted and how hard it was for her to forget for a moment that she was Iraqi and an outsider. She explained how Syrians could always tell by her accent that she was from Iraq, and that this determined her relationship with her surroundings. Sara explained that she felt that Syrians did not like Iraqis because they believed that the Iraqi presence led to increased prices on housing, food, and other commodities. The feeling of not being welcome also influenced her self-esteem and engagement with her surroundings. Sara's story points out the apathy caused by lack of opportunities and how a feeling of temporality affected the way Iraqis like Sara were (not) engaging with the society, and explains the way of life in the urban areas of Damascus where Iraqis settled.

The "Little Baghdads" of Damascus

Despite the limited engagement of some Iraqis, in other areas and suburbs Iraqis developed different ways of engaging and making a living by various kinds of economic activities, ranging from street selling to small clothing manufactures or small grocery shops. These modes of settlement were both connected to the personal itineraries of Iraqi entrepreneurs and the specific urban context in some Damascene neighborhoods. These areas facilitated the development of a wide range of coping strategies for these Iraqi businessmen. In the following we will describe two unique Iraqi areas of Damascus.

---

3. As of the time of writing, they were still waiting.

In Sayda Zaynab, west of Hajjira roundabout, extends the area where a large number of Iraqis resided. The main street was called "Iraqi Street," and many Iraqi-owned businesses developed there. Several travel agencies opened—also very present in Jaramana—selling taxi or bus tickets to the main Iraqi cities. Iraqi taxi drivers offered their services to these agencies and carried passengers, bags, and cartons of goods to Iraq. However, the areas were constantly changing according to circumstances; for example, when after October 2007 Iraqis needed a visa prior to entry into Syria, there was a sharp decrease in traffic.

Numerous small shops were located both in Jaramana and in Sayda Zaynab: popular restaurants offering traditional Iraqi dishes, Iraqi bakeries, and small grocery stores that imported Iraqi food previously not available in Syria. Street vendors offered Iraqi pastries for takeaway, carp for the preparation of the *Masgouf* (grilled carp), or Iraqi tea. Bigger shops were also developed; for example, the pastry shop Al Baghdadi in Sayda Zaynab produced many types of Iraqi pastry, which were sold in other Iraqi neighborhoods in Damascus. In the narrower streets of the two neighborhoods many small shops developed that offered traditional Iraqi clothing such as scarfs and hats, as well as flags marked with the colors of Iraq and the jerseys of the Iraqi football team, which won the Asian Cup of Nations in 2007.

Some parts of the Damascene suburbs deeply changed after the arrival of Iraqi refugees. Iraqi businesses and restaurants as well as travel agencies developed rapidly and locally modified the townscape. Iraqis developed their own activities in the different suburbs of Damascus, ranging from street selling, to small clothing manufactures or small groceries. These economic activities were connected both to entrepreneurs' and workers' personal itineraries and to the rather flexible urban context in which they were situated, which facilitated the adaptation of the newcomers.

Influencing the Atmosphere

Jaramana, known to be the main Druze quarter in Damascus, used to be a quiet suburb with green fields and animals grazing on the outskirts. Later, concrete blocks rose everywhere, many inhabited by newly arrived Iraqis. Also many Christians as well as other groups had settled in the area since the 1970s because of lower rents and liberal atmosphere. In the streets of Jaramana, women's dress was less conservative and there were nightclubs and prostitutes in the streets.

The next case focuses on an entirely different type of refugee from Sara and her family, that of a young man who was not waiting to be resettled via UNHCR but who was one among a large group of mostly young men who saved money in order to be able to pay for the illegal trip to Europe. The men struggled for the dream of creating a better future for themselves and their families, and they felt high pressure to make it to Europe and send back remittances at some point in time. This group of young men had minimal contact with the official refugee apparatus; they were not registered with UNHCR; and they made a living from varying degrees of semilegal enterprises.

This specific group lived in shared apartments with other young men in order to save money. During interviews the men would explain that they had chosen to live in Jaramana because of the more liberal atmosphere where they attracted less attention from the authorities and where the community did not bother too much about their activities. They lived on their own without their families and behaved as they wanted. The men argued that Jaramana was a good place to live because it was easy to find cheap food and there were many places of entertainment. One of the men, Mohammed, twenty-eight years old and from Baghdad, lived with three friends who knew each other from Iraq. They had always made plans to leave Syria, but during the time we conducted interviews with them, they were not successful in carrying out their plans.

Mohammed made a living together with his friends on a very day-to-day basis and spent most days sleeping or waiting in the streets for something to happen. They often went to the streets to look at girls or chat with friends. Mohammed liked Jaramana because the atmosphere was more liberal and the streets were always busy. He explained that he felt less noticed and that he would have found it difficult to live in this way in a more conservative setting like Sayda Zaynab.

The neighboring Syrian families described the Iraqi presence in Jara-mana in a different way. They explained that the Iraqis had influenced the area in a bad way, and mentioned that young Iraqi men had caused increased demand for prostitution and increased consumption of alcohol. The freedom that the young men enjoyed increased Syrians' dissatisfaction with the massive Iraqi presence in some areas. Combined with price inflation and a Syrian infrastructure struggling to keep up with urban expansion, the Iraqi presence caused discontent in the Syrian host populations and, as a result, some Syrians moved from the area.

An Evolving Permanence

The Iraqi settlement in Damascus appeared to become permanent as time passed. This evolving permanence varied from one area to another as did engagement with the host community. In some areas the tension between the populations increased but in others the situation stabilized. Damascus was adapting to the refugees while the image of the city was changing. Because of the increased permanence of the "temporary" settlement, new challenges were being faced both on a personal level and in the different areas. At a personal level the Iraqis who had not yet been offered asylum in a third country started to look at other ways to achieve the future they were hoping for, for example by marriages and family reunions, by illegal migration, or simply by settling more permanently in Syria.

To return to Sara's personal situation, it was hard for her to hold on to her hope of receiving a resettlement permit. In the last interview in early 2010, she emphasized that she was starting to doubt whether resettlement would be good for her in the end. She explained that it had been hard to start a life in Syria, owing to the stress of not being accepted and not being able to live the life that she wanted. In Iraq she had been a young attractive woman, just about to finish her bachelor's degree and about to start her career and perhaps find a husband. Now she felt that because of the restrictions on her life, the "pause" was becoming permanent. She underlined in our conversations that it would be difficult to start all over again in a third country, and therefore she was not sure about wanting to be resettled if she had the chance. Her view of Syria had changed, and she had started to try to establish herself more. The last time we met she explained that almost a year earlier she had started to work and was looking for a husband. She explained that she had started to understand that her life in Syria might not come to an end soon, and she might as well get the best from the situation that she could.

Conclusions and Future Challenges

The Iraqi refugees in Damascus demonstrate the importance of forced migration in an unstable Middle East for the development of the region's cities. The Iraqis' presence in Damascus had, as described, led to changes of the city, more visible in some areas than others. Many of the refugees we studied prior to the uprising expressed their beliefs that they were getting increasingly established and used to living in Syria as time passed and that they were giving up hope of resettlement. As a result, the question of their legal situation would have to be addressed to enable them to access the job market and to give them clear residency rights. In September 2011 more than 122,000 Iraqis were registered in Syria, with more than 1,200 new registrations since January 2011 (UNHCR 2011).

Because of the recent and massive arrival of Iraqis belonging to different social classes and religious or ethnic groups, it was very difficult to assess how long their exile would last. Refugees with temporary statuses can stay for very long periods in their host states, as is the case for some Iraqis in Jordan, or for the Sudanese in Lebanon. Yet well-established refugees, like Palestinians in Kuwait or to a lesser extent in Libya, can be expelled en masse during regional political crises. Migrants in the Middle East are often subject to rapid changes in their situation, and strong local integration (through economic participation, for example) does not always mean integration in the long term. In fact, economic participation can lead to empowerment of the refugees who are thus able to emigrate. Emigration or resettlement strongly depends on access to resources. Most of the Iraqi migrants belong to groups with high connections with the diaspora and the host society.

Comparing the settlement of Iraqis at the regional level, the situation in Damascus is unique. While the presence of migrants and refugees is visible in the public space in some neighborhoods in Beirut, Iraqi migration remains more or less invisible there. In Amman, where hundreds of thousands of Iraqis have settled or transited since 1991, only a few public spaces can be labeled as Iraqi. In Damascus, the mass arrival of Iraqis deeply transformed the periphery of the Syrian capital. The flexible migration policy as well as the tolerance of informal economic activity contributed to this phenomenon. The nature of the migration movement combining asylum, economic migration, and pilgrimage was also important. Finally, the urban dynamic, where internal and international migrations played a leading role, was also a key element in understanding the mode of settlement of Iraqis. They were only the last wave of arrivals in spaces strongly structured by migrations and mobility.

The Syrian uprising may reverse the trend toward permanent Iraqi resettlement in Syria. If the number of Iraqis registered with the UNHCR decreased after the uprising, this was not a new phenomenon and did not, according to UNHCR statistics, initially seem to accelerate. However, opportunities declined and the security situation became more difficult. The development of security checkpoints limited the possibilities for Iraqis to move in the city. Because of economic decline and restrictions on movement, some Iraqis started running out of money, potentially forcing them to migrate again, either back to Iraq, to elsewhere in the Levant, or illegally into Europe. Assistance decreased dramatically and they faced very hard difficulties to survive. On the other hand, UNHCR resettlement procedures in Syria slowed, and refugees who could not go back to Iraq (for security, personal, or economic reasons) were trapped in Syria. Some refugee families who could not leave concentrated in what seemed to be the safest neighborhoods, such as Jaramana. Iraqi refugees seemed caught between the accelerating violence in both their host country and their home state.

13

Hamas's Rhetoric and Mobilization Practices in Palestinian Refugee Camps in Syria

VALENTINA NAPOLITANO

According to Julie Peteet (2005, 25), refugee camps are situated "at the intersection of local, regional, national, and global zones and processes." Because of their status as places supposed to temporarily welcome refugees, camps preserve a link with their land of origin. At the same time they are politically and socially sensitive to the changes within the host country and the surrounding area on which their destiny depends. Multiple local and regional dynamics have to be addressed to understand the political life in refugee camps.

In light of this situation, this chapter aims to understand the major developments that have characterized Palestinian refugee camps in Syria during the decade 2000–2010,[1] encompassing the local, national, and regional levels. It will focus on one phenomenon in particular: the political and social emergence of Hamas since 2000. This movement has been a key political actor in refugee camp life during the years until the outbreak of the Syrian uprising in March 2011.

Hamas's role in Palestinian camps in Syria should be understood from two different perspectives: first, a macro-sociological perspective

---

1. This chapter was first completed in June 2011. Since then many important events have taken place in the Palestinian refugee camps, which will be briefly summarized at the end.

will allow us to understand the regional situation that favored Hamas's rise in Syria and the relationship between the two. Second, a micro-sociological point of view will clarify how Hamas, a movement originally born "inside" Palestine,[2] was received by the Palestinian refugees in Syria, how it adjusted to refugees' attitudes, and what collective action it provoked within the camps. This combination of macro- and micro-analysis will allow us to understand the multiple levels of interaction between the camps and Palestine, Syria, and the surrounding region.

This chapter is based on data obtained from fieldwork I carried out between September 2008 and May 2011,[3] in the Yarmouk refugee camp,[4] which was selected because of its urban, social, and political characteristics. Yarmouk, established between 1954 and 1957 in the south of Damascus, was home to the largest Palestinian community in Syria, with 148,500 inhabitants,[5] and was one of the most populated suburbs of the city. After

2. Hamas was created in 1987 in the Gaza Strip.

3.3 As part of the fieldwork in Yarmouk, I conducted many semistructured interviews with various members of the camp's political and social microcosm. I met representatives and sympathizers of Hamas, Fatah, leftist organizations (the Popular Front for the Liberation of Palestine, the Democratic Front for Liberation of Palestine), and other political factions present in the camp (PFLP-GC, Fatah al-Intifada). I met independent intellectuals, journalists, and social activists. I also participated in more informal conversations between inhabitants of the camp, especially among its youth. During these interviews, which were conducted in Arabic, I tried to understand the most important factors that affected refugees' attitudes and their perspectives of the national cause. During the fieldwork I also observed everyday life in the camp and took part in the events organized by political and social actors based in the camp. This type of activity played a significant role in understanding the messages broadcast by the Palestinian factions and social organizations and the type of people who were taking part.

4. Yarmouk is defined by the UNRWA (United Nations Relief and Works Agency) as an unofficial camp because it was established later than the other camps and at the initiative of the host country.

5. Statistics published by the UNRWA in 2010. This number only refers to Palestinians who arrived in Syria in 1948 and their descendants, but it does not take into account the other waves of immigration following the war of 1967, the "Black September" in 1970, the Israeli invasion of Southern Lebanon in 1982, and the expulsion of the PLO (Palestine Liberation Organization) from the country in 1983.

Damascus's urban expansion, the camp was integrated into the boundaries of the capital. Since the beginning of the "Palestinian revolution"[6] in 1965, Yarmouk became a center of Palestinian activism in Syria, where political groups established their social and political structures.[7]

Owing to its proximity to the Syrian capital and its high number of inhabitants, Yarmouk was selected by Hamas as the principal base for its grassroots movement in Syria. It is here that Hamas built its mobilization structure, composed of numerous social organizations, and it is here that all of Hamas's political and social activities, such as rallies, festivals, and training courses, took place and attracted extensive media coverage.

The remainder of this chapter is divided into four sections. First, it focuses on the relationship between Hamas and Syria; second, on the influence wielded by Palestine and the surrounding area on Yarmouk's refugees favoring Hamas's rise in popularity; third, it looks at the local mobilization strategy adopted by Hamas in the Yarmouk camp; and finally, it discusses Hamas's ability to fulfill refugee expectations and the future of the movement in the camp in light of the subsequent developments affecting the situation in Palestine and Syria.

Hamas and Syria: Reciprocal Regional Interests

Other studies dealing with Hamas focus on the role that this movement acquired in the occupied territories and, more specifically, in the Gaza Strip, where the movement was founded in 1987 and enjoys its largest support (Chehab 2007; Gunning 2007; Hroub 2010; Milton-Edwards and Farrell 2010). But Hamas's activity is not limited to the Occupied Territories. After its formation, the movement developed a network of offices in the countries bordering historical Palestine, first in Jordan and Syria in 1993, then in Lebanon in 2000. These offices became the external wing of the movement, in charge of developing its foreign relations and

6. This term refers to the emergence during the 1960s of Palestinian political factions independent of Arab countries' politics. The principal actor in this process was Fatah.

7. About this subject see Mawed 2006.

collecting funding.[8] Hamas's decision to establish a base outside of Palestine was strategic. The movement needed to escape from isolation and the repressive measures imposed by the Israeli army in the Gaza strip and the West Bank.

Hamas was established in Syria in 1993 when the movement opened a political office under the umbrella of the "Alliance of Ten Palestinian Factions." This alliance, which for the first time brought together Palestinian nationalist, leftist, and Islamist movements in opposition to the Oslo accords,[9] was supported by the Syrian regime in the attempt to foster a substitute for the PLO, which had signed up to the Oslo Accord that Syria opposed.[10] Hamas's headquarters in Damascus acquired a central role in its regional strategy after the expulsion of its leaders from Amman in 1999. Damascus's role was also accentuated by the death of the two most important Hamas internal leaders, Ahmad Yassin and Abdel Aziz al-Rantisi, in 2004, and the consequent emergence of an external leadership.

The alliance of the Syrian authorities with Hamas consolidated in 2000 in a specific regional context. Soon after Bashar al-Asad assumed the presidency, he was in need of legitimacy on both the internal and the regional scene. The alliance with Hamas, Iran, and Hezbollah in the frame of the "Axis of Resistance" represented, on the one hand, an opportunity to keep alive the regional conflict with Israel and hence preserve Syria's leverage in future peace process negotiations.[11] On the other hand, it allowed the regime to renew its influence on the Palestinian scene, from which it had been marginalized as a consequence of Palestinian actors' transfer into

8. Hamas was principally financed by the Gulf countries, Iran, Turkey, Syria, and the Palestinian diaspora. After its break with Syria following the Syrian uprising, it lost Iranian and Syrian funding.

9. This alliance included the Popular Front for the Liberation of Palestine (PFLP), the Democratic Front for the Liberation of Palestine (DFLP), the Popular Front for the Liberation of Palestine-General Command (PFLP-GC), the Palestinian Popular Struggle Front (PPSF), the Palestine Liberation Front (PLF), Fatah al-Intifada, the Palestinian Revolutionary Communist Party (PRCP), and the Saïqa, Hamas, and Islamic Jihad.

10. About this subject see Strindberg 2000.

11. About this subject see Hemmer 2003.

13.1. Bashar al-Asad's picture at one of the entries of the Yarmouk camp. Photograph by V. Napolitano.

the West Bank and Gaza Strip,[12] in 1993. The "Axis of Resistance" allowed Bashar al-Asad to gain a regional role and reaffirm his father's nationalist credentials, according to which Syria was the only Arab country to defend the Palestinian cause and support the resistance against Israel.[13]

Syria's alliance with Hamas allowed the regime to benefit not only regionally but also locally. On the one hand, it enabled the regime to

12. Since the signature of the Oslo Accords in 1993, the majority of Palestinian nationalist actors transferred their political bases as well as military and civil infrastructures into the Palestinian territories.

13. See also Aurora Sottimano's chapter 4 in this volume.

channel, at least for a while, the Islamist opposition and a public opinion sympathetic with the Palestinian cause, against Israel, weakening their potential opposition to the regime. Before massive internal opposition broke out in March 2011, the support accorded by the regime to the Palestinian "resistance" organizations was considered one of the factors that would spare Bashar al-Asad's regime from the protest movements that were spreading throughout the Arab world.

To justify the support accorded to an Islamist movement descended from the Muslim Brotherhood, the main historic opposition to the Ba'th, the Syrian regime adopted a discourse stressing the principle of the common "resistance" against Israel and neglecting the religious dimension of Hamas's ideology. This justification explains why Hamas's mobilization strategy in Syria limited its religious fervor so as not to offend regime sensitivities and tried not to be seen as associated with the Muslim Brotherhood. On the contrary, Hamas's leaders were involved in official Islamic activities sponsored by the regime. Khaled Meshaal, former head of the Political Bureau, used to attend the Friday prayers in mosques of central Damascus.

Owing to Syria's support, Hamas began to manage its foreign relations from its base in Damascus, where it attracted media coverage on its views and activities. Hamas's leaders were free to travel to and from the country, and Syria became a conduit to transfer funding to the movement in the occupied territories. Syrian support was also central to increasing Hamas's popularity in the refugee camps. Compared to other political groups, Hamas enjoyed significant liberty as well as significant financial support that allowed it to create several social organizations in Palestinian refugee camps and to organize their political mobilization.

Hamas's Rise in Popularity in the Yarmouk Camp and Regional Changes

The rise in Hamas's popularity on the grassroots level of the Yarmouk refugee camp must be understood in light of developments that took place in the 2000–2010 period in both the occupied territories and the host region. The outbreak of the second *intifada*[14] in the West Bank and Gaza in 2000 was a key moment for Hamas's consolidation in the camp. The intifada was characterized in Yarmouk by its solidarity with the territories. Demonstrations and debates as well as aid collection were organized mainly by young people who had not experienced the national mobilization of their parents' generation. These young people saw the intifada as their first opportunity to get involved in the national cause. During this period many youth associations and committees defending the right of return were created.[15] This mobilization proved that refugees were willing to take action in support of the national cause and to propose new forms of mobilization, independent of the traditional political movements, such as Fatah, PFLP,[16] and DFLP,[17] with which young people did not identify. In this respect the example of Hazem, a thirty-year-old Palestinian who, during the intifada, participated in the creation of the Jafra Youth Centre, is significant. "The idea of the center was born after the second intifada," Hazem explained. "At that time there were several young people who wanted to get involved in political and cultural activities. After Oslo, all political organizations abandoned the [camp] youth to focus on the internal [West Bank/Gaza] political situation; therefore, they did not have

14. The word *intifada* was used to describe the Palestinian uprising in December 1987 in Gaza and the West Bank. "Second intifada" therefore refers to the uprising in September 2000 triggered by the visit of Ariel Sharon to the Temple Mount in Jerusalem.

15. The right of return is the claim of Palestinian refugees to return to their land of origin. From a legal standpoint, it is based on resolution 194 of the UN General Assembly passed in 1948, which states, "Refugees wishing to return to their homes and live at peace with their neighbours should be permitted at the earliest practicable date, and that compensation should be paid for the property of those choosing not to return and for loss of or damage to property which, under principles of international law or in equity, should be made good by the governments or authorities responsible."

16. The Popular Front for the Liberation of Palestine (PFLP) was established in 1967 by George Habash following the collapse of the Arab Nationalist Movement.

17. In 1969, Nayef Hawatmeh split from the PFLP and established the Democratic Front for the Liberation of Palestine.

confidence in these political organizations."[18] The second intifada in Yarmouk was a time of mobilization for the national cause and constituted an opposition to the old Palestinian leadership accused of having signed the Oslo accords "behind the backs of refugees who played a central role in the creation of the national movement during the Palestinian revolution."[19] Refugees feared the Arafat-led PLO was prepared, after Oslo, to abandon their right of return in order to get a state on the West Bank/Gaza.[20]

For this reason Hamas was seen as an alternative political force capable of fulfilling refugees' hopes for change. Hamas's rise in popularity in Yarmouk was based on its engagement in the armed struggle against Israel, which intensified during the first years of the second intifada. Hamas was perceived as the only organization able to reintroduce armed struggle as a principle tool of liberation, a method established and employed by Palestinian nationalism since its formation in the 1960s. Hamas's resistance strategy mobilized the refugees who felt betrayed by the PLO, which had marginalized them since the Oslo accords.[21]

Hamas's resistance strategy and stance were consolidated in the camp by further changes in the region after 2000. First of all, the Israeli army withdrew from South Lebanon in 2000, which was celebrated by Hezbollah as the only Arab victory against the Israeli army and occupation of Arab land. In this context the war of 2006 was perceived as a second demonstration of Hezbollah's power. This war was followed by an exchange of prisoners between Israel and Lebanon. During this exchange the remains of seventy-four Palestinians from Yarmouk were brought back to the camp. The event was accompanied by a sizeable commemorative ceremony and a huge parade in the camp, at which Palestinian and Hezbollah

18. Interview held with Hazem, member of the Jafra Youth Centre, in October 2010. "Internal" political situation here refers to that in the West Bank and Gaza.

19. Interview held with Abou Basel, leader of the Palestine Liberation Front (PLF), in October 2010.

20. About this subject see al-Husseini and Signoles 2009.

21. The Oslo accords postponed the discussion of the refugee problem to the last phase of peace talks.

flags were waved. Thus Hezbollah victories contributed to the consolidation of Hamas's strategy.

Another regional event that played in Hamas's favor was the American attack on Iraq in 2003. This war influenced refugees' attitudes because "it represented the fall of a country which, like Syria, was close to the Palestinian issue and was among those countries that opposed Israel and the United States."[22] The war on Iraq provoked mobilization among Yarmouk's population. Many refugees, along with other Syrians and Arabs, went to Iraq to participate in the resistance against the American forces. On Iraqi soil they were coordinated by the Islamist groups there. Even if there was no connection between Hamas and the Islamist movements in Iraq, this mobilization showed the readiness of refugees to participate in the armed struggle against two common enemies: the United States and Israel. "When the war on Iraq broke out, as a Palestinian I felt involved because I am the 'son of a cause,' and I know what it means to live with the occupation of a foreign power," said Abed, an independent activist for the defense of the right of return.[23]

Therefore, the image of resistance was the first element of Hamas's politics that attracted refugee support. But it was through their social strategy and the cultivation of grassroots activities that the movement built its network of partisans in the Yarmouk camp.

Social Activities as an Instrument
of Recruitment and Socialization

The importance Hamas attached to its social strategy has been highlighted by many studies dealing with the movement. For instance, Khaled Hroub stated that "grassroots work has always been Hamas's strongest aspect. Its unstoppable rise over the past 20 years and eventual triumph over other Palestinian factions is largely attributed to its success in social work" (Hroub 2010, 68). The attention paid to social activities was an idea

22. Interview held with Hazem, member of the Jafra Youth Centre, in October 2010.
23. Interview held in March 2011.

inherited from the Muslim Brotherhood strategy through which their political project aimed first to Islamize society as a fundamental step toward the establishment of an Islamic state.

Compared with the other Palestinian factions present in Syria, Hamas's engagement in social activities was widespread because of its significant funding resources and the relative freedom it was granted by the Syrian authorities. Starting in 2004, Hamas created a dense social infrastructure in Yarmouk: a sports club, a charity organization, a women's association, an organization promoting the right of return, and a student organization. Hamas's investment in social activities was received very positively by refugees because of the vacuum left by the decline of the other Palestinian factions (Fatah and the leftist organizations), which had previously been the providers of social services in the camps together with humanitarian relief. Fatah was in fact banned from Syria in 1983,[24] and, for those Fatah partisans who had continued to be active unofficially, the movement's attentions turned toward the occupied territories, neglecting the Palestinian diaspora. The leftist organizations such as the PFLP and the DFLP, which during the 1960s and 1970s played an important role in social interaction in Yarmouk, were severely affected by the fall of the Soviet Union and the decline of the Palestinian national project, reducing their activities in the camp.

If Hamas's expansion beyond Palestine was linked to regional political requirements, how can we explain the movement's investment in the social aspect of refugee camps? Hamas's provision of social activities to camps in Syria was justified by the movement as normal assistance provided to Palestinians in the diaspora, who are considered an integral part of Palestinian society (and in fact their special constituency).[25] But it is certainly the case that Hamas's social activities in refugee camps had political objectives as well as charitable ones. The social goals pursued by Hamas in the diaspora were different from those in the occupied territories because of the

24. Fatah in 1983 split into two organizations: the Fatah of Yasser Arafat, which was banned from Syria, and the Fatah al-Intifada, which was supported by Syria and welcomed on its territory.

25. Interview held with Mousa Abou Marzouk, deputy chief of Hamas's Political Bureau, in November 2010.

specific political context and the opportunities that presented themselves. In the territories Hamas's social strategy had the following main objectives: to introduce people to the political and social mindset of the movement, to sign up new recruits for its political and military branches, and to gain popular support that would in turn earn more votes in elections. Social activities organized by Hamas in the refugee camps in Syria had the same goal of socializing people, making its ideas known, and increasing the movement's popular support. But outside of Palestine, Hamas did not aim to integrate refugees into its organizational structure. Hamas's leaders in Syria came all from Gaza, and there were no refugees from Syria who occupied positions of responsibility within the movement. Moreover, Palestinian refugees were not included in the electoral process of the occupied territories. Thus we can infer that Hamas's desire to increase its popular base in the diaspora principally aimed to reinforce its legitimacy among its internal (that is, Gaza) electorate. Hamas's mobilization in the Palestinian diaspora additionally allowed it to present itself as the only organization still interested in the Palestinian refugees and their right of return, in contrast to the other Palestinian factions that neglected them. Hamas's social mobilization in the refugee camps had another central goal: to gain media coverage for the movement. Collective action organized in Yarmouk was very well covered. In fact, refugee camps could be considered as showcases for Hamas's mobilization and beliefs.

Hamas's social strategy adapted according to the needs and expectations of refugees. Its pragmatic attitude allowed the movement to provide social services appropriate to the camp's specific circumstances. One interesting example of this approach was the creation of an organization called Wajeb (meaning "duty" in Arabic) in 2006, which defended the right of return.

Wajeb declared itself an independent organization, as did most of Hamas's social organizations in Yarmouk,[26] but its affiliation to Hamas

---

26. The independent status of Hamas's social organizations in the camp could be linked to security precautions and to the need to attract funding from foreign countries, but it was not possible to investigate this sensitive question in detail.

was noticeable owing to its beliefs and its participation in public protests and parades organized by Hamas in the camp. The will to preserve an independent status could be explained as a strategy to diffuse, in an unofficial way, a political message similar to that of Hamas. This strategy allowed them to sidestep the lack of confidence in political organizations persisting among refugees and enabled them to reach out to a larger number of people.

Wajeb was formed in the wake of the right of return mobilization, which started in Yarmouk in 2000, when more than ten committees were founded to defend the right of return. The majority of these organizations were established by ex-militants from the Palestinian factions (PFLP, the DFLP, and Fatah) and aimed to instill an interest in the preservation of Palestinian culture as well as to propose a new form of participation in the national cause, different from the methods used by the Palestinian factions. Hamas tried to take over this mobilization, proposing its own committee. Wajeb's role was to coordinate activities and information campaigns concerning the right of return, refugee folklore, and living conditions in the camps.

With the creation of Wajeb, Hamas proved that it was able to create a social organization for refugees specifically adapted to the social circumstances of the camp. Other social structures founded by Hamas in Yarmouk were more similar to those in the occupied territories. Hamas created a charity providing assistance to poor people in need of aid, especially during religious celebrations. The above-mentioned women's center was created by Hamas to provide work for women in the traditional embroidery sector, meaning they could play an active role in the protection of Palestinian folklore. The women's center also offered training courses and workshops in education and sanitation, and had a sports club. Hamas also had a student organization aiming at helping young people to complete their studies and at encouraging the best students with monetary prizes. Finally it had a sports club for men that provided sporting activities for a nominal fee.

Among the most significant social events organized by Hamas in Yarmouk was the mass wedding, a charity-funded event, which allows us to understand the social, religious, and political aspects of Hamas's social strategy in the camp. The practice of holding a mass wedding already existed in the occupied territories and grew in importance in Yarmouk. In 2006, the first wedding brought together sixty couples and, in 2010, the couples numbered seven hundred, including refugees from different Palestinian camps in Syria. The mass wedding offered material aid (domestic appliances and financial help) to refugee couples to celebrate their marriage and to build a family. The mass wedding was a huge collective event attended by many people and gaining extensive media coverage. The wedding was accompanied by a ceremony with a very elaborate program (musical performances, traditional dances, religious songs, and theater performance) interspersed by speeches by Hamas leaders and Syrian representatives.

Among the various types of aid, Hamas chose funding mass weddings for several reasons. First, there was a high percentage of youth, and a high rate of unemployment in the refugee camps often forced young people to postpone marriage. Indeed, "Hamas aims to answer a central need of young Palestinians: that of building a family and finding stability."[27] Marriage is thus a practice concurring with the vision of society that Hamas encourages. Marriage is a doctrine of Islam and it is considered to be the foundation of society. As Khaled Meshaal said during his speech at a mass wedding held in October 2010, "marriage has the social role to consolidate society, which is the first step towards the achievement of a larger project: that of national liberation." The link between marriage and the national struggle is also made by the role that reproduction plays in the "demographical fight" against Israel, as was shown by the title given to the ceremony of 2010: "To build the generation of victory and liberation." For Hamas the mass wedding was therefore a charitable, social, and religious event aiding the progression of the national cause.

The mass wedding had other political functions too. It was a tool to reach new supporters. We can assume that, as a result of this help, Hamas obtained the support of the newlyweds and their families. Moreover, during the wedding ceremony Hamas could publicly display its local and

---

27. Interview held with Sadek, a Hamas partisan, in October 2010.

regional allies. For instance, representatives from Syrian institutions and regional leaders participated in the wedding organized in 2010.

Aspirations and Disillusions of Palestinian Refugees

The previous paragraphs showed that Hamas's rise in the Palestinian refugee camps in Syria was based on three factors: the local support accorded to it by the Syrian regime, its "resistance capital,"[28] and its social work. The following paragraph will focus on weak points of the Hamas strategy vis-à-vis refugees. It will reveal the major criticisms voiced by refugees about Hamas and how unfolding Palestinian and regional developments had a negative effect upon Hamas's reputation among refugees.

Hamas's resistance strategy, perceived by refugees as the only way of breathing new life into the Palestinian national struggle, was weakened by its entering into the electoral process in 2005 and 2006 when it participated in the municipal and legislative elections in the Palestinian territories. This change in strategy generated a climate of suspicion toward the movement. Refugees perceived it as a move toward pragmatism, which would negatively impact Hamas's armed resistance tactics. When I asked Mousa Abu Marzouk, deputy chief of Hamas's Political Bureau, how the movement would be able to retain a balance between the principle of resistance, its entry into the Oslo political framework, and the refusal to have relations with Israel, he answered,

> It will be difficult to reconcile the roles of government and resistance, because the first is synonymous with stability and the second, on the contrary, represents a total lack of stability. Concerning negotiations, we refuse them. But if we look at all past agreements, they were the result of negotiations on one hand and resistance on the other. The best strategic move for peoples oppressed and occupied like this was demonstrated by the Vietnamese and Algerians who didn't stop the armed struggle while they negotiated. During the second intifada Yasser Arafat too

---

28. This term, used by Khaled Hroub, refers to the principal component of Hamas's legitimacy represented by its armed resistance (Hroub 2010, 72).

understood his mistake and continued to negotiate on the table and to encourage the resistance under the table! Our strategy must be the rejection of negotiations, the union of the Palestinian people, and the continuation of the armed resistance.[29]

In spite of Hamas's official rhetoric, reasserting their resistance strategy against Israel and comparing the Palestinian struggle to that of other countries, the refugees actually perceived Hamas differently: "Hamas was supposed to represent something new compared to the other organizations because it opposed the Oslo accords which completely excluded refugees from the Palestinian political scene. But finally it demonstrated that it was like the other organizations because it entered the Oslo process through the back door," said Maher, a Palestinian intellectual close to the Islamic jihad.[30] Maher considered the Islamic jihad to be more coherent compared with Hamas because it neither entered the elections nor was involved in the clash between Fatah and Hamas in 2006.

The "national rupture"—the fighting between Fatah and Hamas—and Hamas's consequent seizure of power in the Gaza Strip aggravated suspicions toward it. Hamas was criticized for its interest in power and for stopping the armed attacks. "When Hamas saw that it was stronger on the ground it did not hesitate to take the power in a bloody way. Before, no Palestinian imagined shedding Palestinian blood. If Hamas was not interested in the power it would never have accepted this," said Ali, a leftist writer. He continued,

Hamas said that Fatah was corrupt, but when it took the power it emerged that it was no less corrupt. Moreover, since the seizure of power, those who attacked Israel [the Islamic jihad] are considered traitors. So where is the resistance now? There is a difference between what is said and what is practiced. I think that the national rupture was the worst crisis for Palestinians. This rupture is not only political and ideological

---

29. Interview held with Mousa Abou Marzouk, deputy chief of Hamas's Political Bureau, in November 2010.

30. Interview held in November 2010.

but also geographical and it has serious negative effects on the national question and Hamas has a big responsibility for this situation![31]

Moreover, Hamas was criticized for imposing restrictive social norms in the Gaza Strip against the national liberation project that, according to Hamas's policy, was a priority. Camp inhabitants critical of the religious rigidity imposed by Hamas on Gaza influenced the movement's attitude in the camps. It adopted a soft stance on social issues, as remarked by Aiham, a young leftist, who said, "Before, in Hamas's offices it was forbidden to smoke, now it seems that they are more permissive."[32] Hamas's moderate social attitude in the camp was an attempt to reach a consensus. But Hamas's social work and service allocation were still criticized by refugees for being selective and based mainly on religious factors. The mass weddings, for example, "address[ed] only a certain type of people and not all Palestinians. Refugees [were] in fact selected on the basis of a dossier: they ha[d] to be observant Muslims, they must not smoke and their wife must wear a veil."[33] The mass wedding was also perceived by some as being "completely detached from any patriotic and national work."[34]

Indeed, after the national rupture Hamas lost support in the camp, which could be proved, according to Aiham, by the diminishing number of people who participated in the Friday prayer in the camp's central mosque.[35] But the Israeli war on Gaza in December 2008 and January 2009 allowed Hamas to reinvest in the camp. During the war, daily demonstrations in support of Gaza and Hamas's resistance against the Israeli army were staged in Yarmouk. However, criticism against the movement reemerged some months after the end of the war. In 2010, when the peace negotiations restarted between the Palestinian authority and Israel, Hamas was accused of having ceased all military operations against Israel. Many refugees said they no longer identified with any Palestinian political

31. Interview held with Ali, a leftist intellectual, in October 2010.
32. Interview held in October 2010.
33. Interview held with Mohammad, an independent, in February 2011.
34. Ibid.
35. Interview held with Aiham, a young leftist, in October 2010.

faction and expressed a lack of confidence in them. "We are trapped between Fatah and Hamas. The two organizations do not represent Palestinians' point of view. One [Fatah] has abandoned us, while the other [Hamas] provides a very limited view for the realization of Palestinian ambitions."[36] Palestinian refugees' criticism of Hamas and the political leadership in general proved a discontent rooted in a long-standing state of political marginalization that goes back to the signature of the Oslo accords in 1993. If Hamas was able, for a while, to embody refugees' expectation for change, it could not really answer to their quest of reintegrating the Palestinian political life.

Hamas, the Refugee Camps, and the Syrian Uprising

The popular contestation that broke out in March 2011 against the Syrian regime undermined Hamas's partnership with Syria. Eleven months after the start of the uprising, and under political pressure from many quarters, Hamas finally came out in favor of the Syrian people and broke its relationship with the Syrian regime.[37] Hamas's offices closed and its leaders left Syria for Gaza, Egypt, and Qatar.

At the same time, Palestinian refugees in Syria became massively engaged in the Syrian contestation. In spite of Syria's role in support of the Palestinian cause, the historical relationship between Palestinians and both Hafiz's and Bashar al-Asad's regimes had been marked by the manipulation of Palestinian nationalist actors in Syria's regional policy and instances of their suppression inside and outside Syria. Moreover, Palestinians, like Syrians, endured a climate of political repression for more than forty years. For these reasons refugees became engaged with the Syrian revolution in the same quest for "dignity" and "liberty."

Palestinians first mobilized by joining the peaceful movement (spreading information, participating in demonstrations outside the camps, organizing relief efforts, and so forth) and, second, by getting engaged in the

---

36. Interview held with Maher, partisan of the Islamic jihad, in November 2010.
37. About Hamas's stance on the Syrian uprising, see Napolitano 2013.

armed action under the leadership of the Free Syrian Army and other armed militias. Moreover, Palestinian camps were affected, like most Syrian towns and villages, by Syrian army bombings and by repression by the security services.[38]

Palestinians engaged in the Syrian uprising in the same Syrian quest for democratization. But the local contestation gave also a voice to Palestinians' discontent with their leadership. The PLO has been criticized for its neutral stance and its soft and late reaction to the Syrian regime's violation of Palestinian refugee camps. Hamas was not spared by this criticism because of its initially hesitant stance. Therefore, the movement clearly distanced itself from the regime, and the recent participation of Hamas partisans in the armed struggle and in relief activities demonstrated that the movement undertook concrete actions in favor of the revolutionaries.[39]

Conclusion

Today it seems very hazardous to make any predictions about the future political life of Palestinian refugees in Syria. The country has been ravaged by the brutal war the Syrian regime is waging against its people. The society is shattered and the conflict seems destined to drag on. The humanitarian crisis that affects the Syrian people did not spare Palestinians. By 2013 more than 235,000 of them were displaced inside Syria and a further 62,000 had left the country, fleeing from violence.[40]

The developments in Palestine, Syria, and the region influenced Hamas's rising stance among Palestinian grassroots in Syria, as demonstrated by this chapter. External factors will continue to have a decisive

38. About Palestinian forms of mobilization in the Syrian uprising, see Napolitano 2012–13.

39. Information diffused on social networks stated that Hamas's partisans were involved in armed militia formed in the Yarmouk camp, but the movement did not made any official statements on this subject. The Syrian regime, from its side, accused the movement of being directly involved in supporting the revolutionaries and of acting as a proxy of Qatar.

40. Statistics published by UNRWA, Sept. 6, 2013.

influence on the movement's role in the country, but eventually internal dynamics will be determining. If the Syrian Muslim Brotherhood participates in a future postrevolutionary government, this would facilitate Hamas's restoring its former relations with the country. Hamas was the only Palestinian faction to take a stand in favor of the revolution, albeit somewhat belatedly, and for this reason its chances of being favored by the future authorities are better than those of other Palestinian actors. At the same time, two factors will probably not play in favor of a rapprochement between Syria and Hamas. First, postconflict Syrian authorities will give first priority to rebuilding the country, while regional policy will be of secondary concern. Second, Hamas diversification of its regional alliances could reduce the strategic importance of Syrian support.

Hamas's mobilization in Palestinian refugee camps in Syria will probably not be restored. On the one hand, the movement's actions in Syria were principally linked to the movement's propaganda and not to a genuine concern for Palestinian refugees. On the other hand, the movement will have to face enormous transformations engendered by the Syrian uprising in local social and political life. It is questionable whether the movement will be able to meet Palestinian refugees' new political expectations and to cater to their new needs.

14

The Syrian Uprising and Bashar al-Asad's First Decade in Power

RAYMOND HINNEBUSCH
AND TINA ZINTL

By the end of the first decade of Bashar al-Asad's presidency, the achievements and costs of his "modernizing" authoritarianism could be discerned, but how far it had prepared Syria to face the tsunami of the Arab uprisings was far from predictable. After March 2011, al-Asad's rule quickly changed from a seeming case of successful authoritarian upgrading into a highly repressive regime fighting for its survival. What appeared for a period to be a mass revolution from below, similar to that in Tunisia or Egypt, morphed into a violent civil war. This concluding chapter highlights how the "Bashar decade," as detailed and analyzed by this volume, allows us to cast light on the origins and, to some degree, also on the tangent of the uprising.

The Origins of the Uprising: Factors For and Against

Authoritarian Upgrading and Regime Resilience

Bashar al-Asad had pursued a distinctive version of authoritarian upgrading that retained many of the advantages of the state built by his father, such as its nationalist legitimacy as keeper of the Arab cause against Israel, while addressing key weaknesses, such as the exhaustion of the public sector and the impending decline of oil rents.

While the Ba'th state was constructed with many built-in vulnerabilities, not least a permanent legitimacy crisis owing to the dominant role of the 'Alawite minority in the leadership, under Hafiz these had been contained by assiduous cross-sectarian coalition-building, a populist social contract with the middle and lower classes, and a nationalist foreign policy. This formula, however, could only be sustained with copious amounts of rent, an enduring vulnerability. Thus the most immediate roots of the 2011 crisis can be traced back to the overdevelopment of the Ba'thist state fueled by both foreign aid and petroleum rent, making it vulnerable to rent declines. Periods of rent decline then stimulated efforts to revive the market and private sector and to foster inward investment through polices that necessarily favored investors. This economic liberalization meant that the regime needed to restructure its social base away from its initial populist alliance with the lower-middle and lower classes. Syria began to replicate the transition common across the region from a populist form of authoritarianism to a "post-populist" version wherein authoritarian power was used to pursue economic liberalization and to appropriate public sector assets for presidential families and privileged cronies. In parallel, the regime adopted the techniques of "authoritarian upgrading" by which several Arab post-populist regimes tried to compensate for the risks of abandoning their mass constituencies.

Initially, few thought the uprising would spread to Syria. Syria watchers such as Carsten Wieland (2012), David Lesch (2012), and Bassam Haddad (2011) argued that Syria encountered the Arab uprisings with advantages lacking in other Arab republics: the *balance between grievances against the regime and satisfaction delivered by it* seemed more favorable in Syria than in some other Arab countries. First, unlike his overthrown counterparts, elderly and in power for decades, Bashar was young and, in power for only a decade, still enjoyed the benefit of the doubt and was widely seen as preferable to the plausible alternatives (Lesch 2012, 38–54). The president had earned some respect among parts of the public, having steered Syria through extreme external threat and isolation in the middle of the 2000–2010 decade, while also presiding over a post-populist transition that made the regime more compatible with an age of neoliberal globalization.

Second, Asad's regime enjoyed some nationalist legitimacy from decades of opposition to Israel and Western imperialism (see chapter 4), in sharp contrast to other Arab presidents, most of whom were widely seen as Western clients. The regime sustained nationalist credibility through its stand against the US invasion of Iraq, its tenacity in defending its position in Lebanon, and its support for Hezbollah and Hamas in their confrontations with Israel (in striking contrast to Mubarak's perceived collaboration with Israel against them). This credibility was bolstered through the regime's welcoming position toward Hamas's mobilization efforts in Palestinian refugee camps in Syria (see chapter 13) and toward Iraqi refugees after the 2003 war (see chapter 12). Regional polls showed Asad to be quite popular compared to other Arab leaders[1]—and, interestingly, his nationalist legitimacy did not suffer when he followed a more accommodationist foreign policy after 2008, lifting Syria out of its pariah role in the West (see chapter 11). Moreover, the regime had delivered stability, sparing Syria the sectarian chaos in neighboring Lebanon and especially in Iraq, the showcase of American-imposed democratization, which seemed to allow the regime to discredit the West's democracy discourses among a silent majority that valued stability.

Third, during his first decade, Bashar al-Asad's Syria also successfully diversified its economic relations by forging ties first with Western Europe, and then, as a result of Western hostility and sanctions on the regime in the middle of the decade, cultivating deepened relations with Turkey, Iran, Russia, and Asian countries, relations that, with the exception of Syrian-Turkish relations, would help it withstand renewed Western sanctions after the uprising started. By moving toward a so-called "social market economy," Syria was able to access new economic resources (see chapter 3). In the first half of the decade, the regime enjoyed a boom in oil revenues, enabling the buildup of substantial foreign exchange reserves; in the second half, as oil income declined, the economic opening, including new private banks and a stock market, mobilized substitute Arab and private financial capital, with the proportion of GDP generated in the private

---

1. See presentation by Shibley Telhami, "Annual Arab Public Opinion Survey," 2010, http://www.brookings.edu/%7E/media/Files/rc/reports/2010/08_arab_opinion_poll _telhami/08_arab_opinion_poll_telhami.pdf. Sampling procedures and representativeness of this poll remain, however, opaque.

sector and by foreign investment steadily rising (Abboud 2009; Leverett 2005, 86–87; Haddad 2012; Lesch 2012, 55–68). Investment inflows drove a boom in trade, banking, housing, construction, and tourism in the latter years of the decade. The regime also protected its revenue base by taxing a portion of the new wealth to substitute for declining oil revenues. At the same time, compared to Egypt and Tunisia, Syria's neoliberalism was recent, and it entered the post-populist stage with a low-inequality starting point and shallower mass impoverishment, with the poverty rate actually declining, from 33.2 percent in 1996 to 30.1 percent in 2004 (El-Laithy and Abu-Ismail 2005) and with HDI (Human Development Index), life expectancy, and literacy rates above the Arab world average.

Fourth, Asad developed new constituencies, enabling the regime to balance above a divided society. On the one hand, the regime was able to stimulate new entrepreneurial energies among the upper middle class (see chapter 7); attract back and co-opt foreign-educated Syrians into reformist public agencies and private business (see chapter 6); and launch a new breed of pro-regime development GO-NGOs. In parallel, Bashar pushed ahead Hafiz's détente with "moderate Islam" (see chapter 8). The regime tolerated the proliferation of nonpolitical Islamic schools and charities, concentrated in Damascus and Aleppo, and it co-opted Sufis and 'ulama connected to Damascene businesses prospering on the encouragement of the private sector and influx of Gulf capital, using them against the political Islamists such as the Muslim Brotherhood and the Salafis. The regime also mobilized the 'ulama against the foreign threat (see chapter 8) and even flirted with jihadis, encouraging them to transit to Iraq to fight the US occupation (this strategy would later first boomerang, as these elements returned to fight against the regime after the uprising, and then, whether intentionally or not, helped the regime to exploit divisions between moderate opposition and jihadi fighters). On the other hand, the regime posed as protector of secularists, women, and minorities, and profited by their alarm at the Salafi threat—though this led, occasionally, to a contradiction between its pro-secularist and its Islamic co-optation efforts (see chapter 9). At the same time, the single party and corporatist institutions left over from the populist era were retained, albeit now to demobilize and control rather than to mobilize and empower the regime's mass constituencies (see chapter 2).

Another major set of reasons for thinking the Syrian regime might avoid the Arab uprising was that the *opportunity structure* for successful rebellion against it seemed less favorable than in the other republics. Unlike in Egypt and Tunisia, where the focus of grievances on the president enabled his departure without threatening the whole regime, in Syria the removal of Asad alone would have served no similar safety valve function; the army and the security forces were tightly interlocked with the 'Alawite political elite and controlled by Asad's kin and fellow sectarians, hence could not be readily separated from the top regime elite or easily brought to abandon the president in Tunisian or Egyptian style. They were also far stronger and more cohesive than, notably, Gaddafi's forces in Libya or Salah's in Yemen. The thicker state-society relations in Syria also meant that many more interests would be threatened by the more thorough kind of regime change that happened in Libya; the regime in Syria had much stronger links to society—in particular the regime had worked assiduously to co-opt the business class and the 'ulama, the traditional centers of opposition to the Ba'th (Haddad 2011).

If the regime was cohesive, the heterogeneity of Syrian society was expected to undermine collective action among the opposition or the deprived. Thus hitherto opposition attempts to build larger coalitions, for example through the 2005 Damascus Declaration, were weak and thus either muted by repression or driven abroad (see chapter 5). As for the deprived, the large number of rural-urban migrants, stimulated by the drought in the northeast of Syria, were not only economically disadvantaged but also, for a long time, politically inactive and dispersed (see chapter 10). This atomization was expected to (and perhaps did to an extent) retard the formation of a broad antiregime mobilization comparable to the one that quickly toppled President Mubarak in more homogeneous Egypt. Egypt's larger public space and more developed civil society, opposition parties, and press, which had prepared the ground for collective action, had no parallels in Syria's more repressive political climate and underdeveloped civil society.

The regime was also thought to be a robust authoritarian state that, having contained dissent for decades, would be able to handle new challenges. It combined many mechanisms of co-optation with a pervasive *mukhabarat* (intelligence) network and seemingly had a demonstrated capacity to successfully repress violent opposition, whether by Islamists in the early eighties or by Kurds in 2004. Moreover, peaceful opposition to the regime in Syria had been so successfully managed that in 2010 the "traditional" opposition was thoroughly disillusioned and seemingly marginalized (see chapter 5).

In summary, it appeared from both the balance of grievance/satisfaction and the opportunity structure in 2010 that the spread of the uprising to Syria was not inevitable and, moreover, that any rapid success, comparable to that in Egypt or Tunisia, was never likely. Although "authoritarian upgrading" did not immunize Syria from the so-called Arab Spring as Bashar al-Asad prematurely claimed in an interview in January 2011,[2] it did arguably position the regime to more effectively resist it. The fact that the uprising caught everyone by surprise, including the Syrian regime, demonstrates how convincing his authoritarian modernization efforts had been.

The Roots of Rebellion: The Vulnerabilities of Authoritarian Upgrading

If not inevitable, the uprising *did* spread to Syria and, to a considerable extent, it can be attributed to flaws built into the state at its founding and to the post-populist upgrading strategies pursued by Bashar to "fix" these vulnerabilities. Although meant to resolve certain vulnerabilities in *populist* versions of authoritarianism, post-populism generated powerful mass grievances. Authoritarian upgrading, although meant to contain and compensate for these negative side effects, had also its own cumulative *long-run costs*, generating *new* vulnerabilities. Thus the seeds of rebellion

---

2. "Interview with Syrian President Bashar al-Assad," *Wall Street Journal*, Jan. 31, 2011.

can be identified in the grievances generated by post-populist transition and the inability of authoritarian upgrading techniques to fully compensate for them. These techniques were too weak or they targeted either the "wrong" audiences or audiences that were largely inconsequential for long-term power maintenance. Additionally, other elements of authoritarian upgrading, which had proven more effective, were revoked and nullified by the immediate repressive answer to the first protests in 2011.

To begin with, Asad believed that in order to carry out economic reform he had to concentrate power rather than share it with other regime elites in the Ba'th Party. That Bashar al-Asad's inheritance of the presidency, the first case of republican dynasty (*jumlukiyya*) in the Arab world (with the prospect of permanent Asad family rule) did not initially generate wider and deeper resentment was owing to the fact that the regime was a coalition that reached beyond the Asad family. Yet, during the 2000–2010 years, this coalition was contracting with the removal of several Sunni barons and apparatchiki, whose clientalist networks had incorporated important segments of Sunni society; those Asad co-opted in their place often lacked comparable experience, stature, and clientele networks. The most vulnerable point for neopatrimonial regimes is when they go too far, as Bashar al-Asad arguably did, in centralizing power and patronage in the "royal clan." In parallel, economic liberalization was opening the door toward crony capitalism as new economic opportunities and also corruption became more concentrated and intense among a few insiders. At the same time, in attacking the party apparatus as an obstacle to his reforms, Bashar also debilitated its capacity to incorporate the regime's traditional constituencies, especially in rural areas, once its stronghold among the Sunnis, leaving the rural Sunni population "available" for anti-regime mobilization (see chapters 2 and 10). The regime's incorporated social base was therefore shrinking, leaving it as a result *both* more upper class and more sectarian in social composition.

At the broader level of society, a rising number of Syrians—both winners and losers—pointed to the shortcomings and inconsistencies of economic reform policies. While under Hafiz the regime had balanced between plebeian and bourgeois constituencies, under Bashar, instead of pursuing the balanced "social market economy" promised, the crony bourgeoisie was super-enriched while support for agriculture, health, education, and a social security network contracted (see chapter 3). Instead of encouraging productive capital in industry and agriculture, the regime fostered tertiary capital from crony businessmen and from the Gulf countries. Free-trade agreements opened the country to foreign imports, from Turkey and China particularly, that drove small and medium manufacturers into bankruptcy; indeed some manufacturers turned into traders, seeing trade as more profitable. Tourist and real estate operators also flourished, mainly in the big cities but, while enriching some, drove up the cost of housing for many. Moreover, the predatory activities of crony capitalists and the lack of rule of law still deterred investment in productive assets that could not quickly be liquefied and exported. There were gains from this economic activity but it depended on political stability and thus quickly dissipated after the uprising.

Among the losers of post-populist upgrading, the accumulation of grievances could be said to have reached a tipping point. High birth rates, combined with free education, resulted in a quickly growing number of unemployed educated youth that the labor market could not absorb. In rural areas, population growth on a fairly fixed amount of arable land meant that the younger generation was left without land and needed to enter a depressed job market in the cities. As chapter 10 shows, the neglect, in particular, of the northeast Jezira area, but also the decline of subsidies for agriculture and a change in the agrarian relations law favoring landowners at the expense of tenants and leading to mass expulsions of the latter in certain areas made parts of the countryside hotbeds of grievances. Drought greatly exacerbated the situation and prompted a massive influx of vulnerable people to the suburban informal settlements—where the uprising would gain its most dedicated followers. At the same time, the regime attempted to promote the private sector—privileging investors and further enriching already well-connected elements of the urban bourgeoisie—while it provided no satisfactory safety net for the large group of losers of economic liberalization: 30 percent of the population were living under the poverty line and 11 percent below subsistence, according to a UNDP report (El-Laithy and Abu-Ismail 2005); in addition, the Gini index of inequality increased from 33.7 in 1997 to 37.4 in 2004 (Bibi and

Nabli 2010, 40). Corruption was a long-standing grievance, but as social mobility stalled for the majority while a visible few enriched themselves, it was less tolerable. Even the regime-controlled Syrian General Federation of Trade Unions complained in 2009 that "the rich have become richer and the poor poorer . . . low-income earners who make up 80 percent of the Syrian population are looking for additional work to support themselves."[3]

The unequal treatment of different constituencies meant that the regime's co-optation measures had a differential effect. They were successful enough to persuade significant parts of the population—especially urban, wealthy elements—until well into the uprising that the status quo was favorable to them or at least that there was no viable alternative. But these same strategies largely ignored the majority of society, especially in rural areas and midsized cities like Der'a or Homs.[4] While there were exceptions to this situation, such as the too-little-too-late aid to drought victims and the developmental (GO-)NGOs such as FIRDOS,[5] operative in the poorer countryside, these initiatives remained mere drops in the ocean of increasing unemployment and socioeconomic deprivation. In this regard, the uprising uncovered which elements authoritarian upgrading had failed to address.

Authoritarian upgrading's co-optation measures were also sometimes directed at audiences that proved to be ineffectual for the stability of the authoritarian system. For instance, the Syrian regime's policies that were meant to incorporate both Palestinians living in Damascus and Iraqi refugees—see chapters 12 and 13—paid no dividends during the uprising; the former turned away from, and partly against, the Syrian regime, just as Hamas did; and the latter started to leave Syria, as it became increasingly

3. "Dardari Defends Syria's Economic Reforms," *Syria Today* 56, Dec. 2009.

4. Surprisingly, Homs, as the hometown of the First Lady's Akhraz family, was, in contrast to Damascus or Aleppo, not linked up with the regime by co-optation or favoritism to any meaningful extent.

5. FIRDOS, the Fund for Integrated Rural Development of Syria, was the first GO-NGO initiated by the Syrian First Lady in 2001 and is concerned with rural development through microcredits, skills development, and ameliorating social services.

"Iraqified" and entangled in civil war, to return to their still troubled and insecure native country. Just as the regime's pro-Palestinian and anti-Iraq war rhetoric during 2000–2010, despite accurately expressing the opinion of the Arab masses (see chapter 4), did not secure it enduring support among society at large, so also the support of the particular Palestinian and Iraqi beneficiaries of its policies vanished into thin air. The regime's nationalist legitimizing discourses that had seemed a stable base for authoritarian upgrading proved impotent in the face of the Arab uprisings.

Paradoxically, even the co-optation of the winners of economic liberalization from the other end of the social spectrum proved disappointing from the point of view of the authoritarian regime, for once the popular uprising began, many economically successful upper-middle–class people, among them foreign-educated returnees with contacts abroad (see chapters 6 and 7), had the opportunities and means to leave the country or decided to stay on the sidelines of the revolution, not joining either side. Even the regime's policies vis-à-vis those Islamic actors, such as al-Buti and the Grand Mufti, who were deemed to be important enough to be courted, and thus controlled, by the regime (see chapter 8) did not—and arguably could not—dissuade a much larger mass of religious oppositionists from antiregime activism during the uprising.

Furthermore, the opportunity structure was becoming less unfavorable for antiregime mobilization: although to a much lesser extent than in Egypt, society had become somewhat more empowered on the eve of the uprising. Though unsuccessful in realizing the demands of their advocates, the Damascus Spring (2001) and the Damascus Declaration (2005) provided models and experience of civil society mobilization (see chapter 5) that activists would build on once the uprising started. In the late years of the decade—and paradoxically as part of authoritarian upgrading—the Internet and mobile phones acquired a critical mass: Internet use increased from less than 1 percent in 2000 to 21 percent in 2010, while mobile phone access reached 60 percent.[6] While the regime, in parallel,

<hr />

6. "Percentage of Individuals Using the Internet—Syria," UN Data, http://data.un.org/Data.aspx?q=Syria&d=ITU&f=ind1Code%3aI99H%3bcountryCode%3aSYR;

stepped up efforts to control the electronic media, activists quickly learned how to circumvent these efforts. The Internet was crucial in overcoming the atomization of society, thus enabling mobilization against the regime. Already before 2011, the regime had, for example, underrated society's ability to organize via the Internet when provoked by the government's turning of the reform of the personal status law over to Islamic conservatives, as shown by chapter 9. The opening of the information sphere increased political consciousness and awareness of abuses, spread democracy discourse, and, after the uprising started, was pivotal in sustaining its momentum; the wide availability of phones with cameras in particular allowed the opposition to spread a message of unprovoked regime violence that widely mobilized discontent from both within and without.

Another factor was that during the decade, the arbitrary hand of the security forces had been somewhat eased under Bashar al-Asad's rule and their control capacity weakened. There was, thus, a certain loss of fear, especially among the young who had not experienced the clampdown on Hama in 1982. At the same time, however, there was enough continuing arrest and torture, underlining the nonexistence both of rule of law and of protection of human rights, that the regime got no credit for Bashar's modest reforms of the security forces; such a partial relaxation in repression is arguably the most dangerous strategy for an authoritarian regime. Perhaps most important, the success of the uprisings in Tunisia and Egypt encouraged people to believe that even repressive authoritarian regimes could be driven from power.

Even as society was incrementally mobilizing, the regime's political incorporation was stagnant, even regressing. By repeatedly rebuffing the demands of the moderate opposition for political reform, notably failing to allow party pluralism that could have satisfied many pent-up participation demands, the regime passed up the opportunity to co-opt such groups (see chapter 5). While the regime successfully monitored both the

---

"Mobile-cellular Subscriptions per 100 Inhabitants," UN Data, accessed July 13, 2014, http://data.un.org/Data.aspx?q=Syria&d=ITU&f=ind1Code%3aI911%3bcountryCode%3aSYR.

old secular and the traditional Islamic oppositions, it failed, having debilitated the party's penetration of society, to anticipate the emergence of at-the-time-unknown antiregime activists' networks.

Finally, the attempt to co-opt and foster a politically harmless version of Sunni Islam was always going to be risky for a regime that was, in many ways, a coalition of minorities. The Sunni majority had long felt bitter about privileges that, they felt, were granted to 'Alawite elites; as such, sectarian mistrust was rife under the surface and, as a taboo subject, could not be faced and dealt with openly. The secular Ba'thist ideology of Arabism had marginalized religious identities, and helped integrate the minorities and Sunni majority within a shared identity; but when Arab nationalism and socialism declined after 1990, the identity vacuum was—despite the continuing unifying narrative of secularism—mostly filled by clashing religious identities. In particular, there was a rise of pious Islam, which provoked minorities to follow a defensive religious counter-identity. This rise was aggravated by money from the Gulf countries that helped fund a Salafi revival, ready to transform into jihadism under the right conditions. The regime hoped to ride and control this wave, but it got out of its control.

Agency as a Switching Factor

Structural forces push social dynamics along predetermined paths, much like a rail network, but human agency can operate like switching junctures, determining which of several outcomes prevails. In Syria the structural factors emergent toward the end of the decade, being relatively balanced for and against the possibility and likely success of an uprising, are clearly not enough to explain why it happened, and *agency* is crucial to understanding what tipped the balance.

For one, there would have been no uprising without the agency of dissenters. Determined activists, many of them exiles, systematically set out to spread the Arab uprising to Syria, using the Internet and promoting a discourse of democratization meant to delegitimize the regime. In some instances, the regime was deliberately provoked, when, for example, in sectarian-mixed Banias an uncompromising Salafi shaykh exploited years of anti-'Alawite resentment among Sunnis (which, possibly, also provoked the Banias massacres against the Sunni population two years into the uprising). Furthermore, party headquarters and the officers club were attacked, statues of Hafiz al-Asad and portraits of his son were torn down, and, much earlier than is usually acknowledged, there were armed attacks on the regime's security forces.[7]

How the regime responded to the protests (and provocations) made all the difference for the Syrian tangent; it did not have to overreact with excessive use of force, but it did so. Reportedly, a security committee had judged that rebellion had ousted presidents in Tunisia and Egypt because regimes had used insufficient repression; if so, the overreaction by the security forces was not surprising.[8] Indeed, the regime's actions suggest a security culture within its inner core that believed any tolerance of dissent could quickly snowball but that sufficient repression could defeat it, as it had done in the 1980s. Still, there appears to have been a split within the regime over how to respond, between confrontationists, who assured Asad that the security forces could end the protests, and accommodationists, such as Farouk al-Shara' and Bouthaina Shaaban, who advocated political reforms. Moreover, during the initial protests the president still enjoyed some legitimacy: protests did not target him and urged him to respond positively and even to lead a democratizing transition. Arguably had he opted to lead a renewed reform process, becoming part of the solution rather than the core of the problem, the legitimacy dividend might have enabled him to win a free election, thus legitimizing his office and liberalizing Syria's political system. However, he aligned with the hard-liners, and the soft-liners were marginalized; in fact, the uprising empowered hard-liners such as Bashar's brother Mahar al-Asad and re-empowered some of the security barons who had been retired during the last decade.

7. Robert Worth, "The Price of Loyalty in Syria," *New York Times*, June 19, 2013, http://www.nytimes.com/2013/06/23/magazine/the-price-of-loyalty-in-syria.html ?partner=rss&emc=rss&_r=2&pagewanted=all&.

8. Similarly, Heydemann and Leenders (2011) argue that regime responses to the Arab uprisings changed over time to more violent repression, in a process they call "authoritarian learning."

Thus the deployment of excessive violence against protesters was the factor that tilted Syria into the uprising. Indeed, the trigger was the brutal reaction of the regime to the antiregime graffiti of children in the southern city of Derʿa and the disrespectful treatment by the local security chief of tribal elders seeking to intervene on their behalf. Once the government responded to demonstrations and attacks on public buildings in Derʿa with excessive force, a tit-for-tat process of escalation began.[9] The president failed to reverse this spiral of violence by restraining and calling to account the security forces, and only conceded some of the legitimate demands of the protestors when it was too little, too late. The use of violence against unarmed protestors, rapidly made known by the new media, had the effect of swiftly expanding the initially peaceful protests to other towns and suburbs where the deprived or aggrieved were concentrated.

The turning point in the official regime narrative came with Asad's speech before parliament at the end of March 2011. In this and other speeches and statements by the president, as well as by state media or regime officials, the legitimate demands of protestors were, if at all, only reluctantly conceded and overshadowed by the claim that Syria was the target of an international conspiracy. Repression was paralleled by traditional attempts at appeasement and co-optation, such as pay increases to public employees, stopping the enforcement of regulations, and granting of privileges to tribal, religious, or communal notables. Promises of reform, such as ending the emergency law; giving the Kurds citizenship; and amending the parties law, were insufficient or remained largely on paper; often they were so designed that they indeed helped to maintain regime control, as was the case with the parties law, which still allowed the regime to limit party formation, or the replacement of the emergency law by an antiterrorism law.

The regime's forces, initially lacking training and experience in crowd or riot control, continued to respond with brutality and thus

---

9. For an account on oppositional mobilization in and around Derʿa, with a focus on clan-based and tribal social networks as enabling factors, see Leenders and Heydemann 2012.

multiplied its enemies as funerals became the occasions for more confrontation. If the protests had been unleashed by a breaking of the fear barrier, now the uprising was further driven by the desire for retribution for the deaths or imprisonment of relatives and friends. The regime sought to appease amenable parts of the protesters while hoping prison sentences, torture, and killings would eventually exhaust others. In fact, however, government violence only escalated opposition demands for reform and for democratization to calls for an end to the regime. Though this reaction was not inevitable, it had to a considerable extent been built into the regime's security culture and its illegitimacy among a big part of the population.

The structural situation—namely, the shifting balance between grievances and satisfaction, as well as opportunity structure—in good part helped define the two camps in the uprising. On the one hand, the regime's traditional enemies, such as children of exiles or aggrieved Islamist militants, were natural historic enemies of the regime who took the opportunity to turn the tables on it; while parts of its traditional constituency, particularly the minorities, were naturally wary of the uprising and had a stake in the secular state the regime purported to protect. On the other hand, the regime's fairly successful "authoritarian upgrading" and divide-and-rule tactics also partly helped form the opposing camps. While co-opted, privileged parts of society held out with the regime, those who felt marginalized and deprived by post-populist policies, particularly rural youth lacking a stake in the system, were mobilized by the opposition. The silent majority, caught in the middle, was over time forced either to take sides or to flee the country.

The Tangent of the Uprising

The question remains as to how far the Bashar al-Asad decade, and its inheritances from the Hafiz period, can explain the particular *tangent* that the uprising took in Syria in contrast to the other Arab uprisings—namely the morphing of peaceful civil resistance, which fell short of a revolution *à la tunisienne*, into violent civil war of an increasingly sectarian caste. Arguably, the earlier successes of the authoritarian upgrading strategy with some constituents, on the one hand, together with the disillusionment of others with the empty promises of the Asad years, on the other hand, shaped the uprising in a way poles apart from the other Arab uprisings. Once the civil war began, contrasting perceptions among a divided populace of the first decade of the 2000s help explain both the failure of a tipping point for or against the regime and the inability of the hurting stalemate to open the door (as in Yemen) to a political settlement.

Stalemate I: The Phase of Mass Protest

This phase of the uprising was characterized by massive, unprecedented nonviolent protest, which, however, was contained in the periphery—the villages, suburbs, and medium-sized cities—while the centers of power (Damascus) and business (Aleppo) seemed relatively immune. This rural-urban pattern corresponded precisely to the geographical distribution of benefits and costs of Bashar's post-populist upgrading. The uprising began in the periphery, indeed, in Der'a, an area that had formerly been a base of the Ba'th, but by 2011 was characterized by semisettled tribal elements impoverished by the drought, new rural generations lacking land and connections, and educated yet unemployed youth, who generated the shock troops of rebellion. Parts of central Hama, Homs, and Deir ez-Zor, long bastions of Sunni piety and aggrieved notable or tribal families, also became centers of rebellion. In some instances, Islamic issues, such as the regime's ban on the full-face veil, were stimulants of discontent, and, once the uprising had started, committees centered on mosques constituted a network of opposition in parts of the periphery.

In addition, however, other, mostly middle-class, elements with a history of antiregime attitudes also joined the uprising. The traditional secular activists of the earlier Damascus Spring had also become active again, many seeking to position themselves as mediators between regime and opposition. A key role in spreading discontent by showing images of repression and by propagating the idea of a revolution was played by the Internet activities of Diaspora-based Syrians, often children of those who had been aggrieved by Ba'th rule and exited the country; these were often secular too, but not ready for mediation and compromises. Abroad, also, the exiled Muslim Brothers, who saw their moment arriving, met to constitute themselves as an alternative government, following the Libyan model and gaining Western encouragement.

Inside Syria, from the outset, the uprising mobilized youth, who had limited or no stake in the status quo. The rebellion was conducted by new youth activists, widely dispersed and unknown to the government, who quickly produced new leaders to replace those arrested or killed. Networks of local committees in touch via cell phones and the Internet rather than formal organization, drove the uprising.

There was no obvious unified or alternative leadership to the regime with a road map to power, nor even a program—except "freedom" and "dignity." But a strategy was nevertheless discernible. The opposition's aim was to mobilize such massive numbers of protestors that the security services would be stretched thin and exhausted, hoping that eventually a majority of the population would turn against the regime, that there would be a split within the regime or between the leadership and the army, rendering it an unreliable instrument of repression because of defections—or that foreign intervention would be precipitated by regime repression. Also, the opposition knew it could not win without breaking the alignment between the regime, on the one hand, and the Damascene and Aleppine bourgeoisie and middle classes, on the other hand. At first the opposition thought that the turmoil would paralyze the economy enough to cause the business elites to desert the regime; yet these valued stability and had much to lose economically from the turmoil, therefore choosing to remain on the sidelines of the uprising. The opposition also hoped that international economic sanctions would drain the regime's revenue base and thus its ability to pay salaries and sustain the loyalties of the state administration. Indeed, tourism, inward investment, and money transfers from expatriates on which regime beneficiaries and urban businessmen had thrived dried up, and foreign exchange became scarce. The regime's revenue base suffered from the decline of tax collections and the European ban on purchase of Syrian oil. However, there was no economic collapse and, crucially, the regime proved capable of perpetuating itself financially, often by relying on new rents or loans granted by its regional and international allies such as Iran and Russia. Moreover a new class of business operators benefited from the conflict, enriched through smuggling and monopolies of scarce commodities.

The social base on which the regime relied to survive comprised the crony capitalists, urban government employees, and parts of the minorities, especially of 'Alawites and Christians whom the regime sought to rally by exploiting their fear of Salafi Islam. Few of the rich beneficiaries of the regime could, of course, be expected to actively fight for it. That left parts of the 'Alawites who were mobilized in militias (the *shabbiha*), recruited into the military reserves, and later a pro-regime national guard. 'Alawites, especially the less privileged, may have felt the Asads had roped them into a conflict that did not serve their interests, but increasingly there was no way back for them, as they were sure to face retribution if the regime fell. The military remained largely loyal, and although there was a growing incidence of desertions after the regime resorted to a "military solution," once these disaffected elements had left, the number of defections declined and the military continued to be surprisingly cohesive. The main cities, Damascus and Aleppo, remained largely quiescent in this period although their suburbs were often hotbeds of revolt. The upper middle classes had just gotten a taste of the good Westernized life, for example Terc's young entrepreneurs (chapter 7) or Zintl's educated expatriates (chapter 6) who had made the decision to return to Syria and to invest in the status quo (just as some of those remaining in exile had a stake in regime change). 'Ulama in the main cities remained inactive and some more loyalist ones, such as al-Buti, cautioned Syrians against *fitna* encouraged by outsiders whose intentions and backgrounds were unknown, thus echoing the regime's narrative of a foreign conspiracy. Some social forces remained ambivalent: the tribes were split, for and against the regime. Concessions to the Kurds, together with regime links to Iraqi Kurdish leaders, kept the Kurds on the sidelines. Even a debilitated Ba'th Party had deeper roots in the state establishment and society than did ruling parties in other Arab states. The regime sought to promote itself as a protector of order and to exploit citizens' fear of civil war by referring to the civil war accompanying Iraq's "democratization" or by drawing parallels to the 1980s Syrian insurrection, although its inability to maintain order called its claims into question. The regime also played on fear of foreign interference and raised the Palestine issue by organizing demonstrations on the Golan Heights, although there was as yet no obvious foreign threat, with Israel lying low.

After the start of the uprising, Asad deviated from his previous "authoritarian upgrading" pattern, yet his decade of modernizing (though piecemeal) reforms and legitimizing discourse, resonating at the time with foreign and local reformers as well as with the pro-Palestinian "Arab street," had a legacy that served him well once the uprising began. His image as a closet reformer helped his regime to surmount both domestic and international observers' "shock" at the post-2011 military solution employed against civilian protesters, and, eventually, to maintain his power grip on Syria. There was only a half-hearted continuity of authoritarian upgrading measures during the first year of the uprising—for example, the too-little-too-late reforms such as the parties law, the substitution of emergency law by antiterror legislation, or the new constitution confirmed by "popular" referendum in spring 2012. Yet these policy measures sufficed to buy time, not only with mostly urban, often minority constituencies who were unwilling to give up their belief in slow but steady reforms. Also, Western observers at first restrained their reaction, calling for a continuation of the promised reforms and an end to the security solution. The peaceful protesters thus failed to make a breakthrough during the first months of the uprising, and with the progressing of the crisis and the ensuing spiral of violence, a stalemate on both domestic and international levels set in.

However, there was one element of Asad's authoritarian upgrading that lived on, though in a twisted form, and that shaped the tangent of the uprising in a decisive way. The nationalist discourse of a "resistance front" against Israel was continued and reinforced by a renewed anti-imperialist stance against foreign interference. But most important, the regime also adopted the sloganeering of pro-Western Arab regimes, that of a "fight against terrorism," which not only resonated particularly well with the regime's Russian ally but convinced many in the West that intervention would benefit Islamic terrorism. This demonizing of the opposition, however, made a political solution all the harder.

Stalemate II: The Phase of Armed Insurgency and Sectarian Civil War

The immediate origin of the descent into civil war was the regime's "security solution" to the challenge of civil resistance and its refusal to concede democratization as a legitimate way out of the crisis or to accept the opposition as a legitimate partner. Later, however, opposition groups also became complicit in the escalation of violence. The regime, in turn, responded by escalating its violence to the level of a "military solution."

While, earlier in the uprising, the regime sought to limit its response to those who participated in protests, its violence later turned to indiscriminate striking of whole neighborhoods in small towns and suburbs to deter spread of the uprising to the main cities. The military solution was also meant to prevent a Libya-like scenario in which parts of the country fell into opposition hands, thus providing an opening for foreign intervention. It appears, too, to have been a response to the killing of more than a hundred regime solders and police in the Islamist stronghold of Jisr al-Shaghour in June 2011. The regime's escalation provoked defections from the army and the creation of the Free Syrian Army in summer 2011, while also generating a desire for revenge and gradually legitimizing the notion of armed self-defense among the mostly Sunni opposition. This interaction drove a deepening militarization of the conflict. The regime may have welcomed a militarized opposition as an enemy easier to deal with than mass civil protest.

When the opposition realized that nonviolence would not oust the regime and that foreign intervention was not coming, it had to choose between armed struggle for victory and a negotiated political settlement. The latter was rejected, not only because the opposition was outraged at the killings committed by the government and believed that the government's offers of dialogue were insincere, but also because opposition activists believed that they could only be safe if the regime was removed, since, if it survived, it would certainly seek revenge. On its side, the regime believed that an opposition ready to call for an intervention by Syria's "imperialist" enemies was a fifth column that needed to be eliminated.

Opting for an "all-or-nothing" solution, militant insurgents chose to intensify the conflict in order to turn the main cities against the regime.

Antiregime fighters—since summer 2012 increasingly also of an international jihadist type—brought the front line into Aleppo. Their bombings and armed infiltrations into the big cities also served to show that the regime could not guarantee stability. On the regime's side, the use of heavy weaponry was to signal to Syrians that "armed terrorist groups" should not be tolerated in their midst. When one level of violence failed to stop the uprising, the regime's steady escalation—to tanks, fighter planes, missiles, barrel bombs, and finally chemical weapons—showed that it was ready to overstep all redlines. Numbers of internally displaced people and refugees skyrocketed as the initially uninvolved civilian population sought to flee bombardment, shoot-outs, and a rapidly deteriorating food and medical situation on the ground, thus increasingly leaving the field to the armed factions and accelerating the dynamics from civil resistance to armed struggle.

In parallel to the increase in violence came a sectarianization of the conflict. The weakening of secular Ba'thism as an ideology over the years, the debilitation of the party organization that used to cut across sectarian divisions in villages and neighborhoods, and the regime's reneging on the populist social contract during the first decade of the 2000s meant that it had no ability (aside from co-optation of privileged groups through patronage) to mobilize in its defense supporters on a broader basis (as it had in the 1980s). The regime therefore gauged that, by rallying the minorities and its 'Alawite base and by painting the opposition as radical Islamist jihadists, it could still survive. Despite the high risks for a minority regime of sectarianizing the conflict, the regime chose to frame it as a choice between stability and social peace or terrorists' violence and chaos. Particularly the regime's recruitment and use of mostly 'Alawite militias (shabbiha) fostered sectarianism. The government's success in infusing the conflict with a strong sectarian dimension and in securing the support of minorities, who feared retribution if the regime fell, further mobilized Sunnis against it. While the opposition strategy was initially to emphasize its nonsectarian, secular democratic character in order not to scare secularists or the West and to mobilize maximum civil resistance, once this strategy failed to dislodge the regime, parts of it also had an incentive to sectarianize the conflict. Calculating that a regime of minorities would be vulnerable to a 70 percent Sunni majority, if the latter could be mobilized, this part of the opposition's sectarian discourses sought to turn the whole of the majority community against the minority in power.[10]

This development opened the door to jihadists, including al-Qaida, who saw sectarianizing and militarizing Syria as a perfect arena in which to regain the momentum they had lost when the so-called Arab Spring at first seemed to produce democratic transitions through nonviolent means. Some of them were veterans of the Muslim Brotherhood–led uprising in the early 1980s, members of the radical *talia al-muqatila* (Fighting Vanguard) of the Islamic revolution, who had, after the insurgency in Syria was repressed, morphed into transnational jihadists and, for instance, later played a role in the formation of al-Qaida (Lefèvre 2013, 137–50). Now, often funded and armed by Gulf donors, they returned to Syria and joined other Arab jihadist fighters. Their message was also spread by the Salafi and jihadi networks on the Internet, on satellite TV, and through Arab Gulf-funded preachers depicting the Syrian struggle in sectarian terms. The shift of power within the opposition to Islamist hard-liners deepened the polarization of the conflict.

The sectarian dynamic did not, of course, come out of nowhere: it goes back to the original 1960s alliance against the minoritarian-rural-based Ba'th regime of urban merchants, landlords, and the Muslim Brotherhood that had never accepted the legitimacy of the regime. It was reinforced by the 1980s Muslim Brothers' insurgency, in which terrorist violence against 'Alawites by the insurgents was matched by massive regime violence, notably at Hama. The desire for retribution for these old wrongs by the Islamists and a renewed minority complex by the 'Alawites rapidly resurfaced with the uprising. This time, however, the Islamist challenge was much more potent than in the 1980s. The beginning of the 2000s had seen the further spread of Islamist opinion, particularly to the formerly untouched *rif* (countryside). Asad's neglect of the rural areas provided

---

10. Yet secular Sunnis were deterred by the sectarianization, and also Kurds (7–10 percent of the population) would not be mobilized by this because their ethnic identity was more important to them than their religious identity.

Islamist opposition with a mobilizable mass base they had lacked in the 1980s when the peasantry remained incorporated into the regime via party, peasant union, and cooperative.

After mid-2012, the regime lost control over wide parts of the north and east of the country, but this lack of control did not decisively tilt the power balance toward the insurgents. In these areas, predatory practices, criminal activity, and warlordism became commonplace, and conflicts among antiregime factions, often along moderate-radical Islamic lines and Kurds versus jihadis, eventually broke out. The externally led opposition attempted to restore order by setting up new municipal and regional councils responsible for the provision of health and education, as well as courts, made up of clerics and "free" lawyers, and a substitute police force. For example, the Muslim Brotherhood, dominant in the Syrian National Council, used foreign funding to build clientalist links to communities and armed groups in "liberated" areas as well as in refugee camps. But rival networks were established by the jihadists, such as Jabhat al-Nusra, which controlled areas in the north and east, and by the Kurdistan Workers Party (PKK)–linked Kurdish Democratic Union Party (PYD) in Kurdish areas. As Sunni Islamists consolidated control of eastern regions bordering Iraq, Kurds gained control of northern regions bordering compatriots in Iraq and Turkey, and Asad's troops were confined to controlling a western rump state running from Damascus to the Lattakia heartland of the 'Alawites—with strategic areas sectarian-cleansed of distrusted "others"— a de facto Somaliazation appeared more likely than victory for either side (Dukhan 2013).

Finally, the stalemate at a high level of violence that the insurgency had reached by mid-2012 was in good part owing to the (in)action of external actors fishing in troubled waters. First, early in the conflict the West's discourse of democratization (and financial support for dissidents) had helped generate exile groups that promoted the uprising; the discourse of humanitarian intervention encouraged the opposition to think that the regime could not bring the full force of its repressive capabilities against protestors without provoking foreign intervention, an expectation that kept alive both their resistance and their unwillingness to compromise. Once the uprising began, Turkey, once an Asad ally, played a crucial role in organizing and hosting the opposition, first in the form of the Syrian National Council, then as the Free Syrian Army, and later as the Syrian National Coalition. Funders from the Gulf states, notably Saudis and Qataris, funded and armed the insurgents.

By mid-2011 the regime, isolated from the West and under Western sanctions, appeared to be an international pariah. Western sanctions helped debilitate the regime's capacity to fund state institutions and to maintain its control over wide swaths of the country. However, the West proved unwilling to intervene militarily, even after the usage of chemical weapons in August 2013 marked the clear overstepping of the US president's announced redline, with intervention adverted by a Russian-brokered deal signed to destroy the Syrian regime's chemical weapons arsenal. Furthermore, the West did not provide the opposition with the high-quality weaponry that might turn the battle in its favor for fear these would fall into the hands of jihadists. Yet, as the West raised the discourse of the international criminal court, regime elites realized that, their bridges burned, there was no way back: they would have to stick together and do whatever it took to win.

In parallel, Russia and China, antagonized by the West's use of a UN humanitarian resolution to promote regime change at their expense in Libya in early 2011, moved to protect Syria from a similar scenario. Iran's support for the regime was especially important: it provided crucial financial resources, assistance in electronic warfare, and support in the formation and training of pro-regime militias on the model of the revolutionary guard. At Iran's urging, Iraq provided Syria with cheap oil and declined to isolate Asad's regime. Likewise, by early 2013, Hezbollah stepped in, notably also with special forces in the strategically important town of al-Quseir, to help defend the route between regime-controlled coastal provinces and Damascus. The regime's long practice, under Hafiz and continued by his son, of maximizing and balancing among a multitude of external alliances had positioned it to avoid isolation and to secure the resources to survive the uprising far longer than anyone would have anticipated. The early 2000s narrative of West-centric modernizing reforms had just been an interlude, and Asad later was able to build upon other alliances he had kept on a low flame throughout the decade.

In this sense the regime transited from its original tangent of "authoritarian upgrading" to what might be called "authoritarian persistence at all costs"—a change of direction that, to some extent, had been made possible by its earlier fairly successful politics of authoritarian upgrading but was not easily reversible.

Conclusion

The fragile, multicommunal, artificial Syrian state created by post–World War I Western imperialism had been held together for half a century by a flawed authoritarianism. While the Ba'th regime had constructed the capacity, in organizational and patronage terms, to incorporate a near-majority constituency when the population was eight or ten million, as it grew past twenty million increased numbers were left unincorporated and potentially mobilizable by opposition forces. Once, under the pressure of the uprising, the variegated cement that had held the state together— the regime's monopoly of coercion, its modicum of legitimacy, its cross-sectarian coalition—dissolved, deep cultural and identity fault lines were exposed, burst the bounds of the regime, and even threatened to put the territorial state at risk.

As of the time of writing, there appeared no obvious way out of the crisis. Stalemate was built into the structural situation, notably by the cohesion of the regime and the fragmentation of its opponents, with neither, however, able to defeat the other. Hard-liners came to dominate on both sides, each more interested in destroying the other than in a peaceful solution. From the beginning, the opposition challenged the vital interests of regime elites, who were, in turn, prepared to resort to extreme violence to turn back the threat. Unable to prevail at one level of conflict, each side further escalated the level of violence. There were no credible soft-liners on either side that might come together to marginalize the hard-liners, break the upward spiral of violence, and broker a compromise solution or transition. Quickly, too much blood was spilled by the regime while the opposition went from calling for international intervention to threatening revenge on 'Alawites, each delegitimizing the other. As the security dilemma deepened, neither could trust the other not to seek revenge if one let down their guard, a combustible situation exploited by ever more radical Islamist forces, such as ISIS (Islamic State of Iraq and Greater Syria), who were quickly advancing in 2013 and 2014. At the international level, a renewed Cold War scenario of US-Russian rivalry blocked a breakthrough by either side on the ground or a diplomatic resolution favoring one side over the other; at the regional level the Iran/Hezbollah and the Saudi/Qatari camps also checkmated each other. Both sides still harbored the hope of victory, particularly if their external patrons could be brought to provide them with increased levels of support; and their international patrons, despite ostensibly agreeing on the need for a political solution, were not making their support contingent on their clients' willingness to negotiate in good faith. Three years into the uprising, protracted conflict had become normalized and ever more radical elements have prevailed.

References

About the Contributors

Index

References

ABSP (Arab Bath Socialist Party). 1985. *Taqarir al-mutamar al-qutri al-thamin wa muqarraratihi* [Reports and resolutions of the 8th Regional Congress], 35–58. Damascus: ABSP.

———. 1990. *Taqarir al-mutamar al-qutri al-tassia wa muqarraratihi* [Reports and resolutions of the 9th Regional Congress]. Damascus: ABSP.

Ababsa, Myriam. 2001. "Les Mausolées Invisibles: Raqqa Ville de Pèlerinage Chiite ou Pôle Étatique en Jazîra Syrienne?" *Les Annales de Géographie*, 647–63. Paris: Armand Collin.

———. 2005a. *Privatisation in Syria: State Farms and the Case of the Euphrates Project*. European University Institute, Robert Schuman Centre for Advanced Studies working paper series. http://www.iue.it/RSCAS/WP-Texts /05_02.pdf.

———. 2005b. "Significations Territoriales et Appropriations Conflictuelles des Mausolées Chiites de Raqqa (Syrie)." In *Les Pélerinages au Maghreb et au Moyen Orient: Espaces Publics, Espaces du Public*, edited by Sylvia Chiffoleau and Anna Madoeuf. Beirut: IFPO (Presses de l'Institut français du Proche-Orient).

———. 2009. *Raqqa: Territoires et pratiques sociales d'une ville syrienne*. Beirut: IFPO (Presses de l'Institut français du Proche-Orient).

———. 2010. "Agrarian Counter-Reform in Syria." In *Agriculture and Reform in Syria*, edited by Raymond Hinnebusch. St. Andrews, Scotland: St. Andrews Papers on Contemporary Syria, distributed by Lynne Rienner Publishers.

Ababsa-Al-Husseini, Myriam. 2002. "Mise en valeur agricole et contrôle politique de la vallée de l'Euphrate (1865–1946): étude des relations État, nomades et citadins dans le caza de Raqqa." *Bulletin d'Etudes Orientales* 53–54:459–88. Damascus: IFEAD.

Abboud, Samer. 2009. "The Transition Paradigm and the Case of Syria." In *Syria and the Transition Paradigm*, Samer Abboud and Ferdinand Arslanian. St.

Andrews, Scotland: St. Andrews Papers on Contemporary Syria, distributed by Lynne Rienner Publishers.

———. 2010. "Syrian Trade Policy." In *Syrian Foreign Trade and Economic Reform*, Samer Abboud and Salam Said. St. Andrews, Scotland: St. Andrews Papers on Contemporary Syria, distributed by Lynne Rienner Publishers.

Adler, Nancy J. 1981. "Re-Entry: Managing Cross-Cultural Transitions." *Group and Organization Studies* 6, no. 3:341–56.

Aita, Samir. 2010a. "Al-zamah al-ijtimaeeah wa al-takhteet al-iqleemee fi al-mantaqah al-sharqeeah" [The social crisis and territorial planning in the eastern region]. Lecture at Syrian Economic Society, Damascus, Syria, Jan. 12.

———. 2010b. "Hal hunak ichkalia ziraiat fi surya?" [Is there a problem with agriculture in Syria?]. http://annidaa.org/modules/news/article.php?storyid=3873.

Ajemian, Pete. 2008. "Resistance Beyond Time and Space: Hizbullah's Media Campaigns." *Arab Media and Society* 5 (Spring).

Al-Ali, Nadje. 2004. *The Relationship between Migration within and from the Middle East and North-Africa and Pro-Poor Policies*. A Report by the Institute of Arab and Islamic Studies, University of Exeter for the Department for International Development. https://eprints.soas.ac.uk/4888/2/migrationMENAreport-1.

———. 2007. "Iraqi Women in Diasporic Spaces: Political Mobilization, Gender and Citizenship." *Revue des mondes musulmans et de la Méditerranée* 117–18:137–53.

Bamyeh, Mohammad. 2011. "Anarchist, Liberal, and Authoritarian Enlightenments: Notes from the Arab Spring." July 30. www.jadaliyya.com.

Bauer, Susanne. 1990. *The Euphrates Development Scheme in Syria. Social Impact, Production, Organisation and Linkages*. Berlin: German Development Institute.

Beetham, David. 1991. *The Legitimation of Power*. Basingstoke, UK: Macmillan.

Bibi, Sami, and Mustafa K. Nabli. 2010. "Equity and Inequality in the Arab Region." *Policy Research Report*, no. 33, Economic Research Forum, Feb.

Böttcher, Annabelle. 1997. "Le Ministère des Waqfs." *Monde Arabe: Maghreb/Machrek* 158:18–30.

Bourdieu, Pierre. 1997. *Outline of a Theory of Practice*. Cambridge, UK: Cambridge Univ. Press.

Brown, Oli, and Alec Crawford. 2009. *Rising Temperatures, Rising Tensions: Climate Change and the Risk of Violent Conflict in the Middle East.* Winnipeg, Canada: International Institute for Sustainable Development.

Brumberg, Daniel. 2002. "The Trap of Liberalized Autocracy." *Journal of Democracy* 13, no. 4:56–68.

Brun, Catherine. 2001. "Reterritorializing the Relationship between People and Place in Refugee Studies." *Geografiska Annaler* 83, no. 1:15–25.

Bush, R., ed. 2002. *Counter-Revolution in Egypt's Countryside: Land and Farmers in the Era of Economic Reform.* London: Zed Books.

Chatelard, Géraldine. 2005. "L'émigration des Irakiens de la guerre du Golfe à la guerre d'Irak (1990–2003)." In *Mondes en mouvements. Migrants et migrations au Moyen-Orient au tournant du XXIe siècle*, edited by H. Jaber and F. Métral, 113–55. Beirut: IFPO (Presses de l'Institut français du Proche-Orient).

Chehab, Zaki. 2007. *Inside Hamas: The Untold Story of Militants, Martyrs and Spies.* New York: Tauris.

Chiffoleau, Sylvia, ed. 2006. "La Syrie au Quotidien: Cultures et Pratiques du Changement." *Revue des Mondes Musulmans et de la Mediterranée* (REMMM) 115–16.

Clerc, Valérie. 2006. "Beyrouth: l'influence du foncier et des plans d'urbanisme sur la formation des quartiers irréguliers de la banlieue sud." *Mappemonde* 84, no. 4.

Cornand, Jocelyne. 1994. *L'entrepreneur et l'État en Syrie: Le Secteur Privé du Textile à Alep.* Paris: Harmattan.

Dawisha, Adeed. 1978. "Syria under Asad, 1970–1978: The Centres of Power." *Government and Opposition* 13, no. 3.

DIS and ACCORD (Danish Immigration Service and Austrian Center of Country of Origin and Asylum Research and Documentation). 2010. "Human Rights Issues Concerning Kurds in Syria." http://www.nyidanmark.dk/NR/rdonlyres/FF03AB63-10A5-4467-A038-20FE46B74CE8/0/Syrienrapport2010pdf.pdf.

Donker, Teije Hidde. 2010. "Enduring Ambiguity: Sunni Community–Syrian Regime Dynamics." *Mediterranean Politics* 15, no. 3:435–52.

Doraï, Mohamed Kamel. 2009. "L'exil irakien à Damas. Modes d'insertion urbaine et reconfiguration des réseaux migratoires." *EchoGéo*, no. 8. http://echogeo.revues.org/index10976.html.

Drieskens, Barbara, and Franck Mermier. 2007. "Introduction: Towards New Cosmopolitism." In *Cities of the South. Citizenship and Exclusion in the*

Twenty-first Century, edited by Barbara Drieskens, Franck Mermier, and Heiko Wimmen, 10–19. London: Saqi.

Droz-Vincent, Philippe. 2001. "Syrie: La Nouvelle Generation au Pouvoir." *Monde Arabe: Maghreb-Machrek* 173:14–38.

———. 2004. *Moyen Orient: Pouvoirs Autoritaires, Sociétés Bloquées.* Paris: Presses Universitaires de France.

Drysdale, Alasdair. 1979. "Ethnicity in the Syrian Officer Corps: A Conceptualization." *Civilisations* 29, no. 3–4:359–73.

Dukhan, Haian. 2103. "Syria and the Risk of Somalisation." *Open Democracy.* www.opendemocracy.net/author/haian-dukhan.

Dupret, Baudoin, Zouhair Ghazzal, Youssef Courbage, and Mohammed al-Dbiyat, eds. 2007. *La Syrie au Présent: Reflets d'une Société.* Arles, France: Actes Sud.

FAO. 2008. *Drought Appeal 2008.* http://www.fao.org/emergencies/tce-appfund /tce-appeals/appeals/emergency-detail0/en/item/7857/icode/?uidf=6095.

Fábos, Anita, and G. Kibreab. 2007. "Urban Refugees: Introduction." *Refuge* 24, no. 1:3–10.

Fadil, Mahmoud Abdel. 2004. "Squatter and Slum Areas in Syria: The Face of New Urban Poverty." In *Macroeconomic Policies for Poverty Reduction: The Case of Syria,* 149–54. Damascus: UNDP.

Faist, Thomas. 2000. *The Volume and Dynamics of International Migration and Transnational Social Spaces.* Oxford, UK: Clarendon Press.

Fargues, Philippe. 2009. Introduction to *CARIM Mediterranean Migration Report, 2008–2009.* Robert Schuman Centre for Advanced Studies, San Domenico di Fiesole (FI), 19–38. Fiesole, Italy: European Univ. Institute.

Foster, Darren. 2006. "Syria's Delicate Balancing Act." *World Dispatches,* Sept. 22. www.pbs.org/frontlineworld.

Gelvin, James. 1997. "The Other Arab Nationalism: Syrian/Arab Populism in Its Historical and International Contexts." In *Rethinking Nationalism in the Arab Middle East,* edited by James Jankowski and Israel Gershoni. New York: Columbia Univ. Press.

George, Alan. 2003. *Syria: Neither Bread nor Freedom.* New York: Zed Books.

Ghadbian, Najib. 2001. "The New Asad: Dynamics of Continuity and Change in Syria." *Middle East Journal* 55, no. 4 (Autumn): 624–41.

———. 2006. *Addawla al-Assadiyya al-Thaniyya: Bashar al-Asad wal Furas al-Dhai`a* [The second Asad regime: Bashar of lost opportunities]. Jeddah, Saudi Arabia: Dar al-Rayyah.

Ghazzal, Zoheir, et al. 2009. "Civil Law and the Omnipotence of the Syrian State." In *Demystifying Syria*, edited by F. H. Lawson. Beirut: Saqi, in association with London Middle East Institute at SOAS, Univ. of London.

Glasser, Bradley Louis. 2001. *Economic Development and Political Reform: The Impact of External Capital on the Middle East.* Cheltenham, UK: Edward Elgar.

Guazzone, Laura, and Daniela Pioppi. 2009. *The Arab State and Neo-liberal Globalization: The Restructuring of the State in the Middle East.* Reading, UK: Ithaca Press.

Gunning, Jeroen. 2007. *Hamas in Politics: Democracy, Religion, Violence.* London: Hurst and Co.

al-Habash, Muhammad. 2005. *Dirasa fiqhiyya liltahaffuthatal-lati wadaaha al-marsum al-tashri liam 2002 ala ittifaqiyyat mukafahat kull ashkal al-tamyiz didd al-mara.* [An Islamic jurisprudence study of the reservations laid by the 2002 legislative decree on the Cedaw]. Damascus: markaz al-dirasat al-islamiyya and al-haya al-suriyya li-shuun al-mara.

Haddad, Bassam. 2007. "Sharks and Dinosaurs: State-Business Relations in Syria." *Global Studies Review* 3, no. 2 (Summer).

————. 2011. "Why Syria Is Not Next—So Far." Mar. 9. http://www.jadaliyya.com /pages/index/844/why-syria-is-not-next-.-.-.-so-far_with-arabic-translation-.

————. 2012. *Business Networks in Syria: The Political Economy of Authoritarian Resilience.* Stanford, CA: Stanford Univ. Press.

al-Haj Saleh, Yassin. 2011. "A Tense Syria in a Changing Arab World." In *Perspectives, Special Issue: People's Power—The Arab World in Revolt.* May 2. Beirut: Heinrich Böll Foundation.

Hannoyer, J. 1982. *Campagnes et pouvoirs en Syrie, l'étude de Deir ez Zor.* Dissertation, École des Hautes Études en Sciences Sociale, Paris.

Heck, Paul L. N.d. *Religious Renewal in Syria—The Case of Muhammad Al-Habash.* Damascus: dar at-tajdid.

Hemmer, Christopher. 2003. "I Told You So: Syria, Oslo and the Al-Aqsa Intifada." *Middle East Policy* 10, no. 3 (Sept.): 121–35.

Heydemann, Steven. 2004. *Networks of Privilege in the Middle East: The Politics of Economic Reform Revisited.* New York: Palgrave Macmillan.

————. 2007. *Upgrading Authoritarianism in the Arab World.* Analysis Paper no. 13. Washington, DC: Saban Center for Middle East Policy at the Brookings Institution.

Heydemann, Steven, and Reinoud Leenders. 2011. "Authoritarian Learning and Authoritarian Resilience: Regime Responses to the 'Arab Awakening.'" *Globalizations* 8, no. 5:647–53.

Hinnebusch, Raymond. 1989. *Peasant and Bureaucracy in Bathist Syria. The Political Economy of Rural Development.* Boulder, CO: Westview Press.

———. 1990. *Authoritarian Power and State Formation in Bathist Syria; Army, Party and Peasant.* Boulder, CO: Westview Press.

———. 1995. "Syria: The Politics of Peace and Regime Survival." *Middle East Policy* 3, no. 4:74–87.

———. 2001. *Syria. Revolution from Above.* London: Routledge.

———. 2006. "Authoritarian Persistence, Democratization Theory and the Middle East: An Overview and Critique." *Democratization* 13, no. 3 (June).

———. 2008. "Modern Syrian Politics." *History Compass* 6, no. 1:263–85.

———. 2009a. "The Political Economy of Populist Authoritarianism." In *The State and the Political Economy of Reform in Syria*, Raymond Hinnebusch and Søren Schmidt. St. Andrews, Scotland: St. Andrews Papers on Contemporary Syria, distributed by Lynne Rienner Publishers.

———. 2009b. "Syrian Foreign Policy under Bashar al-Asad." *Ortadoğu Etütleri* 1, no. 1 (July).

———. 2010. "Syria under Bashar: Between Economic Reform and Nationalist Realpolitik." In *Syrian Foreign Policy and the United States: From Bush to Obama*, Raymond Hinnebusch, Marwan J. Kabalan, Bassma Kodmani, and David Lesch. St. Andrews, Scotland: St. Andrew Papers on Contemporary Syria, distributed by Lynne Rienner Publishers.

Hroub, Khaled. 2009. "The Arab System after Gaza." *openDemocracy*, Jan. 27. www.opendemocracy.net.

———. 2010. *Hamas. A Beginner's Guide.* London: Pluto Press.

Hsu, Carolyn L. 2007. *Creating Market Socialism: How Ordinary People Are Shaping Class and Status in China.* Durham, NC: Duke Univ. Press.

Al-Husseini, Jalal, and Aude Signoles. 2009. "Construction nationale, territorialité et diasporisation: le cas palestinien." *Maghreb-Machrek* 199 (Spring): 23–42.

Huuhtanen, Heidi. 2008. *Building a Strong State: The Influence of External Security and Fiscal Environment on Syrian Authoritarianism.* PhD thesis, Univ. of Durham, UK.

ICG (International Crisis Group). 2008. *Failed Responsibility: Iraqi Refugees in Syria, Jordan and Lebanon.* Middle East Report no. 77, July 10. http://www.crisisgroup.org/home/index.cfm?id=5563&l=1.

————. 2009. *Reshuffling the Cards: Syria's Evolving Strategy (I)*. Middle East Report no. 92, Dec. 14.

————. 2011. *Popular Protest in North Africa and the Middle East (VI): The Syrian People's Slow Motion Revolution*. Middle East Report no. 108, July 6.

IDMC (Internal Displacement Monitoring Centre). 2007. *Syria: Forty Years On, People Displaced from the Golan Remain in Waiting*. Oct. 31. Geneva: IDMC.

IMF (International Monetary Fund) 2009. *Syrian Arab Republic: 2008 Article IV Consultation—Staff Report; Staff Statement; Public Information Notice on the Executive Board Discussion; and Statement by the Executive Director for the Syrian Arab Republic*. IMF Country Report No. 09/55. Washington, DC: IMF.

Ismael, Salwa. 2006. "Authoritarian Civilities and Syria's Stalled Political Transition." Paper presented at the American Political Science Association meeting, Philadelphia, Aug. 31–Sept. 3.

————. 2009. "Changing Social Structure, Shifting Alliances and Authoritarianism in Syria." In *Demystifying Syria*, edited by F. H. Lawson. Beirut: Saqi, in association with London Middle East Institute at SOAS, Univ. of London.

Itri, M. 2006. *Qanun al-ahwal ash-shakhsiyya*. [The personal status law—issued by legislative decree no. 59, 1953, amended by law 43, 1975, with some legal interpretations issued by the Syrian High Court]. Damascus: Muassasat al-Nouri.

Kabbani, Nader. 2009. "Why Young Syrians Prefer Public Sector Jobs." *Middle East Youth Initiative Policy Outlook*, Mar. 18, 1–8.

Kagan, M. 2007. "Legal Recognition in the Urban South: Formal v. *de facto* Refugee Status." *Refuge* 24, no. 1:11–26.

Kassem, Maye. 2004. *Egyptian Politics: The Dynamics of Authoritarian Rule*. Boulder, CO: Lynne Rienner Publishers.

Kawakibi, Salam. 2009. "Syria's Mediterranean Policy." In *Mediterranean Politics from Above and Below*, edited by Isabel Schäfer and Jean-Robert Henry, 237–50. Baden-Baden, Germany: Nomos.

Khader, B. 1984. *La question agraire dans les pays arabes. Le cas de la Syrie*. Louvain, Belgium: ciaco éditeur.

Khalaf, S. 1981. *Family, Village and Political Party: Articulation of Social Change in Contemporary Rural Syria*. PhD diss., Univ. of California at Los Angeles.

Khatib, Line. 2011. *Islamic Revivalism in Syria: The Rise and Fall of Bathist Secularism*. London: Routledge.

King, Stephen. 2009. *The New Authoritarianism in the Middle East and North Africa*. Bloomington: Indiana Univ. Press.

El-Laithy, H., and Abu-Ismail, K. 2005. *Poverty in Syria: 1996–2004. Diagnosis and Pro-Poor Policy Considerations*. United Nations Human Development Program. http://www.undp.org.sy.

Leenders, Reinoud. 2008. "L'adieu aux armes: la politique des réfugiés irakiens et son impact sécuritaire sur la région." *Maghreb-Machrek* 198:93–122.

Leenders, Reinoud, and Steven Heydemann. 2012. "Popular Mobilization in Syria: Opportunity and Threat, and the Social Networks of the Early Risers." *Mediterranean Politics* 17, no. 2:139–59.

Lefèvre, Raphael. 2013. *Ashes of Hama: The Muslim Brotherhood in Syria*. London: Hurst.

Lesch, David. 2005. *The New Lion of Damascus: Bashar al-Asad and Modern Syria*. New Haven: Yale Univ. Press.

———. 2012. *Syria: The Fall of the House of Assad*. New Haven: Yale Univ. Press.

Leverett, Flynt. 2005. *Inheriting Syria: Bashar's Trial by Fire*. Washington, DC: Brookings Institution Press.

Lewis, Norman. 1987. *Nomads and Settlers in Syria and Jordan, 1800–1980*. London: Cambridge Univ. Press.

Lipset, Seymour. 1960. *Political Man*. New York: Doubleday.

Lobmeyer, Hans Gunter. 1994. "Al-dimqratiyya hiyya al-Hall? The Syrian Opposition at the End of the Asad Era." In *Contemporary Syria: Liberalization between Cold War and Cold Peace*, edited by Eberhard Kienle. London: British Academic Press.

Lund, Aaron. 2013. "The Baath Party and the War in Syria: An Interview with Sami Moubayed." *Carnegie Endowment*, no. 17 (Nov.). http://carnegieendowment.org/syriaincrisis/?fa=53490&reloadFlag=1.

Lust-Okar, Ellen. 2004. "Divided They Rule: The Management and Manipulation of Political Opposition." *Comparative Politics* 36, no. 2.

———. 2006. "Reform in Syria: Steering between the Chinese Model and Regime Change." *Carnegie Endowment*, no. 69 (July).

Maktabi, Rania. 2006. "På nett for syriske kvinner" [On the net for Syrian women]. *Klassekampen*, Dec. 27.

———. 2010. "Gender, Family Law and Citizenship in Syria." *Citizenship Studies* 4, no. 5.

Malkki, Liisa. 1995. "Refugees and Exile: From Refugee Studies to the National Order of Things." *Annual Review of Anthropology* 24:495–523.

Mawed, Hamad Said. 2006. *Mukhayyam al-Yarmouk* [The Yarmouk camp]. Damascus: Dâr al-Shajara.

Mayer, Ann Elizabeth. 2003. "Islamic Law as a Core for Political Law: The Withering of an Islamist Illusion." In *Shaping the Islamic Reformation*, edited by B. A. Roberson. London: Frank Cass.

Mervin, Sabrina. 1996. "Sayyida Zaynab: Bainlieu de Damas où Nouvelle Ville Sainte Chiite?" *Cahiers d'Etudes sur La Mediterranée Orientale et le Monde Turco-Iranien* 22:149–62.

———. 2002. "Quelques Jalons pour une Histoire du Raprochement (Taqrîb) des Alaouites vers le Chiisme." In *Islamstudien Ohne Ende: Festschrift fur Werner Ende*, edited by Rainer Brunner, Monika Gronke, Jens Laut, and Ulrich Rebstock. Wurzburg, Germany: Ergon Verlag.

Meyer, Günter. 1990. "Rural Development and Migration in Northeast Syria." In *Anthropology and Development in North Africa and the Middle East*, edited by P. Salem, M. Murdock, and S. M. Horowitz. New York: Westview Press.

Middle East Watch. 1991. *Syria Unmasked: The Suppression of Human Rights by the Asad Regime*. New Haven: Yale Univ. Press.

Milton-Edwards, Beverley, and Stephen Farrell. 2010. *Hamas: The Islamic Resistance Movement*. Cambridge, UK: Polity Press.

Ministry of Irrigation. 2001. *Statistics of the General Administration for the Development of the Euphrates Basin (GADEB)*. May. Damascus: Ministry of Irrigation.

Moors, Annelies. 1999. "Debating Islamic Family Law: Legal Texts and Social Practice." In *Social History of Women and Gender in the Modern Middle East*, edited by Margaret Meriwether and Judith E. Tucker, 141–75. Boulder, CO: Westview Press.

Moubayed, Sami. 2005. "Syria: Reform or Repair?" Carnegie Endowment for Peace, *Arab Reform Bulletin* 3, no. 6 (July). http://www.carnegieendowment.org.arb.

Mouffe, Chantal. 2005. *The Return of the Political*. London: Verso.

Napolitano, Valentina. 2012–13. "La mobilisation des réfugiés palestiniens dans le sillage de la 'évolution' syrienne: s'engager sous contrainte" [Palestinian mobilization in the frame of the Syrian "Revolution": Engaging under constraint]. *Cultures & Conflicts* 87 (Winter): 119–37.

———. 2013. "Hamas and the Syrian Revolution: A Difficult Choice." *Middle East Policy* 20, no. 3 (Fall): 73–85.

Nasr, Seyyed Vali. 2006. *The Shia Revival*. New York: Norton.

Nejmeh, Elias. 2003. *"Al-siyaasat al-maleeah fi suryeeah"* [Finance Policy in Syria]. Lecture at Syrian Economic Society, Damascus, Syria, Oct. 23.

Noe, Nicholas, ed. 2007. *Voice of Hezbollah: The Statements of Sayyed Hassan Nasrallah*. London: Verso.

Nome, Frida. 2006. *Strained Harmony—Religious Diversity in Syria*. A Report for the Norwegian Ministry of Foreign Affairs. Oslo: International Peace Research Institute.

OBG (Oxford Business Group). 2003. *Syria Report*. Vol. 40.

OCHA (Office for the Coordination of Humanitarian Affairs). 2009. *Syria Drought Response Plan*. http://www.un.org.sy/Syria_Drought_Response_Plan_2009.pdf

———. 2010. *Syria Drought Response Plan, 2009–2010, Mid-Term Review*. http://www.unocha.org/cap/appeals/syria-drought-response-plan-2009-2010.

Pace, Joe. 2005. "Interview with Ayman Abdel Nour, Editor-in-Chief of 'All-4Syria.'" *Syria.comment*, July 21. www.joshualandis.com/.

Pace, Joe, and Joshua Landis. 2009. "The Syrian Opposition: The Struggle for Unity and Relevance, 2003–2008." In *Demystifying Syria*, edited by Fred H. Lawson. Beirut: Saqi in association with London Middle East Institute at SOAS, Univ. of London.

PECAD (Production Estimates and Crop Assessment Division). 2008. "SYRIA: Wheat Production in 2008/09 Declines Owing to Season-Long Drought." http://www.pecad.fas.usda.gov/highlights/2008/05/Syria_may2008.htm.

———. 2010. "Middle East: Yellow Rust Epidemic Affects Regional Wheat Crops." http://www.pecad.fas.usda.gov/highlights/2010/06/Middle%20East.

Perthes, Volker. 1995. *The Political Economy of Syria under Asad*. New York: I. B. Tauris.

———. 2004. *Syria under Bashar al-Asad: Modernization and the Limits of Change*. London: Oxford Univ. Press.

Peteet, Julie. 2005. *Landscape of Hope and Despair. Palestinian Refugee Camps*. Philadelphia: Univ. of Pennsylvania Press.

Petran, Tabitha. 1972. *Syria: Nation of the Modern World*. London: Ernest Benn.

Pierret, Thomas. 2008–9. "Les Cadres de l'Élite Religieuse Sunnite: Espaces, Idées, Organisations et Institutions." *Maghreb-Machrek* 198:7–18.

———. 2009. "Sunni Clergy Politics in the Cities of Bathi Syria." In *Demystifying Syria*, edited by Fred H. Lawson. Beirut: Saqi in association with London Middle East Institute at SOAS, Univ. of London.

———. 2013. *Religion and State in Syria: The Sunni Ulama from Coup to Revolution*. Cambridge, UK: Cambridge Univ. Press.

———. Forthcoming. "Merchant Background, Bourgeois Ethics: The Syrian Ulema and Economic Liberalization." In *Syria under Bashar al-Asad, 2000–2010: Culture, Religion and Society*, edited by Christa Salamandra and Leif Stenberg. Syracuse, NY: Syracuse Univ. Press.

Pierret, Thomas, and Kjetil Selvik. 2009. "Limits of 'Authoritarian Upgrading' in Syria: Private Welfare, Islamic Charities, and the Rise of the Zayd Movement." *International Journal of Middle East Studies* 41, no. 4:595–614.

Poidebard, Antoine. 1927. "La Haute-Djezireh (notes de voyage)." *La Géographie* 47, no. 1:191–206.

Pripstein-Pousousny, Marsha. 2005. "Multiparty Elections in the Arab World: Election Rules and Opposition Responses." In *Authoritarianism in the Middle East: Regimes and Resistance*, edited by Marsha Pripstein-Pousousny and Michelle Penner Angrist. Boulder, CO: Lynne Rienner Publishers.

Rabil, Robert. 2005. "Baath Party Congress in Damascus: How Much Change in Syria?" *Washington Centre Policy Watch #1000*. June 2. Washington, DC: Washington Institute.

Rabo, Annika. 2005. *A Shop of One's Own: Independence and Reputation among Traders in Aleppo*. London: I. B. Tauris.

Raphaeli, Nimrod. 2007. "Syria's Fragile Economy." *Middle East Review of International Affairs* 11, no. 2:34–51.

Rondot, Pierre. 1938) "Les Kurdes." *Cahiers du Centre des Hautes Etudes sur l'Afrique et l'Asie Modernes CHEAM*, no. 1411:1–16.

Salloukh, Bassel F., and Pete W. Moore. 2007. "Struggles under Authoritarianism: Regimes, States, and Professional Associations in the Arab World." *International Journal of Middle East Studies* 39, no. 1:53–76.

Saad-Ghorayeb, Amal. 2002. *Hizbullah: Politics and Religion*, London: Pluto Press.

SAR (Syrian Arab Republic). 2009. *Statistical Abstract*. Damascus: SAR.

SAR/CBS (Syrian Arabic Republic/Central Bureau of Statistics). 2009. *Statistical Yearbook 2009*. Damascus: SAR/CBS.

SAR/MoHE (Syrian Arabic Republic/Ministry of Higher Education). n.d. *Achievements in Higher Education under the Glorious Correctionist Movement, 1970–1996*. Damascus: SAR/MoHE.

Sarkis, Fernández. 2011. "El contrato es la ley: estado, economía y políticas de la responsabilidad en la agricultura Siria." In *Antropología de la Responsabilidad*, edited by Ignasi Terradas Saborit. A Coruña, Spain: Universidade da Coruña.

Sassoon, Joseph. 2009. *The Iraqi Refugees. The New Crisis in the Middle East*. London: I. B. Tauris.

Schedler, Andreas. 2006. *Electoral Authoritarianism: The Dynamics of Unfree Competition*. Boulder, CO: Lynne Rienner Publishers.

Seale, Patrick. 1988. *Asad: The Struggle for the Middle East*. Berkeley: Univ. of California Press.

Seifan Samir. 2008a. "Seeasat tawseegh qaadah al-dakhl fi iqtisaad al-souq al-ijtameeah" [Policies for increasing base revenues in the social market economy]. Lecture at Syrian Economic Society, Feb. 19, Damascus, Syria.

————. 2008b. "Reform Paradox in Syria." Paper presented at the Conference on Economic Transition in Syria, St. Andrews, Scotland, Apr. 11–12.

————. 2010a. *Syria on the Path of Economic Reform*. St. Andrews, Scotland: St. Andrews Papers on Contemporary Syria, distributed by Lynne Rienner Publishers.

————. 2010b. "Al-ather al-ijtameeah al-seeaset al-iqtisad fi suryeeah" [The social consequences of economic policies in Syria]. Lecture at Syrian Economic Society, Feb. 9, Damascus, Syria.

Selvik, Kjetil. 2009. "It's the Mentality, Stupid. Syria's Turn to the Private Sector." In *Changing Regime Discourse and Reform in Syria*, Kjetil Selvik and Aurora Sottimano. St. Andrews, Scotland: St. Andrews Papers on Contemporary Syria, distributed by Lynne Rienner Publishers.

Seurat, Michel. 1980. "Les populations, l'Etat et la Societe." In *La Syrie d'Aujourd'hui*, edited by A. Raymond. Paris: CNRS.

SHRC (Syrian Human Rights Committee). 2008. *Seventh Annual Reports on Human Rights Status in Syria*. http://www.shrc.org/en/?cat=10.

————. 2009. *Eighth Annual Reports on Human Rights Status in Syria*. http://www.shrc.org/en/?cat=10.

————. 2010. *Ninth Annual Reports on Human Rights Status in Syria*. http://www.shrc.org/en/?cat=10.

Sid-Ahmad, Mohammed. 2005. "Change in Syria?" *Al-Ahram Weekly On-line*, June 16–22. weekly.ahram.org.eg/.

St. John, Ronald Bruce. 2005. "New Syria Acts, Looks Like Old Syria." *Foreign Policy in Focus*, June 20. http://www.fpif.org/.

Sottimano, Aurora. 2009. "Ideology and Discourse in the Era of Bathist Reforms: Towards an Analysis of Authoritarian Governmentality." In *Changing Regime Discourse and Reform in Syria*, Aurora Sottimano and Kjetil Selvik.

St. Andrews, Scotland: St. Andrews Papers on Contemporary Syria, distributed by Lynne Rienner Publishers.

Strindberg, Anders. 2000. "The Damascus-Based Alliance of Palestinian Forces." *Journal of Palestine Studies* 29, no. 3 (Spring): 60–76.

Sukkar, Nabil. 2006. *Developing Options for Surplus Labor in Syria*. Damascus: Institutional and Sector Modernisation Facility.

SYEA (Syrian Young Entrepreneurs Association). 2010. "Syrian Young Entrepreneurs Association." www.syea.org.

Szkudlarek, Betina. 2010. "Reentry—A Review of the Literature." *International Journal of Intercultural Relations* 34:1–21.

Tabutin, Dominique, and Bruno Schoumaker. 2005. "The Demography of the Arab World and the Middle East from the 1950s to the 2000s. A Survey of Changes and a Statistical Assessment." *Population* 60, no. 5–6:505–615.

Tejel, Jordi. 2009. *Syria's Kurds: History, Politics and Society*. London: Routledge.

UNDP (United Nations Human Development Program). 2005. *Arab Human Development Report: Toward Freedom in the Arab World*. New York: UNDP.

UNGA (United Nations General Assembly). 2011. *Report of the Special Rapporteur on the Right to Food, Olivier De Schutter. Mission to the Syrian Arab Republic*. New York: UNGA.

UNHCR (United Nations High Commissioner for Refugees) 2009. *Surviving the City—A Review of UNHCRs Operation for Iraqi Refugees in Urban Areas of Jordan, Lebanon and Syria*. Evaluation Report, July. New York: United Nations High Commissioner for Refugees.

———. 2011. *Statistical Report on UNHCR Registered Iraqis and Non-Iraqis. Iraq, Egypt, Iran, Jordan, Lebanon, Syria, Turkey, and the GCC Countries*. September. New York: UNHCR.

Valter, Stéphane. 2002. *Construction Nationale Syrienne: Légitimation de la Nature Communautaire du Pouvoir par le Discours Historique*. Paris: CNRS.

Van Hear, Nicholas. 2005. "The Impact of the Involuntary Mass Return to Jordan in the Wake of the Gulf Crisis." *International Migration Review* 29, no. 2:352–74.

van Leeuwen, Richard. 1999. *Waqfs and Urban Structures: The Case of Ottoman Damascus*. Boston: Brill.

Velud, Christian. 1985. "Régime des terres et structures agraires en Jézireh syrienne durant la première moitié du vingtième siècle." In *Terroirs et Sociétés au*

Maghreb et au Moyen-Orient, série EMA, no. 2, 161–94. Lyon: Publications de la Maison de l'Orient.

———. 1991. *Une expérience d'administration régionale en Syrie durant le Mandat Français: conquête, colonisation et mise en valeur de la Gezira (1920–1936)*. Thèse de Doctorat d'Histoire, Université de Lyon.

Wedeen, Lisa. 1999. *Ambiguities of Domination: Politics, Rhetoric and Symbols in Contemporary Syria*. Chicago: Univ. of Chicago Press.

Westlake, Mike. 2001. "Strategic Crops Sub Sector (Syria)." *FAO Report*. http://www.fao.org/world/syria/gcpita/pubs/policystudies/StrategicCrops-En_1-70.pdf.

Wieland, Carsten. 2006a. *Syria—Ballots or Bullets? Democracy, Islamism, and Secularism in the Levant*. Seattle, WA: Cune Press.

———. 2006b. *Syria at Bay: Secularism, Islamism, and Pax Americana*. London: Hurst.

———. 2012. *Syria: A Decade of Lost Chances: Repression and Revolution from Damascus Spring to Arab Spring*. Seattle, WA: Cune Press.

Wikas, Seth. 2007. *Battling the Lion of Damascus: Syria's Domestic Opposition and the Asad Regime*. Washington, DC: Washington Institute for Near East Policy.

Witson, Sara Leah. 2010. "Syria: Repression Grows as Europe, US Avoid Discussing Rights." *Human Rights Watch*, Mar. 11. http://www.hrw.org/en/news/2010/03/11/syria-repression-grows-europe-us-avoid-discussing-rights.

Zintl, Tina. 2009. "Modernisierungspolitik durch Kompetenztransfer? Syrische Remigranten mit deutschem Hochschulabschluss als Katalysatoren von Brain Gain in Syrien unter Bashar al-Assad." In *Volkswirtschaftliche Diskussionspapiere Nr. 104*, edited by Dieter Weiss and Steffen Wippel. Berlin: Klaus Schwarz Verlag.

———. 2012. "Modernization Theory II: Western-Educated Syrians and the Authoritarian Upgrading of Civil Society." In *Civil Society and the State in Syria: The Outsourcing of Social Responsibility*, Laura Ruiz de Elvira and Tina Zintl. St. Andrews, Scotland: St. Andrews Papers on Contemporary Syria, distributed by Lynne Rienner Publishers.

———. 2013. "Syria's Reforms under Bashar al-Asad. An Opportunity for Foreign-Educated Entrepreneurs to Move into Decision-Making?" In *Business Politics in the Middle East*, edited by Steffen Hertog, Giacomo Luciani, and Marc Valeri, 159–82. London: Hurst.

Zorob, Anja. 2006. "Abdallah ad-Dardari, Stellvertretender Premierminister für wirtschaftliche Angelegenheiten in Syrien." *Orient* 47, no. 3:323–33.

Websites

All4Syria. http://all4syria.info/.
Basma. http://www.basma-syria.org/.
JCI (Junior Chamber International). www.jci.cc.
MoEX (Ministry for Expatriate Affairs). http://ministryofexpatriates.gov.sy/.
SDT (Syria Trust for Development). http://syriatrust.org/.
SYEA (Syrian Young Entrepreneurs Association). www.syea.org.
Syria Comment. Blogspot by Joshua Landis. www.joshualandis.com.
Tharwa Community, http://tharwacommunity.typepad.com/.

Newspapers and News Agencies

Al-Ahram Weekly On-line
Al-Akhbar
Arab Reform Bulletin
al-Arabiya
Associated Press
al-Bath
Bloomberg
Chicago Tribune
Christian Science Monitor
Daily Star
The Economist
Financial Times
Foreign Policy in Focus
Forward Magazine
al-Hayat
The Independent
IRIN (Integrated Regional Information Networks)
Jadaliyya.com
Los Angeles Times
Middle East Intelligence Bulletin
Middle East International
al-Nahar
the National
National Public Radio
New Yorker online
New York Times online
NZZ-Online
openDemocracy
Perspectives
Qantara.de
Al-Rai al-Aam
SANA (Syrian Arab News Agency)
spiegel-online
Syria Times
Syria Today
The Telegraph
al-Thawra
Tishreen
UPI
World Dispatches
Yalibnan.com

About the Contributors

Myriam Ababsa is an associate research fellow and social geographer at the French Institute for the Near East (Institut français du Proche Orient) in Amman. Her work has focused on the impact of public policies on regional and urban development in Jordan and Syria. Her PhD thesis, "Ideologies and Territories in Syria: Raqqa and the Euphrates Project," Tours University, 2004, received the Honorable Mention of the Best Dissertation Prize (Syrian Studies Association). It was published in French in 2009 and is available online. She published *Amman de pierre et de paix* in 2007; *Raqqa: territoires et pratiques sociales d'une ville syrienne* in 2009; co-edited with Rami Daher *Cities, Urban Practices and Nation Building in Jordan. Villes, pratiques urbaines et construction nationale en Jordanie* in 2011 (online); and with Baudouin Dupret and Eric Denis *Popular Housing and Urban Land Tenure in the Middle East. Case Studies from Egypt, Syria, Jordan, Lebanon, and Turkey* in 2012. In 2013 she published an *Atlas of Jordan. History, Territories and Society. Atlas al Urdunn. Al-tarikh, al-ardh, al-mujtama'* with a team of forty-eight scholars.

Samer N. Abboud is an associate professor of international studies at Arcadia University. He received his doctorate in Arab and Islamic Studies at the University of Exeter, where he completed a dissertation entitled "The Political Economy of Marketization in Syria." In 2013 he was a fellow in the Arab Transformation Project at the Institute for International and Security Affairs (SWP) in Berlin, where he completed a project on Syria's business elites during the uprising. His current research is concerned with Syrian capital flight in the context of the uprising.

Mohamed Kamel Doraï is a researcher at the CNRS (the French National Centre for Scientific Research) currently based at MIGRINTER, University of Poitiers (France). His work focuses mainly on asylum and refugees in the Middle

East, new migrations and geopolitical reorganization in the Middle East, and migration and transnational practices within the Palestinian diaspora. He is currently conducting research on Iraqis in Syria as well as on the urbanization process of Palestinian refugee camps in Lebanon. The comparative study between refugees residing in and out of camps as well as the analysis of their migratory experience and spatial practices provide an account of the refugees' socio-spatial dynamics in exile and of relationships between the camp refugees and their urban environment.

Najib Ghadbian is an associate professor of political science and Middle East studies at the University of Arkansas. He is the author of *Democratization and the Islamists Challenge in the Arab World* (English 1997; Arabic 2002). His second Arabic book, *The Second Asad Regime: Bashar of Lost Opportunities*, was published in 2006. He translated Lisa Wedeen's book, *Ambiguities of Domination: Politics, Rhetoric, and Symbols in Contemporary Syria*, into Arabic. Najib has published book chapters, reviews, essays, and articles in journals including *New Political Science, Middle East Journal*, and *al-Mustaqbal al-'Arabi*. Najib is active in Syrian dissent as an independent academic.

Raymond Hinnebusch is a professor of international relations and Middle East politics as well as director of the Centre for Syrian Studies at St. Andrews University, Scotland. He is the author of numerous articles and books on Syria including *Syria: Revolution from Above* (2001) and "Modern Syrian Politics" (in *History Compass* 6, no. 1 [2008]), and of *Turkey-Syria Relations: Between Enmity and Amity*, co-edited with Ozlem Tur, 2013.

Rania Maktabi is an associate professor of international relations and comparative politics at Østfold University College in Norway, and a researcher at the New Middle East Project, Department of Culture Studies and Oriental Languages (IKOS), University of Oslo. She has a PhD in political science from the University of Oslo with a dissertation entitled "The Politicization of the Demos in the Middle East: Citizenship between Membership and Participation in the State" (2012). Citizenship-related issues in the Middle East and North Africa region are her main research field. Her publications include "The 1932 Census Revisited: Who Are the Lebanese?" (*British Journal of Middle Eastern Studies* 26, no. 2 [1999]); "Gender, Family Law and Citizenship in Syria" (*Citizenship Studies* 14, no. 5 [2010]); and "Female Citizenship in the Middle East: Comparing Family

Law Reform in Morocco, Egypt, Syria and Lebanon" (*Middle East Law and Governance* 5, no. 3 [2013]).

Valentina Napolitano is a PhD candidate in political studies in the EHESS (École des Hautes Études en Sciences Sociales) of Paris under the supervision of Dr. Hamit Bozarslan. Her research focuses on political mobilization and engagement in the Palestinian refugee camps in Syria. Among her previous publications are "Hamas and the Syrian Uprising: A Difficult Choice," *Middle East Policy* 20, no. 3 [Autumn 2013]: 73–85; and "La mobilisation des réfugiés palestiniens dans le sillage de la 'révolution' syrienne: s'engager sous contrainte," *Cultures et Conflits*, no. 87, Autumn 2012.

Paulo G. Pinto has a PhD in anthropology from Boston University. He is a professor of anthropology at the Universidade Federal Fluminense, Brazil, where he is also director of the Center for Middle East Studies. He did ethnographic fieldwork in Syria in various periods from 1999 to 2010. He also has done fieldwork with the Muslim communities in Brazil since 2003. In 2012–13 he did ethnographic fieldwork of the *ziyara al-arbaʻiyyn* in Najaf and Karbala, Iraq. He has authored articles and books on Sufism and other forms of Islam in contemporary Syria, as well as on Arab ethnicity and Muslim communities in Brazil. His recent publications include *Ethnographies of Islam: Ritual Performances and Everyday Practices*, 2013, which he co-edited with Baudouin Dupret, Thomas Pierret, and Kathryn Spelman-Poots. He is co-editing, with John Karam and Maria del-Mar Logroño-Narbona, *Crescent of Another Horizon: Islam in Latin America, the Caribbean and Latino USA* (forthcoming).

Aurora Sottimano holds a PhD degree in politics from the School of Oriental and African Studies, University of London, funded by the British Academy. Her research focuses on Syria and Middle East politics; the political economy of development and liberalization; authoritarianism and governmentality; labor unions and mobilization; discourse analysis. She is a fellow of the Centre for Syrian Studies at St. Andrews University, Scotland, and lecturer at the British University in Egypt.

Mandy Terc received her PhD in linguistic anthropology from the University of Michigan in 2011. From 2007 to 2009, she lived in and conducted research in Damascus. Her dissertation, "Syria's New Neoliberal Elite: English Usage,

Linguistic Practices and Group Boundaries," examines the socioeconomic ramifications of Syria's implementation of neoliberal economic policies. She is currently a lecturer in Middle Eastern studies and anthropology at Northwestern University.

Carsten Wieland studied history, political science, and philosophy at Humboldt University in Berlin (PhD in 1999), at Duke University in North Carolina, and at Jawaharlal Nehru University in New Delhi. Since 2011, he has worked in the German Foreign Office. Between December 2013 and June 2014 he was seconded to the UN in Geneva as political advisor of the Joint Special Representative for Syria of the United Nations and the Arab League, Lakhdar Brahimi. Before he entered the diplomatic career, he worked as a political consultant, analyst, author, and journalist and spent several years in the Middle East. A Syria expert for more than a decade, he published numerous articles and books on the Levant, among them: *Syria—A Decade of Lost Chances: Repression and Revolution from Damascus Spring to Arab Spring* (2012). Carsten previously worked at the Goethe Institute in Cairo and Munich and as a country representative for the Konrad Adenauer Foundation in Colombia. He was a correspondent for the German Press Agency (DPA) in Washington, Tel Aviv, and Colombia, as well as DPA head of corporate communications and public affairs in Berlin. He is a guest professor for international relations at the Universidad del Rosario in Bogotá and was a fellow at the Public Policy Department at Georgetown University in Washington, DC (www.carsten-wieland.de) His chapter does not represent the opinion of any institution.

Martine Zeuthen holds a BA in social anthropology and an MSc in anthropology from the University of Copenhagen. During her MSc she conducted eight months of fieldwork while living with Iraqi refugee families in the suburbs of Damascus. Martine then worked in Damascus for a Danish NGO focusing on reconciliation and creation of activities to keep Iraqi, Palestinian, and Syrian children and youth off the streets in refugee-dominated areas of Damascus. Martine has published papers looking at urban displacement as well as at protection and humanitarian assistance in authoritarian regimes. Martine is currently based in Kenya, working on conflict transformation issues in the Horn of Africa.

Tina Zintl is an academic coordinator and lecturer in Middle East and comparative politics at the University of Tübingen, Germany. She holds a PhD from the

University of St. Andrews, Scotland ("Syria's Authoritarian Upgrading, 2000–2010: Bashar al-Asad's Promotion of Foreign-educated Returnees as Transnational Technocrats," 2013), where she also worked at the Centre for Syrian Studies. She graduated with a master's degree in political science, economics, and geography from the University of Erlangen-Nuremberg, Germany. Her research focuses on economic and political transformation, state-society relations, and elite composition in Arab countries, as well as on international migration and development cooperation. Tina has presented her research at numerous conferences and contributed several book chapters, for instance "Syria's Reforms under Bashar al-Asad: An Opportunity for Foreign-educated Entrepreneurs to Move into Decision-making?" in *Business Politics in the Middle East*, edited by Steffen Hertog, Giacomo Luciani, and Marc Valeri, 2013. She published an article, with Laura Ruiz de Elvira, about charities and social benevolence in Bashar al-Asad's Syria in the *International Journal of Middle East Studies* 46, no. 2.

Index